LIFE WRITING AND SPACE

Life Writing and Space

Edited by

EVELINE KILIAN
Humboldt-Universität zu Berlin, Germany

and

HOPE WOLF
University of Sussex, UK

with the assistance of

KATHRIN TORDASI
Humboldt-Universität zu Berlin, Germany

ASHGATE

Published by
Ashgate Publishing Limited
Wey Court East
Union Road
Farnham
Surrey, GU9 7PT
England

Ashgate Publishing Company
110 Cherry Street
Suite 3-1
Burlington, VT 05401-3818
USA

www.ashgate.com

British Library Cataloguing in Publication Data
A catalogue record for this book is available from the British Library

The Library of Congress has cataloged the printed edition as follows:
Kilian, Eveline / Wolf, Hope. / Tordasi, Kathrin.
  Life writing and space / edited by Eveline Kilian and Hope Wolf ; with the assistance of
    Kathrin Tordasi.
    Includes bibliographical references and index.
  ISBN 9781472427946 (hardback) – ISBN 9781472427953 (ebook) –
  ISBN 9781472427960 (epub) 1. LCSH: Space in literature. 2. Self in literature.

PN56.S667 L54 2016
809/.9335–dc23

2015022852

ISBN 9781472427946 (hbk)
ISBN 9781472427953 (ebk – PDF)
ISBN 9781472427960 (ebk – ePUB)

Printed in the United Kingdom by Henry Ling Limited,
at the Dorset Press, Dorchester, DT1 1HD

Contents

List of Plates

List of Contributors

James Attlee has published four non-fiction books: *Gordon Matta-Clark: The Space Between* (with Lisa Le Feuvre, Nazraeli Press, 2003), *Isolarion: A Different Oxford Journey* (University of Chicago Press, 2007), *Nocturne: A Journey in Search of Moonlight* (Penguin, 2011) and *Station to Station: Searching for Stories on the Great Western Line* (Guardian Books, 2015). He has appeared at many literary and cultural festivals in the UK, including Hay and Edinburgh, and was the recipient of awards from The Author's Foundation in 2008 and 2012. He is currently editor at Large for the University of Chicago Press in the UK.

Clare Brant is Professor of Eighteenth-Century Literature and Culture at King's College London, where she also co-directs the Centre for Life-Writing Research. Her book *Eighteenth-Century Letters and British Culture* (Palgrave 2006) won the ESSE Book Award for 2008, and she is the author of numerous articles on literature, culture and gender.

Matthew Ingleby is Lecturer in Victorian Studies at Queen Mary University of London. Before that he taught at University College London, where he completed his doctorate, which contributed to the Leverhulme-funded 'Bloomsbury Project'. He is writing a monograph that explores the role of fiction in the social production of Bloomsbury between the 1820s and 1904. His research attends to both ends of the long nineteenth century and largely addresses the politics of the cultural representation of urban and coastal space. He has published essays on topics including Victorian building plots, locality in utopia, and bachelor domesticity. He co-edited (with Matthew Beaumont) *G. K. Chesterton, London and Modernity* (2013), and is currently preparing a new critical edition (for Anthem) of R. L. Stevenson's *Dr Jekyll and Mr Hyde*.

Elizabeth H. Jones is Lecturer in French at the University of Leicester. Her research focuses on the relationship between literature and space, as well as contemporary French and Francophone life writing. Her publications include *Spaces of Belonging: Home, Culture and Identity in 20th Century French Autobiography* (Rodopi, 2007), 'The Space between Geography and Literature'(2008) and 'Autofiction: A Brief History of a Neologism' (2009).

Eveline Kilian is Professor of English Literature and Culture at Humboldt-Universität zu Berlin. Her major research areas are: metropolitan cultures, modernism and postmodernism, trans/gender and queer theory, gender and ethics. Her book publications include: *Queer Futures: Reconsidering Ethics, Activism and the Political* (ed. with Elahe Hashemi Yekani and Beatrice Michaelis, Ashgate 2013), *London: Eine literarische Entdeckungsreise* (Wissenschaftliche Buchgesellschaft, 2008), *GeschlechtSverkehrt: Theoretische und literarische Perspektiven des gender-bending* (Helmer, 2004) and *Momente innerweltlicher Transzendenz: Die Augenblickserfahrung in Dorothy Richardsons Romanzyklus Pilgrimage und ihr ideengeschichtlicher Kontext* (Niemeyer, 1997).

Martin Klepper is Professor of American Literature and Culture at Humboldt-Universität zu Berlin. His publications include: *Pynchon, Auster, DeLillo – Die amerikanische Postmoderne zwischen Spiel und Rekonstruktion* (Campus, 1996), *The Discovery of Point of View: Observation and Narration in the American Novel 1790–1910* (Winter, 2011) and *Rethinking Narrative Identity: Persona and Perspective* (ed. with Claudia Holler, John Benjamins, 2013). He has also co-edited books on modernism, cybercultures and American economies and has written several essays on postmodernism, visuality and nineteenth-century American literature, American cinema and critical narratology.

Frédéric Regard is Professor of English Literature at the Sorbonne, in Paris. He is the author of books on William Golding, George Orwell and Virginia Woolf. His publications also include collections of essays on life writing (*La Biographie littéraire en Angleterre*, 1999 ; *L'Autobiographie littéraire en Angleterre*, 2000 ; *Mapping the Self: Space, Identity, Discourse in British Auto/Biography*, 2003), on exploration narratives (*British Narratives of Exploration: Case Studies on the Self and Other*, 2009), and on early Arctic voyages (*The Quest for the Northwest Passage: Knowledge, Nation and Empire, 1576–1806*, 2012 ; *Arctic Exploration in the Nineteenth Century*, 2013). His latest book, a monograph on English feminist activist Josephine Butler, was published in 2014.

Anne-Julia Schoen studied Psychology, English and American Literatures and History in Hamburg and at Humboldt-Universität zu Berlin. She is an assistant researcher at the Department of English and American Studies at the HU and at the Department for Jewish Studies at Halle University. Her research interests are modernist art and literature, Anglo-Jewish and First World War literature and art, life writing, gender studies and Jewish scepticism. She is currently finishing her PhD thesis on aspects of form and the formless in Anglo-Jewish literature and art between 1910 and 1937. She has written conference reports and reviews and has co-worked on an English edition of the early modern Rabbi Simone Luzzatto's writings.

Helga Schwalm is Professor of English Literature at Humboldt-Universität zu Berlin. Her current research interests focus on eighteenth- and nineteenth-century life writing, topography and life writing, sympathy and literature, and eighteenth-century aesthetics and criticism. Among her publications are: *Dekonstruktion im Roman. Erzähltechnische Verfahren und Selbstreflexion in den Romanen von Vladimir Nabokov und Samuel Beckett* (1991), *Das eigene und das fremde Leben. Biographische Identitätsentwürfe in der englischen Literatur des 18. Jahrhunderts* (2007), 'The Lake Poets/Authors: Topography, Authorship and Romantic Subjectivities' (2009), 'Lives of the Physicians – Samuel Johnson, Medicine and Biography' (2013) and 'Women's Contemporary Arctic Narratives' (2013).

Andrew Thacker is Professor of Twentieth-Century Literature at Nottingham Trent University. He is the author or editor of several books on modernism, including the three volumes of *The Oxford Critical and Cultural History of Modernist Magazines*, and the monograph *Moving Through Modernity: Space and Geography in Modernism* (2003). He was a founder member and the first Chair of the British Association for Modernist Studies and is an editor of the long-running interdisciplinary journal *Literature & History*.

Kathrin Tordasi studied English and German Literature at the University of Tübingen, Germany. She has published on queer masculinities in mainstream cinema, gendered beach culture, and oblivion as a narrative strategy to subvert rigid gender models. She is an associated member of the Centre for Transdisciplinary Gender Studies in Berlin and teaches English Literature and Cultural Studies at Humboldt-Universität zu Berlin. Her research interests include gender and space, theories of liminality and transgression, modern literature and queer theory. She is currently writing her PhD thesis on 'Women by the Waterfront: Gender, Body and Identity on the Liminal Shore'.

Neil Vickers is Reader in English Literature and the Medical Humanities at King's College London. He is interested in the relationship between autobiographical writing and medicine. His book *Coleridge and the Doctors 1795–1806* (OUP, 2004) examines Coleridge's participation in the medical culture of his time. The book's fundamental claim is that Coleridge's intellectual development cannot be understood independently of his medical endeavours. He has published widely on Romantic psychology and medicine and on the history of the British psychoanalytic movement.

Alexandra Wagner studied Booktrade and Publishing, German Literature and American Studies in Leipzig, Berlin and Seattle, and completed her dissertation at Humboldt-Universität zu Berlin in the field of North American literature and culture with a book about narrative knowledge production in autobiographical texts (*Wissen in der Autobiographie*, Wissenschaftlicher Verlag Trier, 2014). Her research interests include life writing, narrative and genre theory, and literature and culture of the 1930s and 40s.

Hope Wolf is a Lecturer in British Modernist Literature at the University of Sussex. Previously, she held a Research Fellowship in English at Girton College, University of Cambridge. She has research interests in modern and contemporary literature and culture, and has written about, and made, collections of life writing. Her most recent publication, co-edited with Sebastian Faulks, is *A Broken World: Letters, Diaries and Memories of the Great War* (Hutchinson, 2014). Her contribution to this volume draws on her experiences of working, while a researcher at King's College London, on *Strandlines*: a Centre for Life-Writing Research project about lives on the Strand – past, present and creative.

Acknowledgments

This book is the outcome of a long-standing international collaboration between King's College London and Humboldt-Universität zu Berlin, and it brings together chapters written by scholars both from within and outside of these institutions. We would like to thank all the participants for their valuable contributions; these not only made for an extremely pleasurable and fruitful exchange but also crucially advanced our thinking about life writing and space. We would like to extend our thanks to the DAAD, Humboldt-Universität and King's College London for their generous funding of our activities, and to the Ashgate team, especially Katy Crossan and Margaret Younger, for their unfailing support. Hope Wolf would like to thank all participants in *Strandlines* for their contributions to the archive that made her chapter in this collection possible, also Clare Brant, the Director of the project, David Green and the rest of the *Strandlines* team, The Cabinet of Artists, The Connection at St Martin-in-the-Fields, Peabody Bruce House Centre, Age UK Westminster, the City of Westminster Archives Centre, King's College London Archives and the project funders: JISC, AHRC, LCACE, the Edward Harvist Trust and King's College London. We are both grateful to Colden Drystone, artist in residence at Girton College Cambridge for 2013–2014, who generously let us use two photographs of his installation 'Believing in Time Travel', one for the book cover and one to complement our introduction; thanks also go to the photographer, Tim Smyth. Gratitude is also due to Kathrin Tordasi and Julia Schulz for their meticulous preparation of the manuscript and index.

The editors are much obliged to publishers for granting permission for the reproduction of material listed below: excerpts from *Giving up the Ghost* are reprinted by permission of HarperCollins Publishers Ltd © 2003 Hilary Mantel; excerpts from *Isolarion: A Different Oxford Journey*, University of Chicago Press © 2007 by James Attlee, all rights reserved; excerpts from *Nocturne: A Journey in Search of Moonlight*, University of Chicago Press, © 2011 by James Attlee. All rights reserved; a quotation (used as an epigraph) from *The Poetics of Space* by Gaston Bachelard, translated by Maria Jolas, copyright © 1958 by Presses Universitaires de France; translation copyright © 1964 by The Orion Press, Inc., used by permission of Viking Penguin, a division of Penguin Group (USA) LCC; images from *Portrait de Jacques Derrida en Jeune Saint Juif*, Hélène Cixous, 2001, reproduced by kind permission of Éditions Galilée.

Eveline Kilian and Hope Wolf

Introduction:
The Spatial Dimensions of Life Writing

Eveline Kilian and Hope Wolf

Life writing can hardly be thought of without its connection to space: Who we are, and how we narrate ourselves, depends on our ability, our desire or failure, to locate our identities within space and with respect to certain places. Formation of the self often relies on spatial movement, on (re)locating the self in different places and social spaces. Consequently the journey is one of the most common narrative tropes in life writing, with the physical journey corresponding to an inner, metaphorical journey of the self. This is a pattern autobiography shares with the bildungsroman (see Marcus 1994: 171–72), which typically requires the protagonist to leave home (Buckley 1974: 17) and embark upon 'an uncertain exploration of social space ... through travel and adventure, wandering and getting lost' (Moretti 2000: 4). So, in his *Autobiography*, John Stuart Mill describes the beneficial influence his year's residence in France had on his intellectual and political education, leaving its imprint way beyond his adolescent years; he particularly emphasises the self-reflexive impulse afforded by spatial distance, and how 'the free and genial atmosphere of Continental life' (1989: 62) increased his awareness of the English propensity for emotional aloofness and indifference. In her *Testament of Youth,* Vera Brittain pits the stuffy and restricted life of 'Buxton young-ladyhood' (1978: 71) in provincial Derbyshire against the purposeful work and freedom that an Oxford university education promises; and this horizon then drastically expands when she becomes a VAD nurse during the First World War in London, Malta and France, an experience which fuels her later professional and political engagement as a journalist, feminist and pacifist. The trope of the journey is also made productive in hybrid genres such as the autobiographical novel, which frequently combines autobiographical features with the bildungsroman and/or the Künstlerroman. James Joyce's *A Portrait of the Artist as a Young Man*, for example, ends with the protagonist's departure from Ireland, his 'home' and 'fatherland' (1977: 222), as the only possible way to find the freedom he needs to pursue his vocation as a writer.

Despite the importance of spatial parameters, life writing is predominantly mediated through time: A life story has traditionally been thought of as a chronological movement, a narrative that unfolds over time and meaningfully connects events, thereby constructing continuity and coherence. Paul Ricoeur's concept of narrative identity, for instance, is primarily based on time and the transformation of 'time as passage' (meaning the mere succession of events) into 'time as duration' (that is, their ordering into a meaningful configuration) (1991: 22). The conceptual horizon of auto/biography has typically been the lifespan and its phases: from youth to maturity, from sensitive child to poet or artist, from birth to death. The Enlightenment legacy that underlies most of its modern forms links linearity to development and aligns individual with social and historical progress. However, the events of the last century have done much to problematise such narratives. War, violence and continued economic and social inequalities presented a challenge to teleological representations of history. The 'spatial turn' in the Humanities (see Bachmann-Medick 2006: 284–328; Warf and Arias 2009) can be aligned with increasing scepticism about their validity. Drawing on Bertrand Westphal's suggestions about the impact of the Second World War and its aftermath, Robert T. Tally Jr, writes: 'Critical theorists, historians, philosophers, and geographers certainly would now hesitate to proclaim much faith in the universal progress of history in the wake of such destruction, and a changing view of temporal movement may have opened the way to those who demanded that greater attention be paid to spatial concerns' (2013: 12).

While Michel Foucault's diagnosis of a shift from an obsession with time and history in the nineteenth century to an 'epoch of space' in the twentieth is debatable (see Soja 1989: 10), his take on contemporary self-perceptions does anticipate and reflect more recent concerns in life-writing studies: 'our experience of the world is less that of a long life developing through time than that of a network that connects points and intersects with its own skein' (Foucault 1986: 22). When teleological structures and the bildungsroman model become untenable, space acts as a node around which experiences can cluster. Lives are mapped spatially, and this in turn provokes explorations of the interdependencies between spaces and selves and the extent to which selves are constituted through the spaces they traverse, inhabit or move away from. Frédéric Regard calls our attention to the significance of space when he provocatively claims that 'when it comes to self writing, the question is not so much "who am I?" as "where am I?"' (2003: 16). This could also be the motto of the recently published topographical biography of the Viennese writer Hugo von Hofmannsthal, *Hofmannsthal. Orte*, a study in twenty essays centring on the places that shaped his life and work. The editors derive their choice of form from Hofmannsthal's own conscious use of places to develop the different facets of his personality, as they explain in the preface: 'Hofmannsthal pursued this form of permanent self-invention through strategically chosen changes of place throughout his life' (Hemecker and Heumann 2014: 11; our translation).

This is not to suggest that space presents a stable and unproblematic alternative to time. The spatial turn might also be viewed as a response to spatial transformations resulting from historical upheavals and technological developments. And these too can be seen to have left their mark on life writing. Fragmented forms can express, and register the impact of, displacement. As Edward W. Said says of Palestinian writing: 'Our characteristic mode ... is not narrative, in which scenes take place *seriatim*, but rather broken narratives, fragmentary compositions, and self-consciously staged testimonials, in which the narrative voice keeps stumbling over itself, its obligations, and its limitations' (1999: 38). The need to respond to enforced spatial change – as a result of war, economic necessity or the need of relief from cultural oppression – shaped much of the life writing discussed in this book. Globalisation and digital technologies, as some chapters point out, have also impacted upon how space is experienced and imagined. Doreen Massey has commented on the repercussions of these massive shifts: 'In the context of a world which is, indeed, increasingly interconnected the notion of place (usually evoked as 'local place') has come to have totemic resonance' (2005: 5). Given the importance of the experience of relocation to the authors whose works are discussed in *Life Writing and Space*, nostalgia becomes an important theme, whether for irreplaceably lost cities or houses. It is detectable not only in autobiography and memoir, but also in critical writing on space. Henri Lefebvre describes how the idea or '*memory*' of the House, 'a merely historico-poetic reality rooted in folklore', imbues both 'urban reality' and 'the work of its critics' (he specifically refers to Bachelard and Heidegger) with a 'nostalgic aura' (1991: 120, 121).

Such nostalgia about places resonates with phenomenological studies that associate place with rootedness, security, personal significance and identity, as opposed to space to which they attribute qualities like openness, freedom and the uprooting of established values. As Yi-Fu Tuan puts it: 'Place is security, space is freedom: we are attached to the one and long for the other' (1977: 3; see also Relph 1976: 65). Critical geographers have problematised such a neat separation, however, on account of its implicit ideology. Massey, writing from a feminist perspective, and suspicious of dichotomies that are all too often mapped onto gender binaries, has rejected the dualism of space as flow and place as stasis, and has argued that places are also 'unfixed, contested and multiple' as well as 'open and porous' (1994: 5). Indeed, in most spatial theories currently used by scholars, the place/space distinction is blurred and gives way to a much more complex exchange. Some chapters in this book, for instance, draw on the work of Michel de Certeau, who joins place and space in a dynamic relationship. For him, place is brought to life and appropriated by the individual through spatial practices: '*space is a practiced place*. Thus the street geometrically defined by urban planning is transformed into a space by walkers' (1984: 117). This crucially links space and place to movement and to 'vectors of direction, velocities, and time variables' (117).

To movement, and to spatial practices more generally, de Certeau attributes a potentially subversive effect.[1] This idea is echoed in Tim Cresswell's description of mobility as 'a kind of superdeviance', 'a basic form of disorder and chaos' (Cresswell 1996: 87). Movement decentres places, just as it decentres selves and their place-related identities. Hence mobility initiates a dynamic of (re)creation and decreation of the self, one that is explored in several of the following chapters and that is intimately linked to the ideological forces inherent in spaces as well as places and the subject's ability to engage with, and resist, them. The conjunction of the fluidity of spaces, places and selves that is suggested here can form the basis of a self-reflexive autobiographical practice. Rosi Braidotti's book *Nomadic Subjects* comes to mind here, which connects the autobiographical experience of migration with a specific type of knowledge production. She introduces the figure of the nomadic subject who, having 'relinquished all idea, desire and nostalgia for fixity', is defined by transitions and multiple connections (2011: 57). It embodies a decidedly critical epistemology (derived from Deleuze and Guattari) that 'resists settling into socially coded modes of thought and behavior' (26).

Representations of space and place as dynamic and politically charged have often taken inspiration from Lefebvre's notion of the social production of space. Taking a Marxist perspective, Lefebvre argues that any given society's space emerges from its specific modes of production and reproduction and is maintained by spatial practice. The concept of spatial practice not only provides a link between space and place, as outlined above, but also between space and subject: It determines the form of their mutual constitution in an ongoing balancing of social forces and individual agency. In this model, space is seen as radically relational, 'constituted through interactions' and 'always under construction', as Massey has pointed out (2005: 9).

---

[1]   This becomes clear in his intermittent use of terms like 'stubborn resistances' or 'the tactics of users' (1984: 94). This vocabulary seems to at least partly contradict his claim that pedestrians write an urban 'text' through their spatial practices 'without being able to read it' (93), however. Cresswell's distinction between transgression, which does not rest on intent but merely on the effect it creates, and resistance, which is a form of intentional transgression (1996: 23), is helpful to clarify this point.

From Lefebvre and other studies influenced by his work, space emerges as a product of social relations and cultural practices. It becomes a force field of mechanisms of power and control, of inclusions, exclusions and social hierarchies (Soja 1996: 161, Keith and Pile 1993: 220). Postmodern geographer Edward Soja and Marxist geographer David Harvey are two scholars that have most extensively adopted the framework laid out by Lefebvre. Soja shares Lefebvre's belief in the transformative potential of 'lived space' as the level at which ideologies and power relations are negotiated and where 'the real and the imagined intertwine' (1996: 68). For Harvey, lived space is dominated by the 'imagination' and linked to the production of alternative spaces in the form of 'utopian plans', 'imaginary landscapes' or 'spaces of desire' (1995: 221). This is of course where literature and life writing as spaces in their own right come in. Narratives of the self modulate the interrelation between physical and mental spaces and constitute a kind of 'heterotopia' (Foucault 1986) in which alternative configurations of social spatiality and individual subjects' engagements with spatial parameters can be experimented with (see Kilian 2014). Some chapters in this book take up this idea of the text as 'heterotopia', or choose alternative figures (the 'doppelgänger', for instance), in order to explore what happens when versions of the self are projected into remembered or fictionalised representations of physical spaces. They consider how life writing might be motivated by the desire to imagine lives differently.

On a more basic level the ways in which selves are constituted through spatial operations can be seen in the textual emplacement of the subject through deixis. Spatial schemata are tied to the human body and to bodily orientations (left-right, front-back, here-there etc.; see Tuan 1977: 6, 35), which in linguistic terms correspond to indexical pronouns and adverbs (I/here – you/there), that is to the way utterances are tied to a specific location of enunciation. The autobiographical subject becomes the centre of enunciation and organises the world around that centre, an operation that bestows a certain degree of spatio-political agency which is first and foremost textual, and therefore subject to the laws of language.[2] The

---

[2]   Furthermore, the spatio-political aspect is tied to questions of which subjects can occupy the centre and which subjects are relegated to the margins: Who can appropriate the space to claim the position of the I/here? And who is displaced as a result of it? These issues are highly relevant in colonial and postcolonial contexts. Russell West-Pavlov's *Spaces of Fiction/Fictions of Space*, for instance, identifies three modes of spatial representation and deictic activity: the metropolitan writing of imperial space that is firmly located 'in European-speaker-centred deixis' (2010: 13); a diametrically opposed 'post-independence celebration of indigenous space' (115) that reiterates the speaker-centred structure of deixis but transfers it to the newly independent nation; and, finally, texts that in turn critique post-independence nationalism by endowing space and nature with a kind of agency of their own, thus acknowledging 'the debt of writing to the spaces which it portrays' (115).

concept of textual 'space' is strongly motivated by de Certeau's equation of stories with spatial practices and of narrative structures with spatial syntaxes (1984: 115). His 'rhetoric of walking' in which figures of walking translate into figures of speech (100) provides the rationale for Frédéric Regard's bringing together of topology and tropology (2003: 26) in his reflections on the double emplacement of the autobiographical subject as geographical as well as linguistic and discursive – what he calls the 'poetic spacing of the self' (16). Based on a poststructuralist understanding of language and signification, this implies that the subject in language is always displaced, never coincides fully with itself (18), and is, in short, always wandering, always in motion. It is these textual manoeuvrings that the chapters in *Life Writing and Space* address just as much as their autobiographical subjects' physical trajectories and material groundings, or the 'syntax of social relations' (Braidotti 2011: 8) they participate in.

The image of the autobiographical subject always eluding itself has a parallel in how the biographical subject has been represented by recent biographers and life-writing scholars. Where autobiographers have drawn attention to the gap between writing and written subject, biographers have foregrounded the impossibility of capturing their biographees. In *The Old Ways: A Journey on Foot*, for example, Robert Macfarlane follows in the footsteps of nature and war poet Edward Thomas both metaphorically and literally. He took inspiration from Thomas's 'retreading of ancient footpaths and hidden lanes' (a quotation from his wife Helen's recollections, 2012: 309), but also 'set out to know Thomas by walking where he had walked' (326). This desire for origins was ultimately frustrated: Thomas 'mostly eluded me', Macfarlane reflects (326). He remembers how Richard Holmes, adopting a similar method in his 1985 book *Footsteps: Adventures of a Romantic Biographer*, realised that the biographer 'only encountered at best … glimpses of after-glow, retinal ghosts, psychic gossamer' (326). This should not be cast in terms of failure, however. Admitting from the outset the inability to 'know' his subject, the writer not only gives himself considerable creative and indeed spatial freedom – the license to ramble – but also makes space for others to attempt to track his subject (a comprehensive portrait might remove the need). And attempts they must remain. As Jacques Derrida writes in *Archive Fever* (another book that describes the desire for, and impossibility of, uniting footprint with foot): 'the technical structure of the *archiving* archive … determines the structure of the *archivable* content' (1996: 17). Any taxonomy – whether spatial or temporal – imposed upon subjects will exclude aspects of their lives, and, as outlined above, those lives will also always already be mediated by language.

* * *

Engaging both life-writing texts and spatial theory, this book investigates their manifold connections. It shows how concepts of subjectivity draw on spatial ideas and metaphors, and how the grounding or uprooting of the self is understood in terms of place. Scholars have drawn on different vocabularies to distinguish and discuss the relationship between spaces and places: 'country' and 'city' (Williams 1973), 'place' and 'infinity' (Jameson 1990), 'global' and 'local' (Appadurai 1996), 'anthropological places' and 'non-places' (Augé 2008), 'bubbles', 'globes' and 'foams' (the three terms constitute the volume-titles of Peter Sloterdijk's *Spheres* trilogy: 2011, 2014, and 2004), to name a few. While some of these taxonomies are cited in this book, the chapters also draw out the specificities of particular locations. They include comparisons of nineteenth-century Bloomsbury and Marylebone, modernist Berlin and stifling Cambridge, the contemporary thoroughfare and the suburbs. There are also in-between spaces: margins, temporary homes, botanical gardens hosting horticulture from different parts of the world, and the train. This book explores the ways in which life writing is shaped by such spaces, and in turn how life writing might contribute to the ways in which those spaces are imagined and engaged with. Some chapters are particularly concerned with the politics of space: how racial, social or sexual topographies are navigated in autobiographical writing. Others focus on our psychological and phenomenological experiences of space. While most contributions present sustained reflections on the relationship between life writing and space, combining close textual analysis with spatial, postcolonial, psychoanalytic or deconstructionist theory, some more experimental essayistic pieces intersperse critical and autobiographical writing, providing theoretically informed literary explorations of the subject. The book is divided into four parts, each focusing on a different aspect of the spatial dimension of life writing. The principle ideas investigated in each chapter will be outlined in the following sections: Relocating and Reimagining the Self; Traversing Spaces and Texts; Contested Spaces, Precarious Lives; and Space and the Form of Life Writing.

I Relocating and Reimagining the Self

It has already been suggested that the ability to move not only loosens the subject's connection to specific places but also enables them to transcend their present condition (Tuan 1977: 52), in other words: to embark on a journey of the self, which is necessarily accompanied by a sense of displacement. This section explores the ways in which relocation might enable or force a reimagining of the self. The relocation can be textual as well as physical. Changes are parried, managed, responded to and enacted by means of textual emplacement. In his chapter, Matthew Ingleby investigates the uses nineteenth-century writer Anthony Trollope made of fiction, autobiography, and a mixture of the two. He introduces ideas of 'multiple occupancy' and the 'doppelgänger' to think about the phenomenon of writers incorporating past homes and neighbourhoods in their fictional works. He shows how, in Trollope's *Orley Farm*, the author and his fictional characters are made to co-habit. Here, he complicates the idea that returning to 'a site of childhood' is straightforwardly a nostalgic act, whereby space becomes a means of resisting the passing of time. Ingleby acknowledges that correspondences between Trollope's life and writing suggest a 'homesick self', yet he also emphasises that nostalgic urges did not lead him to preserve the spaces of his early life in a fixed state. Ingleby shows how revisiting childhood homes in fiction 'breaks open the Bachelardian shell': Drawing on Lefebvre's interpretation of the 'social contestedness of space', he argues that transposed, fictional homes are places where different 'versions of the authorial self' can be 'tested'. Rather than containing, stabilising and sealing away spaces and selves, the heterogeneous form of life writing discussed in this chapter becomes a means by which bonds between the author and his past might be loosened.

All chapters in this section are concerned with the ways in which life writing mediates feelings about spaces no longer inhabited. Places left behind often accompany subjects on their journeys as welcome or unwanted baggage and infiltrate other places, creating a kind of palimpsest of spatial meanings – as Bachelard writes: 'An entire past comes to dwell in a new house' (1994: 5). Andrew Thacker discusses how two modernist writers represented – at a spatial and temporal distance – their memories of Berlin prior to the accession to power of National Socialism. He describes how the complex intermingling of physical and psychic spaces produced what British novelist and critic Bryher called 'geographical emotions'. Berlin, she writes, catalysed a 'release' of her unconscious; she claims to have 'found herself' in this passionate city. Bryher's writing is compared with two memoirs written about the city by the philosopher and writer Walter Benjamin. The importance of space to his life writing can be seen in how he contemplates 'setting out the sphere of life – bios – graphically on a map'; also in the way in which he rethinks conventional autobiographical form, with its chronological narrative structure; instead, *Berlin Childhood Around 1900* 'relies, like much lyric poetry, upon *images*'. Both Bryher and Benjamin must come to terms with losing Berlin, and the consequent loss of aspects of themselves this entails. As with Ingleby's chapter, the theme of nostalgia becomes important. Thacker describes how Benjamin, preparing himself for a life in exile, sought to 'inoculate' himself against the 'pull of childhood nostalgia' by means of writing.

Spaces of memory, and particularly childhood memory, are also revisited in the memoir Neil Vickers discusses in his chapter: contemporary writer Hilary Mantel's *Giving Up the Ghost*. He notes that every chapter of this book, apart from one, is set in a different house, and explores Mantel's different outlooks or styles of thinking in each location. He describes her 'synaesthesic' perceptions in her grandmother's house, and, drawing on Bachelard, considers how Mantel uses different parts of this house to reflect 'aspects of herself as a child'. He goes on to describe her 'supernatural' experience of her environment and femininity when she moved into her parents' home. A 'succession of non-places' are featured in the final chapter of the memoir, an account of Mantel's life after the diagnosis of her endometriosis. Vickers shows how space and place become metaphors that give expression to difficult experiences in Mantel's life. He develops Foucault's reading of the impact of Galileo's ideas: his decentering of the earth and declaration that 'space was infinite'. Mantel seeks to shelter from the anxiety-provoking qualities of space (which she links with the supernatural) in places: so, for instance, she attempts to 'circumscribe' space by building physical barriers. Moreover, she seeks to 'locate' herself through the process of writing. Drawing on both Foucault and Regard, Vickers casts the memoir as a textual space to rival the testing geographical spaces she inhabited. Where Ingleby shows how the 'dialogism' of fiction undermines the fixity of past spaces, Vickers suggests that Mantel sought to reconcile herself with her past by giving the 'characters in her heterotopia' a belated stability.

II Traversing Spaces and Texts

Movement is also a common denominator of the chapters in this section. They deal with narratives that are structured by the mobility of their protagonists and their traversing of physical spaces as well as literary texts and genres. De Certeau seems a good starting-point to reflect on the specific nexus of these components. He associates the surveying of space with its reading or deciphering and considers walking a spatial practice analogous to writing (Certeau 1984: 92–3). This effectively turns spatial configurations into texts to be written and read. Helga Schwalm's contribution develops this idea further by multiplying the textual levels. She brings together the spatial practice of walking, the literary shaping of places and the creation of the poetic self in the concept of peripatetic life writing. In the texts she discusses, the physical experience of traversing a certain landscape is semantically charged by literary precursors that serve as models for the self-fashioning of the subject. From picturesque travel narratives to Wordsworth's poetic landscapes to de Quincey's autobiography, a rich tapestry of intertextual references unfolds that shape individual topographical experience. Intertextuality produces a form of literary spatialisation, as Julia Kristeva has argued (Kristeva 1986: 35–7), which is superimposed on the spatial movement performed by the walker. Schwalm further unfolds how twentieth-century writers attempted to escape the layering of cultural inscriptions, as in the case of Laurie Lee who placed himself in a topography seemingly devoid of meaning, that is a landscape (the Galician mountains) he could imagine as 'semantically empty' and 'unwritten' because he was oblivious to its cultural meanings. Lee's choice presupposes a profound cultural dislocation from his familiar environment which mirrors the dislocation of identity generated by the 'geopoetical peripatetics' discussed in Schwalm's chapter. Her autobiographical subjects traverse spaces but are not rooted in any place; they are in a state of perpetual motion, a condition best captured in the image of the vagrant self.

In her chapter on Christopher Isherwood's autobiographical and autofictional writings, Eveline Kilian elaborates on geographical and textual displacement as a mode of existence and self-construction. According to Regard, the discursive decentring of the subject, what Butler calls the 'dispossession of the "I"' (2004: 16), is inevitable, since discourse must always already adhere to 'the law of the other, or the law of elsewhere' (Regard 2003: 23). The autobiographical subject of Isherwood's life writing turns this predicament to his own advantage by losing and reinventing himself in and through a series of texts. Isherwood's protagonists are driven by an urge to get away from themselves, from their past and, in terms of geographical and social space, from England, from Englishness, from sexual closetedness and upper-middle-class behaviour. Kilian demonstrates that the systematic merging of the autobiographical and the fictional is vital to this project in that Isherwood achieves the effacement of his old self by creating a series of interconnected but different personae distributed across a network of autofictional intertexts whose protagonists do not coincide. Geographical movement (from England to Berlin to other European countries, to China and, finally, to America) is accompanied by textual spatialisations that disperse the autobiographical subject beyond containment and gradually divest him of his extra-textual moorings. Kilian shows how the subject's movements from place to place are as much instrumental in the shedding of his former self as they are in the construction of a new identity. The textual meanderings of the self go hand in hand with a vision he has of himself as a permanent foreigner and of the space of unbelonging as his true destination.

In Martin Klepper and Alexandra Wagner's chapter on life writing during the Depression era, the protagonists' intertextual engagements are situated on the level of genre. The autobiographical subjects of Jerre Mangione's *An Ethnic at*

Large and Richard Wright's *Black Boy (American Hunger)* appropriate existing cultural scripts for the description of their life journeys (the bildungsroman and, in Wright's case, also the slave narrative) and map them onto politically charged axes of power. Klepper and Wagner rely on Bakhtin's concept of the chronotope as a nodal point that connects time, space, crisis and genre and that reflects on genre as a specific configuration of knowledge production. Spatial configurations function as cognitive maps in these texts with certain spaces signifying access and social mobility and others exclusion, especially in times of racial segregation. In contrast to Isherwood in the previous chapter, who starts out from a comfortable and privileged background, the social position of these subjects is much more precarious. Mangione, the son of Sicilian immigrants, and the African American Wright are socially and economically on the margins of society. Their journeys are as much about finding and pursuing their vocation as writers as they are about navigating the 'obstacles and gateways' of American society as outsiders and achieving a state of belonging. Their aim is certainly not a (further) decentring of the self, because this has always been their existential condition and remains a threat throughout. The term 'critical topographies' Klepper and Wagner employ points to the importance of a precise contextual and material grounding of any analysis of spaces and selves. In their readings, the autobiographical pattern of crisis and resolution is linked to a very specific economic crisis, the Great Depression, which triggers the 'quest for a safe and sustaining space' as well as a critical questioning of the social inequalities encoded by spaces.

III   Contested Spaces, Precarious Lives

Foucault's work on power and resistance as ubiquitous concomitants not only of discourse but also of social relations has had a lasting impact on the view of space as a contested field of differently motivated constructions. In recent decades, the gendering of spaces has come into focus, as in the work of feminist geographers Gillian Rose (1993), Doreen Massey (1994) and Linda McDowell (1999). It is discussed in various collections of essays (for example Higonnet and Templeton 1994, Nast and Pile 1998; see also the periodical *Gender, Place & Culture: a Journal of Feminist Geography*) and studies of specific periods or individual authors (e.g. Wilson 1992, Duncan 1996, Frank 2003, D'Souza and McDonough 2006, part I of Snaith and Whitworth 2007); other critics more specifically deal with the queering of spaces (see Ingram et al. 1997, Delaney 1999, Bell and Valentine 2005, Chisholm 2005, Abraham 2009). And practically every book on postcolonialism or transnational migration more generally (see e.g. Jackson, Crang and Dwyer 2011, Ponzanesi and Merolla 2005) addresses the politics of space with respect to ethnicity. Although Said, one of the most prominent postcolonial critics, did not rely on the spatial theories discussed above, his writings correspond very closely to the notion of space as expressive of a specific cultural and political order. A central tenet of his early study *Orientalism* is that 'the Orient' is a (Western) construction predicated on the opposition between 'Orient' and 'Occident' with the relationship between the two being one of 'power, of domination, of varying degrees of a complex hegemony' (1991: 5). And in *Culture and Imperialism* he states even more succinctly: 'Just as none of us is outside or beyond geography, none of us is completely free from the struggle over geography' (1994: 6). When it comes to postcolonial life writing, questions of locatedness, of geographical placement and displacement, of spatial belonging and struggles over the meaning of places and spaces are of paramount importance (Moore-Gilbert 2009: 53) and are reflected in the 'politically invested cartography' (Braidotti 2011: 4) these texts present. Given that subjects are constituted across different axes of differentiation (ethnicity, gender, class, sexuality, age etc.), an intersectional analysis that takes into account the manifold interactions of these categorisations and the 'kinds of power differentials and/or constraining normativities' they bring forth (Lykke 2010: 50; see also Bhabha 2004: 2), suggests itself as a productive method to approach the reciprocal mapping of selves and spaces.

While social markers such as class, sexuality or ethnicity will have already figured in the previous chapters, they are foregrounded in this section which specifically engages with gender, ethnicity, migration and/or the condition of (post)coloniality in life-writing texts in different historical and cultural contexts. Elizabeth H. Jones draws on both postcolonial studies and feminism in her discussion of two Algerian women's autobiographical texts that are set against the backdrop of the post-Independence era. She shows how material spaces are shaped by power relations, notably with respect to cultural identity and gender hierarchies. Especially for women, a conflictual terrain of contradictory alliances opens up in a context where the wish for female empowerment is faced with an increasing gender conservatism, which reinforces spatial restrictions of women and their bodies. However, space can also be turned into a tool of resistance, as Jones demonstrates with Malika Mokeddem's *Mes Hommes*, whose protagonist engages in 'out of place' bodily performances and tries to inhabit a state of 'foreignness' by maintaining a distance from both Algerian and French societies. For the authors discussed in this chapter, the literary text and its spatial mappings allows for an imaginative balancing of the autobiographical subjects' different strands of affiliation and identification. Jones reads these texts as examples of a postcolonial literary cartography that has both an existential and a political function. They not only provide a space for these subjects to locate themselves through literature but they also intervene in the country's ideological struggles over cultural self-definitions.

Kathrin Tordasi's chapter on Katherine Mansfield, a New Zealand writer of British heritage, focuses on another kind of liminal subject who tries to negotiate the in-between space of coloniser/colonised. Her reading of the topography of the self in Katherine Mansfield's notebooks and letters dwells on Mansfield's self-placements at the intersection of different, and in a sense competing, places and spaces (New Zealand and London; the colonised parts of New Zealand and the New Zealand bush and Māori culture), all steeped in colonial history. She describes the autobiographical subject as a threshold where self and other converge and where distinctions are blurred and suspended, a process mirrored in the numerous depictions of merging landscapes in Mansfield's notebooks. Tordasi uses the photographic metaphor of double exposure to capture this specific spatial production of the self, an arrangement which superimposes body and landscape in the text. We could say that in postcolonial terms, Mansfield's construction of a liminal self highlights the historical and political reality of a 'nation split within itself' and becomes a marker of both the otherness within and the heterogeneity of New Zealand's population (Bhabha 2004: 212–15). In feminist terms, the crossing of borders and the merging of sides prefigures the more radical epistemological position of the '*mestiza* consciousness' (Anzaldúa 1999: 102), whose unruly force uproots dualistic thinking. Its creative energy derives from not belonging to any country and is instrumental in imagining and building cross-cultural networks – with all the conflicts and contradictions that this might entail.

Anne-Julia Schoen addresses the intersection of class and ethnicity in her chapter on Isaac Rosenberg, the son of Jewish immigrants whose family settled in London's East End. Based on a close analysis of his letters from 1911 until his death in 1918, Schoen traces Rosenberg's attempts to overcome the material and spatial restrictions of his home and his job at an engraver's workshop in the City by projecting poetry as an intellectual space that transcends these limiting parameters. She evokes the 'compartmentalised cultural map' of London and Rosenberg's outsider status on the margins of the literary market. She argues that he used his letters to friends and potential supporters as a means to procure greater access to this coveted cultural field from which he felt excluded. The reasons for his exclusion may have been more complex than Rosenberg suggested, however. Schoen demonstrates that his own self-stylisation as a multiply deprived artist did not match the frequent support he received from his friends and family to further his literary and artistic aspirations. There is similarly a telling gap between the freedom and creativity he imagined a change of location would bring about and the actual outcome of his stay in Cape Town, which did not result in an outburst of creativity. A little like Isherwood, he seemed to find it difficult to shed the habits, mental imprints and patterns of feeling associated with his 'home' when moving to another place.

IV   Space and the Form of Life Writing

Chapters in this section show how a focus on space, rather than time, has impacted upon the form of life writing; some also consider how different types of life writing have the capacity to change the ways in which spaces are imagined and used. The extent to which the foregrounding of space has left its mark on life-writing research can be seen in the emergence of hybrid terms for describing new textual forms that blend life writing with space, some of which are listed in Schwalm's chapter: 'autobiogeography', 'psychogeobiography' and 'eco-autobiography'. This volume also discusses experimental forms of life writing that do not align neatly with any of these more recent genres, such as digital forms using new technologies.

Frédéric Regard's chapter considers marginalia (material written in the margin of a book or manuscript), showing how under-recognised forms of, and spaces for, life writing might yet be found in paper media. Hélène Cixous's annotations of an unpublished manuscript by Jacques Derrida in her *Portrait of Jacques Derrida as a Young Jewish Saint* are shown to re-voice the biographee, drawing attention to aspects of the text that might not otherwise have been heard. Through the use of marginalia 'the dead and the living are summoned on the same stage'. Making space for ghosts is an ethical act. The biographer does not replace the lost object with another; instead, she allows it to return. The equation of biography with the burying of the biographee was famously made in Lytton Strachey's 1918 volume of biographical sketches, *Eminent Victorians*. Of the weighty Victorian biographies against which he compared his briefer book he surmised: 'They are familiar as the *cortège* of the undertaker, and wear the same air of slow, funereal barbarism' (2003: 6). Virginia Woolf, in *Orlando: A Biography*, similarly linked the writing of biography with death: 'the first duty of the biographer ... is to plod, without looking to right or left, in the indelible footprints of truth; unenticed by flowers; regardless of shade; on and on methodically till we fall plump into the grave and write *finis* on the tombstone above our heads' (1928: 62). Might a focus on space halt this funeral procession? Regard argues that 'deconstructionist literary portraiture' might preclude the ritual burials of biography. It is, he argues, in 'marginalia' that 'revenants find an appropriate space'.

Where Regard's spatial focus offers new ways of thinking about the archive (and also the relationship between margin and centre, biographer and biographee), the two chapters that follow are explicitly concerned with the structuring of archives around spatial taxonomies. Hope Wolf reflects on the burgeoning of digital local life-writing archives in recent years. She focuses on one contemporary example: a collection of life writing (textual, visual, sonic and filmic) contributed by people who live and/or work on the Strand (a Central London thoroughfare). She offers a critical analysis of this project (*Strandlines*) and readings of the material collected in order to consider what the future of this and similar enterprises could be; here, she is particularly interested in their capacity to transform spatial practices. Wolf considers what effect the privileging of certain forms of life writing, and of certain methods of collecting, might have on how space is represented in the archive. One of her central arguments is that the premium placed upon the 'story' and upon digital means of generating life writing risks producing material that is complicit with the status quo. Drawing attention to the quantity of stories of eccentricity and encounter in the *Strandlines* archive, she suggests that while they implicitly oppose demands for efficiency and uniformity placed upon the subject in an urban working environment, they can also be seen to detract from more alienating aspects of life in that context. However, she goes on to argue that the archive seems less complicitous if it is viewed as a counter-site, showing what living and working on the Strand might be like were the kinds of incidents described to happen with greater frequency. This considered, Wolf argues that archivists should not only experiment with the forms of life writing they request, and with the spaces for life writing offered to potential contributors, they should also turn their attention to reimagining the function of the archive – as a space that looks to the future as well as to the past.

Wolf's chapter, and also those that follow, James Attlee's and Clare Brant's, reflect upon the position of the researcher and writer. So doing their work aligns with recent attempts to fuse autobiographical reflection with critical practice (see Jolly 2011; also Rendell 2010). In his work, and in his chapter, Attlee shows openness to the influence of spatial contexts. Using Iain Sinclair's terminology, he describes himself as a 'ped' rather than a 'pod'. Writing takes place not in the tightly sealed shell of the home; rather, material is gathered by means of movement and relocation. This was an essential part of a process that culminated in a book about Cowley Road in Oxford (*Isolarion: A Different Oxford Journey,*

2007), and another that charted his search of moonlight (*Nocturne: A Journey in Search of Moonlight*, 2011). He is now the First Great Western Writer on the Train, and is exploring the possibility of using digital technologies to connect others with this project. Foregrounding how space impacts upon the form of his life writing, Attlee notes that he begins his chapter from a park bench: a space in which distractions can 'find their way onto the page, become part of the work'. This decision enables him to resist conveying the impression that he is presenting a final, objective description of his method – noting that his chapter has been written at a specific time and from a specific place, he makes space for later re-visitings of his subject. Close attention to his immediate environment has further advantages. Attlee reflects on how it enables him to 'travel in depth'. The spatial focus of his research allows him to make and perceive powerful associations between images and stories from different historical moments: 'strange resonances that echo down the centuries'.

Clare Brant's closing literary meditation on a lost house also interweaves autobiographical with topographical reflection. 'The professor' writes from a space between a house once occupied (destroyed by fire) and a future home that is in the process of being rebuilt. Loss and rebuilding are shown to prompt questions that are both philosophical and personal: for instance, what constitutes a 'home'? Interpretations of experience, theory, literature and life writing are combined to answer such questions, and to reconsider the relationship between spaces and selves. The form of the chapter shows the difficulties of rebuilding – considered symbolically, as well as materially. If there is a split between the 'home self' and the 'fire self', how is it possible to use the autobiographical 'I'? 'The professor' is observed from a distance, although the chapter is punctuated by her thoughts. Returning to Regard's idea of haunting, this elegiac piece is critically aware of the gap between description and lost object. Perhaps this is why it begins with a nod to storytelling: 'On a dark and winter's night'. It struggles with the idea that terrible beauties might spring from destruction, but also recognises the need for the consolations of narrative, poetry and language. In this way, Brant's chapter, which is both a work about and of life writing, not only reflects upon the way in which the burned house becomes a series of memories, but also enacts this transformation.

* * *

The cover image of this book, and the image that concludes this introduction, are photographs of an installation by artist Colden Drystone (formerly Tom Barnett) called 'Believing in Time Travel' (2014). Although the title suggests a temporal focus, his work resonates with some of the main spatial themes of this volume that will be briefly revisited here by way of conclusion. He completed the work while artist in residence at Girton College Cambridge (where one of the editors of this book was also residing). Over the course of a year he covered the walls of the cottage in which he was living and working with clay. On the walls, and in the numerous paintings and sketches he worked on during the residency, he recorded, as if keeping a diary, everyday inspirations, some of which were immediately outside (animals), some of which came from further afield (a cricket score, for example, heard on the radio). 'I've brought something of the world into the studio', he wrote in the booklet accompanying the exhibition of the installation (Drystone/Barnett 2014). This was epitomised by his decision to cover the floor of the house/studio with grass and to paint in watercolour the sky on the ceiling. However, the outside that had been brought in was ostensibly transformed: the laid turf was much more pristine than the wild grass outside; the blue was bluer than any Cambridge sky. The in-between space was gold, blurring distinctions between the paintings displayed (some were also gold) and the surfaces on which they were hung.

Life Writing and Space explores how mental space transforms physical space, and the ways in which alternative realities are imagined in creative spaces. As the autobiographical 'I' attaches coherence to the nebulous subject (even the most documentary forms of life writing involve distortion – art and non-art blur), so the cloudy sky and wild grass were abstracted in Drystone's installation. In some respects he treated the house like a Bachelardian house: memories were literally inscribed upon its walls. Yet it is also clear that he did not choose to make it a shelter from the world outside. Inside and outside were inverted. This was a deviant space. Chapters in this book are also interested in deviant spaces. They discuss how the built environment might produce certain kinds of behaviour, but also the ways in which spatial practices veer from norms and imperatives – and how life writing might encourage such practices. Drystone's use of the house was not conventional. Owned by an institution, needing to be passed on to the next tenant, it had to be painted white at the end of the residency; there was a limitation to modifications that could be made to the structure of the building and its fittings. Yet the house, a contested space, was also a studio: a site for experimentation, for creative and personal exploration. Can a transformation of the self take place without a spatial transformation? To return to the 'journey' metaphor this introduction began with: If it is necessary to stay in one place, then must one find other ways of relocating the self? Life writing need not have a linear, progressive structure; lives can be organised spatially, around images and episodes. This will not replace time with space, but will rather constitute a shift of focus and perspective, a reimagining of the one in relation to the other. So, to view the walls of Drystone's house, a kind of palimpsest of lived experience, was to begin to believe in time travel.

References

Abraham, J. 2009. *Metropolitan Lovers: The Homosexuality of Cities.* Minneapolis: University of Minnesota Press.

Anzaldúa, G. 1999. *Borderlands – La Frontera: The New Mestiza* [1987]. San Francisco: Aunt Lute Books.

Appadurai, A. 1996. *Modernity at Large: Cultural Dimensions of Globalization.* Minneapolis: University of Minnesota Press.

Augé, M. 2008. *Non-Places: An Introduction to Supermodernity* [1992], translated by J. Howe. London: Verso.

Bachelard, G. 1994. *The Poetics of Space* [1958], translated by M. Jolas. Boston: Beacon Press.

Bachmann-Medick, D. 2006. *Cultural Turns: Neuorientierungen in den Kulturwissenschaften.* Reinbek bei Hamburg: Rowohlt.

Bell, D. and Valentine, G. (eds.) 2005. *Mapping Desire: Geographies of Desire.* London, New York: Routledge.

Bhabha, H. 2004. *The Location of Culture* [1994]. London and New York: Routledge.

Braidotti, R. 2011. *Nomadic Subjects: Embodiment and Sexual Difference in Contemporary Feminist Theory.* 2nd Edition. New York: Columbia University Press.

Brittain, V. 1978. *Testament of Youth: An Autobiographical Study of the Years 1900–1925* [1933]. London: Virago.

Buckley, J.H. 1974. *Season of Youth: The Bildungsroman from Dickens to Golding.* Cambridge, Massachusetts: Harvard University Press.

Butler, J. 2004. *Undoing Gender.* New York and London: Routledge.

Chisholm, D. 2005. *Queer Constellations: Subcultural Space in the Wake of the City.* Minneapolis and London: University of Minneapolis Press.

Cresswell, T. 1996. *In Place/Out of Place: Geography, Ideology and Transgression.* Minneapolis and London: University of Minnesota Press.

D'Souza, A. and McDonough, T. (eds.) 2006. *The Invisible Flâneuse? Gender, Public Space, and Visual Culture in Nineteenth-Century Paris.* Manchester and New York: Manchester University Press.

De Certeau, M. 1984. *The Practice of Everyday Life* [1980], translated by S. Rendall. Berkeley: University of California Press.

Delany, R. 1999. *Times Square Blue, Times Square Red.* New York and London: New York University Press.

Derrida, J. 1996. *Archive Fever: A Freudian Impression* [1995], translated by E. Prenowitz. Chicago: University of Chicago Press.

Drystone, C. (formerly Tom Barnett). 2014. *Believing in Time Travel.* Booklet accompanying the exhibition 'Believing in Time Travel' by Tom Barnett hosted by Girton College, Cambridge.

Duncan, N. (ed.) 1996. *BodySpace: Destabilizing Geographies of Gender and Sexuality.* London and New York: Routledge.

Foucault, M. 1986. Of other spaces [1967 and 1984], translated by J. Miskowiec. *diacritics: a review of contemporary criticism*, 16(1), 22–7.

Frank, S. 2003. *Stadtplanung im Geschlechterkampf: Stadt und Geschlecht in der Großstadtentwicklung des 19. und 20. Jahrhunderts.* Opladen: Leske + Budrich.

Harvey, D. 1995. *The Condition of Postmodernity: An Enquiry into the Origins of Cultural Change* [1990]. Oxford: Blackwell.

Hemecker, W. and Heumann, K. (eds.) 2014. *Hofmannsthal. Orte: 20 biographische Erkundungen*, edited with the assistance of C. Bamberg. Wien: Paul Zsolnay Verlag.

Higonnet, M.R. and Templeton, J. (eds.) 1994. *Reconfigured Spheres: Feminist Explorations of Literary Space.* Amherst: University of Massachusetts Press.

Ingram, G.B. et al. (eds.) 1997. *Queers in Space: Communities, Public Places, Sites of Resistance.* Seattle: Bay Press.

Jackson, P., Crang, P. and Dwyer, C. (eds.) 2011. *Transnational Spaces* [2004]. London and New York: Routledge.

Jameson, F. 1990. Modernism and Imperialism, in *Nationalism, Colonialism and Literature*, edited by T. Eagleton, F. Jameson and E. W. Said. Minneapolis: University of Minnesota Press, 43–66.

Jolly, M. 2011. Life writing as critical creative practice. *Literature Compass*, 8(12), 878–89.

Joyce, J. 1977. *A Portrait of the Artist as a Young Man* [1916]. St. Albans: Triad/Panther.

Keith, M. and Pile, S. 1993. *Place and the Politics of Identity.* London and New York: Routledge.

Kilian, E. 2014. Literarische Heterotopien: Ermöglichungsräume für intergeschlechtliche Subjekte, in *Inter*geschlechtliche Körperlichkeiten: Diskurs/Begegnungen im Erzähltext*, edited by A. Baier and S. Hochreiter. Wien: Zaglossus, 39–66.

Kristeva, J. 1986. Word, dialogue and novel [1966], translated by A. Jardine, T. Gora and L.S. Roudiez, in *The Kristeva Reader*, edited by T. Moi. New York: Columbia University Press, 35–61.

Lefebvre, H. 1991. *The Production of Space* [1974], translated by D. Nicholson-Smith. Oxford: Blackwell.

Lykke, N. 2010. *Feminist Studies: A Guide to Intersectional Theory, Methodology and Writing*. New York and London: Routledge.

Macfarlane, R. 2012. *The Old Ways: A Journey on Foot*. London: Hamish Hamilton.

Marcus, L. 1994. *Auto/biographical Discourses: Theory, Criticism, Practice*. Manchester and New York: Manchester University Press.

Massey, D. 1994. *Space, Place and Gender*. Cambridge: Polity.

Massey, D. 2005. *For Space*. London: Sage.

McDowell. L. 1999. *Gender, Identity and Place: Understanding Feminist Geographies*. Cambridge: Polity.

Mill, J. S. 1989. *Autobiography* [1873]. London: Penguin.

Moore-Gilbert, B. 2009. *Postcolonial Life-Writing: Culture, Politics and Self-Representation*. London and New York: Routledge.

Moretti, F. 2000. *The Way of the World: The Bildungsroman in European Culture* [1987], translated by A. Sbragia. London: Verso.

Nast, H.J. and Pile, S. (eds.) 1998. *Places through the Body*. London and New York: Routledge.

Ponzanesi, S. and Merolla, S. (eds.) 2005. *Migrant Cartographies: New Cultural and Literary Spaces in Post-colonial Europe*. Lanham: Lexington Books.

Regard, F. 2003. Topologies of the self: Space and life-writing, in *Mapping the Self: Space, Identity, Discourse in British Auto/Biography*. Saint-Étienne: Publications de l'Université de Saint-Étienne, 15–30.

Relph, E. 1976. *Place and Placelessness*. London: Pion Limited.

Rendell, J. 2010. *Site-Writing: The Architecture of Art Criticism*. London: I.B. Tauris.

Ricoeur, Paul. 1991. Life in quest of narrative, in *On Paul Ricoeur: Narrative and Interpretation*, edited by D. Wood. London and New York: Routledge, 20–33.

Rose, G. 1993. *Feminism and Geography: The Limits of Geographical Knowledge*. Cambridge: Polity.

Said, E.W. 1991. *Orientalism: Western Conceptions of the Orient* [1978]. London: Penguin.

Said, E.W. 1994. *Culture and Imperialism* [1993]. London: Vintage.

Said, E. W. and Mohr, J. 1999. *After the Last Sky: Palestinian Lives* [1986]. New York: Columbia University Press.

Sloterdijk, P. 2004. *Schäume, Sphären* III. Frankfurt am Main: Suhrkamp.

Sloterdijk, P. 2011. *Bubbles, Spheres*, Volume 1: *Microspherology* [1998], translated by W. Hoban. Los Angeles: Semiotext(e).

Sloterdijk, P. 2014. *Globes, Spheres*, Volume 2: *Macrospherology* [1999], translated by W. Hoban. Los Angeles: Semiotext(e).

Snaith, A. and Whitworth, M.H. (eds.) 2007. *Locating Woolf: The Politics of Space and Place*. Basingstoke and New York: Palgrave Macmillan.

Soja, E. W. 1989. *Postmodern Geographies: The Reassertion of Space in Critical Social Theory*. London and New York: Verso.

Soja, E. W. 1996. *Thirdspace: Journeys to Los Angeles and Other Real-and-Imagined Places*. Cambridge, Massachusetts and Oxford: Blackwell.

Strachey, L. 2003. *Eminent Victorians* [1918]. Oxford: Oxford University Press.

Tally Jr., R. T. 2013. *Spatiality*. Abingdon and New York: Routledge.

Tuan, Y.-F. 1977. *Space and Place: The Perspective of Experience*. Minneapolis and London: University of Minneapolis Press.

Warf, B. and Arias, S. (eds) 2009. *The Spatial Turn: Interdisciplinary Perspectives*. London and New York: Routledge.

West-Pavlov, R. 2010. *Spaces of Fiction/Fictions of Space: Postcolonial Place and Literary DeiXis*. Basingstoke and New York: Palgrave Macmillan.

Williams, R. 1973. *The Country and the City*. London: Chatto and Windus.

Wilson, E. 1992. *The Sphinx in the City: Urban Life, the Control of Disorder, and Women*. Berkeley: The University of California Press.

Woolf, V. 1928. *Orlando: A Biography*. London: Hogarth Press.

Plate 1   'Believing in Time Travel'
Source: © Colden Drystone, 2014. Photography: © Tim Smyth.

I
RELOCATING AND
REIMAGINING THE SELF

Chapter 1

Multiple Occupancy:
Residency and Retrospection in Trollope's
Orley Farm and *An Autobiography*

Matthew Ingleby

In the nineteenth century authors frequently incorporated autobiographical sites into their fiction, as Anthony Trollope did in *Orley Farm* (1862). A text that thematises the legal contestation of space, its characters' residences resemble or are coincidentally located within houses and neighbourhoods the author knew early on in his life. Unlike some other examples of this practice, however, Trollope 'outs' this autobiographical spatiality of *Orley Farm* in his posthumously published *Autobiography* (1883), drawing attention to the material parallel of the property named in the book's title. Thus, the later writer signals the way his earlier novel had already participated through its spatial compass in a veiled form of life writing, and seems to open up his fiction to the speculation of biographically minded critics. But the re-use of childhood homes does not straightforwardly unlock the door to the past: rather the act breaks open these remembered sites within the retrospective authorial imagination and submits them to the dialogism of fiction. These sites become, in the process, 'multiply occupied', by fictional characters as well as past authorial selves, the stories and personalities obtaining to each interacting with and affecting one another. In subjecting sites that are usually sealed off in the nostalgic dream-world of autobiography to the social plurality of fiction, a species of life writing is borne, which, in the interstices between genres, evades the strictures of both. Trollope's acknowledgement of the spatial intertextuality he had practiced illumines a cryptic form of life writing between the two publications quite different to that we tend to associate with this period. Reading into the residential coincidences we encounter an unannounced, revisionary, experimental form of writing the self, which incorporates alternative fates and dreamt possibilities; a form in which selfhood is dispersed and where the borderlines of self and other are productively redrawn.

Residential Coincidence

It was a relatively common phenomenon in the nineteenth century for authors to make use of avatars of homes and neighbourhoods known intimately to them in order to house characters in their novels. Such residential requisitions occur in all but the most geographically exotic or speculative of texts, and can be found in historical, gothic and science fiction, as well as realism and naturalism.

At times, the narrator makes some nod to the reader to acknowledge the autobiographical derivation of settings. For instance, in *Old Saint Paul's* (1841), a historical novel set in the 1660s by William Harrison Ainsworth, the hero Leonard Holt and his friends harbour from the plague in Kensal Green, where the author was residing at the time of writing. In the original edition, Ainsworth included a prefatory note with the following address appended: 'Kensal Manor House, Harrow Road'. Thus the author quietly writes himself into the space he fictionally reproduces. More often, however, the spatial connection to the author's life is entirely concealed from the reader. In *Vanity Fair* (1848), references to Amelia Sedley shopping on Southampton Row covertly commemorate the part of William Makepeace Thackeray's childhood which he spent there in his aunt's house. The placing in that novel of the Todds in Great Coram Street, meanwhile, faintly recalls the years between 1838 and 1843 in which the author let a house on the same road. When she was living unmarried in Mecklenburgh Square with the publisher John Maxwell, Mary Elizabeth Braddon wrote a series of novels including *Eleanor's Victory* (1863) and *The Lady's Mile* (1865) that make use of the immediate locality, culminating in *Birds of Prey* (1867) and *Charlotte's Inheritance* (1868). In these sensation fictions, with which she launched her own periodical *Belgravia*, Braddon makes the residential trajectory of characters closely mirror her own from inner-London Bloomsbury to the south-west suburbs of Richmond and Wimbledon, where she had recently bought a house with the proceeds from her bestselling *Lady Audley's Secret* (1862). In none of these cases do the texts announce in any way what we might call the multiple occupancy of these sites within the authorial imagination: the way they are peopled not only with fictional characters but also with spectral versions of the past or present self.

Towards the *fin de siècle*, the appropriation of places of residence within imaginative literature proliferates. In George Gissing's semi-naturalist *Workers in the Dawn* (1880), the extent to which the story of an idealistic young man's disastrous marriage to a prostitute named Carrie Mitchell is a transcription from the author's own life with Nell Harrison seems to be confirmed by the strict coincidence of lodging houses in which Gissing stayed in the 1870s and those inhabited by Arthur Golding, the tragic hero. William Morris's utopian romance *News from Nowhere* (1890) traces a very thorough itinerary around most of the places with which the author was intimately associated, including Hammersmith, Bloomsbury, and Oxford. The geographies of all three of George du Maurier's occult fictions, *Peter Ibbetson* (1891), *Trilby* (1894) and *The Martian* (1897), extensively parallel the author's lived experience of specific sites in London, Paris and elsewhere in Europe. The narrator of the extra-terrestrial invasion thriller *The War of the Worlds* (1898) lives in Woking, the same town in which H. G. Wells resided, when he was writing the book.

There are many examples, but this selection serves to demonstrate the commonness of the practice in the period and thus renders surprising the fact that it has as yet received no substantial critical attention from scholars as a pervasive yet quite distinct mode of life writing. This lack of analysis is perhaps unsurprising in that one naïve understanding of realism which is a cliché of popular literary criticism assumes fiction writers make use of whatever 'comes to hand'; that they standardly write about what they 'know' from primary experience. Applying this empiricist principle to the production of imagined geographies, writers would be expected to write first and foremost about the places in which they are residing or have at some point resided. But the retrospective quality of this latter form of appropriated spatiality suggests an authorial agenda that exceeds the purely pragmatic and involves in addition some kind of nostalgic impulse.

According to Svetlana Boym, nostalgia bears an intrinsic connection to spatiality: tracing the concept's origins in the enlightenment medicalisation of homesickness or *maladie du pays*, she argues that the feeling classically relates to some kind of 'elsewhere': 'Nostalgia (from *nostos* – return home, and *algia* – longing) is a longing for a home that no longer exists or has never existed' (2001: xiii). Past homes, neighbourhoods and countries are the prime objects of this retrospective longing. According to Boym, however, the yearning of the exile or the nostalgic for another space is actually a reprocessing of a more insoluble feeling of *temporal* dislocation. Homesickness is a strategy for coping with the alienating temporalities of modernity:

> At first glance, nostalgia appears to be a longing for a place, but it is actually a yearning for a different time – the time of our childhood, the slower rhythms of our dreams. In a broader sense, nostalgia is a rebellion against the modern idea of time, the time of history and progress. The nostalgic desires to obliterate history and turn it into private or collective mythology, to revisit time like space, refusing to surrender to the irreversibility of time that plagues the human condition. (Boym 2001: xv)

Retrospective attention to and longing for previously inhabited homes and neighbourhoods is, then, a product of and 'coeval with' (Boym 2001: xvi) modernity, and might be seen as an attempt to slow down or reverse time, spatiality affording a kind of flexibility or reversibility temporality disallows. In this light, the nineteenth-century practice of cryptically writing past places into fiction appears to constitute a symptomatic expression of the wider cultures of nostalgia that operated in the shadows of Victorian modernity (see Dames 2001).

But transcription into fiction of spaces of nostalgia imposes generic mutations upon the autobiographical material. Borrowing spaces from one's past to redeploy in the plurally populated and dialogic domain of fiction constitutes a risky operation, with unpredictable consequences.[1] Just as sharing space in material reality involves both negotiation and contestation, each new intervention into imagined space implicitly heralds not only harmonious concord and resonance with what is already there, but also friction and contention.[2] Turning back to our small survey of examples from nineteenth-century literature, in many cases, it seems likely that this friction is precisely what has attracted the writer to the setting in the first place. These undeclared fictionalisations of autobiographical space might function as partial doppelgängers of the originals, the apparent replication enabling a revision or inversion of the self to be acted out. Whereas in more straightforwardly autobiographical novels, such as instances of the *Künstlerroman*, fictionalised versions of lived space can be claustrophobically restricted by the conservative demands of genre, the more pervasive and more open-ended residential coincidences between fiction and the lives of authors offer us much more ambivalent fragments of a submerged life writing, pertaining to alternative fates dreamt rather than actual experiences lived.

Via the 'multiple occupancies' that operate in cryptically autobiographical fictional spaces, sites become modulated through the narratives staged in them, performing variations upon what we can glean from biographical sources was the author's lived experience of the house or neighbourhood. Thus, some of Thackeray's fictional neighbours carry through with the legal training he himself abandoned; Gissing's sensitive fictional fellow lodging-house tenant kills

---

[1]   My understanding of the novel as structurally dialogic derives, of course, from Mikhail Bakhtin (1981), especially the essay 'Discourse in the Novel' (1934–5), which explains how fiction is made up of different voices, none of which can claim absolute authority.

[2]   As Henri Lefebvre's *The Production of Space* (originally published in 1974) argues, space is defined by contestation. Rendering autobiographical space in fiction entails intervening in a live field, inscribing a new story upon a pre-existing palimpsest of cultural narratives and everyday practices.

himself before managing to escape the difficulties of his youth. There are also extreme cases: Morris's dreamer wakes up in his very own post-revolutionary London to discover a kind of social wish-fulfilment has taken place; Du Maurier's metropolitan man of letters, Barty Josselin, is granted super-powers, enabling him to transcend ordinary physical dimensions, such as the localities he co-habits with his author, in order to commune with aliens; Wells's alter-ego watches much more bellicose Martians ravage Earth. In these cases, it can be seen that the spatially autobiographical quality of these fictions allows for inflated, diminished, distorted, or distended versions of the authorial self to be tested, smuggled in as they are without narratorial declaration of the authorial geographies they mirror. Past regrets and ambitions are revived and rehearsed; nightmarish failures or utopian triumphs are recapitulated. In these re-used sites, we witness the covert exercise or exorcism of alternative selves.

For Bachelard, intimately known space has a universal phenomenological significance and is the 'not-I that protects the I' (1994: 5). A kind of 'shell' (4) that separates the self from the universe, this habitat becomes sedimented into the psyche of the resident; indeed, there is an 'interminable dialectic' between residence and resident, as 'the sheltered being gives perceptible limits to his shelter' (5), each carrying the imprint of the other. Because of this tight organic fit the shell-homes of our past, and particularly of our childhood, follow us around in our dream-life even after we have left them – in a physical sense – behind. These imagined houses of nostalgia are enduring but difficult to put into words:

> ... the real houses of memory, the houses to which we return in dreams, the houses
> that are rich in unalterable oneirism, do not readily lend themselves to description.
> To describe them would be like showing them to visitors. We cannot perhaps tell
> everything about the present, but about the past! The first, the oneirically definitive
> house, must retain its shadows. (Bachelard 1994: 13)

Writing about sites intimately known to the author appears deliberately to transgress some kind of taboo by showing visitors around; it might introduce foreign material to contaminate the sealed environment and interfere with the streamlined self-universe relations Bachelard imagines. Fictional appropriations of lived space, indeed, might disrupt the shelter-sheltered dialectic more fundamentally than welcoming a temporary visitor would, the additional fictional residents making the site rather messier and overcrowded in the authorial imagination, more like the shared space of boarding houses than the hermetic solitude invoked in *The Poetics of Space*. Fictional characters and the traces of past or present selves there might mingle; rub off on one another; draw out something mutually new from an encounter. What is more, they might collide or clash in these plural, multiply occupied, imagined spaces.

What kind of life writing might we be able to discern if we chose to listen out for and transcribe the implicit dialogue between the multiple occupants of one intertextually imagined space? These coincidental geographies suggest a highly ambivalent variety of life writing-between-the-lines, which can be found in the interstices between fictional and autobiographical genres. In *The Radical Aesthetic*, Isobel Armstrong affirms the value of Bachelard's spatial thinking because of its openness to the complex affective currents of our interior lives, but she also argues its incompleteness, finding in Lefebvre's account of the social contestedness of space a kind of corrective complement. *The Production of Space* provides what she calls the 'realism' the phenomenologist's 'paradigm requires' (2000: 223). A critical bridge between these apparently incommensurable theories is necessary, Armstrong argues, if we are to understand the self as both a phenomenological and a social entity. Bridging Bachelard and Lefebvre seems relatedly necessary for a fuller appreciation of the more covert ways in which that entity might write itself. As Laura Marcus has eloquently explained, autobiography has long been treated as a structurally precarious and unstable genre, and the 'auto/biographical' (1994: 11) can best be understood as a much wider discourse, in which a number of forms of writing, including the novel, participate. Attending to the multiple occupancy of shared spaces between autobiographical and fictional writing therefore reveals wider continuities between discursive modes whose generic integrity has already been highly problematised of late. It moreover suggests a cryptic or even semi-conscious way of writing the self in the nineteenth century that has been largely unnoticed as such, one more alive to the multiplicity and open-endedness of that task than more prominent positivistic records of past thoughts or deeds.

I address one particularly interesting example of this multiple occupancy of space, which occurs in the life and fiction of one of the most prolific writers of the period. Trollope's sixth novel, *Orley Farm* (1862), places a number of its characters in settings that strongly resemble houses and neighbourhoods the author and his family knew early on in his life. Unlike the majority of the novelists whose appropriations of lived space are surveyed briefly above, Trollope's posthumously published autobiography 'outed' the cryptic lifewriting he had embedded in his earlier fictional geographies, announcing the non-fictional derivation of the farmhouse named in the book's title. While in his roughly contemporaneous novel *The Small House at Allington* (1864) Trollope makes narrative use of the actual practice of multiply occupied residency by situating Johnny Eames in Mrs

Roper's boarding house in Burton Crescent, in *Orley Farm* the author himself shares imagined spaces of significant nostalgic value with fictional characters, and later lets his readers in on the phenomenon of this cohabitation. The very obliqueness with which Trollope implicates himself into the texture of his fiction is worth noting, in part because, as Stephen Wall has argued, this novelist was so vocal about the separate identity of the characters he had invented from his own: 'he thought of the world of his novels as autonomous, discontinuous with his own life, and free from autobiographical undertow' (1998: 6). But Trollope's novel is interesting to consider in relation to matters of life writing and space also because of the way its narrative associates the key shared sites with loss, and thus quietly gestures to its submerged autobiographical work. In staging the spatial nostalgia of fictional characters, *Orley Farm* reflects Trollope's affective relation to the absent childhood homes he has appropriated for fiction, and in the process opens up a space of closed memory to the dialogism of an open-ended form.

'the director of her destiny and of ours'

Anthony Trollope's *An Autobiography* (1883) introduces space prominently in its first chapter and treats it as a kind of agent in the human chronicles that follow:

> I was born in 1815, in Keppel Street, Russell Square; and while a baby, was carried down to Harrow, where my father had built a house on a large farm ... That farm was the grave of all my father's hopes, ambition, and prosperity, the cause of my mother's sufferings, and of those of her children, and perhaps the director of her destiny and of ours. (1883 Vol. 1: 2–3)

Fixing on the farm as the 'director' of the family's 'destiny', the author casts it as a kind of compensation for his father Thomas's practice as a Chancery barrister in 'almost suicidal chambers' (1883 Vol. 1: 3). At the time of Anthony's birth, Thomas is buoyed up enough to feel himself 'entitled to a country house' in addition to the Bloomsbury home, but in this exuberant expenditure overreaches himself: things go 'much against him', the farm proves 'ruinous', and the landlord features in the family's collective imagination as 'a cormorant ... eating [them] up': 'My father's clients deserted him ... Then, as a final crushing blow, an old uncle, whose heir he was to have been, married and had a family' (Trollope 1883 Vol. 1: 4). This ironic catastrophe reverses the Trollope family's upward social mobility and provokes a residential move to match, which functions in the autobiography as a kind of traumatic primal scene.

Towards the end of the narration of this passage about the decline in the immediate family fortunes, Trollope exposes the way his fiction had borrowed its geographies from that troubled early period in his life:

> The house in London was let; and also the house he built at Harrow, from which we descended to a farmhouse on the land, which I have endeavoured to make known to some readers under the name of Orley Farm. This place, just as it was when we lived there, is to be seen in the frontispiece to the first edition of that novel, having had the good fortune to be delineated by no less a pencil than that of John Millais (1883 Vol. 1: 4–5)

Here the 'good fortune' of having secured one of the nation's greatest painters for *Orley Farm*'s illustrations stands in for the larger upswing in the writer's fortunes to which this autobiography attests. Turning to the frontispiece of the first edition of one of his books reminds us, moreover, that there have been other editions, that the author's career has been a successful one. In drawing our attention to this space of childhood held in common between fictional and biographical worlds, we witness Trollope inscribing it not only with retrospective longing but also a sense of the boy's future destiny as a popular writer. The house he renames Orley Farm is implicitly a material determinant for his turn to the literary profession. The farm can be best interpreted as the 'director' of his mother Frances's fate, after all, if we infer that without the social decline it embodied she would have never taken up her pen to earn money. Had the father been successful, and the Trollope family stayed in the big house at Harrow instead of downsizing to the more humble one on its land, we are led to ponder whether Anthony would ever have thought of writing for a living himself.

Other novels by Trollope have been subject far more frequently to autobiographical readings than *Orley Farm*. *The Three Clerks* (1858) and *The Small House at Allington* both reflect aspects of Trollope's circumstances at a slightly earlier point in his life via their portrayals of the respective hobbledehoys (or aspiring young male characters), Charley Tudor and Johnny Eames (see Langbauer 2011: 124). Although Margaret F. King (1980) has drawn some interesting comparisons between *Orley Farm*'s putative heir, Lucius Mason, and Trollope's father, the autobiographical impulse in the novel in question has been generally neglected by critics, being more obliquely present than in those other texts from the same period, diffused and dispersed as it is through its redeployment of spaces the author borrowed from previous everyday experience.

While the other fictions make liberal use of Trollope's youthful years at the faltering beginning of a career in the Civil Service, *Orley Farm* builds a story which, revolving around a contested will and probing the relationship of legal procedure to truth-telling and natural justice, on the surface has little to do with Trollope's life.

In the backstory to the central plotline, we learn that the widow of an aristocrat, Lady Mason, had been forced to defend her own claims and those of her baby Lucius to the farm, immediately after her husband died. Twenty years later, mother and son are presented living happily in the home that has been declared rightfully theirs when the case re-emerges, after an aggrieved ex-tenant, Samuel Dockwrath, seeks and finds evidence to suggest that the codicil on which the current proprietors' legal status hangs might have been a forgery. Lady Mason comes to London to defend herself and her interests in court, and is declared innocent of any crimes, by virtue of some very nifty and seemingly unscrupulous legal advocacy. Orley Farm is finally given up by the pair towards the end of the novel only after the mother suffers from pangs of conscience sufficient for her to relinquish her claims voluntarily after all legal threat has died away.

From the time of its initial reception to current academic scholarship (including, most recently, Albert Pionke's 2010 article on legal realism in Trollope's work), the lion's share of discussion about *Orley Farm* has focussed on its depiction of the principles and practice of English law. But this novel is simultaneously about space: about the friction that might arise between one's habitual sense of home-as-shell and the contested field of property rights. It is Lucius's eviction of Samuel Dockwrath, after all, that provokes the ex-tenant to dredge up the past and seek to re-open the Orley Farm case. Lucius's vainglorious desire to manage directly the land Dockwrath had long leased in order to try out new agricultural methods brooks no dissent. The young heir apparent pays no heed to those informal privileges accorded to tenants, which had always tempered the hierarchies intrinsic to the rural semi-feudal social structure. As in Hardy's *The Woodlanders* (1887), the eviction of old tenants by a moderniser serves to exemplify a wider social phenomenon: that of the replacement of a complex web of unwritten spatial compromises and accommodations with a hard-headed legalism. Unlike the victims of circumstance in Hardy's fatalistic universe, however, Trollope's wronged ex-tenants fight the forces of spatial modernisation with modernity itself, in the form of legal challenge. Finding evidence of Lady Mason's twenty-year-old fraud that would have otherwise gone undiscovered, Dockwrath takes revenge on those who are taking his home away from him by attempting to do the same to them. The final chapter of *Orley Farm* terminally separates the Masons from their former home by sending mother and son into self-imposed exile in Germany. After six months living in a small German town, Lucius decides to put even more distance between himself and his murky past, and leaves for Australia. Trollope, meanwhile, exerts an authorial revenge upon Dockwrath too, the new owner of Orley Farm successfully defeating the ex-tenant's ambition to be reinstated in the much-coveted land. Placed at the very centre of this novel's narrative structure, the property generates, through the legal case, much of its plot; at first attracting the conflicting claims of a number of parties, it concludes by casting them off, centrifugally, to the margins.

As might be expected in the representation of such an important space, the narrator's introduction of it is both elaborate and suggestive. The narrator takes us on a kind of tour, anatomising the various rooms to an unusual level of detail. This meticulous mapping is inflected diachronically. The house is shown to have expanded over time, being adapted by every generation to suit the changing needs of its successive residents. The original is 'gradually added to' and 'ornamented ... till it [is] commodious, irregular, picturesque, and straggling' (1862 Vol. 1: 6), as it appears in Millais's illustration. In this faux-organic form the house is constructed as a kind of record to the selves that have inhabited it, corresponding quite closely to Bachelard's house-as-shell. Trollope's seemingly excessive description of the place and his implicit insistence on a kind of psychic fit or symbiosis between dwellers and dwelling can be partly justified within the dynamics of the plot. With *Orley Farm* being essentially about a legal dispute over the ownership of this property, it is to a certain extent unsurprising that the narrator lingers over the task of mediating such a key space to the reader. Recalling Armstrong's point about the necessary though difficult complementariness of phenomenological and social understandings of space, we might infer, indeed, that it is precisely *because* this is a novel about contestation over property that the organic rhetoric becomes so necessary. To sympathise fully with Lady Mason's plight requires us to recognise her sense of the shell-like quality of the property, her claim to which hangs in the balance for much of the novel. If we imagine the old 'straggling' farmhouse as an inalienable extension of and protection for Lady Mason and her son, and not only the materially contested subject of wills and codicils, it becomes easier to comprehend how an otherwise morally conventional individual could commit fraud and perjury.

Having encountered Trollope's *Autobiography*, the pedantic delineation of 'large kitchen, ... bake-house, laundry, dairy, and servants' room, all of fair dimensions [etc.]' (1862 Vol. 1: 6) reads differently, however, bearing covertly an autobiographical function that accompanies and complicates the descriptive passage's role within the plot. Alongside the fictional story, which implicitly mobilises a sense of Bachelardian rootedness in order to ramp up our appreciation of the covetedness of the contested property, there is, at once wistful and regretful, the memory of the novelist's childhood home. It is not that the latter trumps the former, or that the 'Orley Farm' we know in hindsight through the autobiographer's representation of it somehow supplants for the critic the novel's own explicit narrative use for the site. Rather, readers are prompted to think through and account for the cohabitation of both constructions, letting each reflect upon and open up the other. As a shared space in the authorial imagination, encompassing remembered selves as well as fictional characters, the 'Orley Farm' we read between the novel and the autobiography invites a fuller analysis for the way it enables a submerged form of life writing to take place.

'those happy days in Keppel Street'

Trollope's novel is actually more autobiographical in its spatial reference than the *Autobiography* explicitly acknowledges. In addition to the key property of Orley Farm, Bloomsbury's Keppel Street also crops up as the previous home of Mr Furnival, Lady Mason's lawyer, in which the character lived at an earlier stage in his career. Never appearing as a setting for episodes that occur within the present time-frame of the narrative, the town-house Thomas Trollope had to give up soon after his son was born nonetheless performs an important role within the fictional text. In contrast to Trollope Sr's forced relinquishment of the extravagant townhouse, which marks a crisis in his family's social status, Furnival's residential trajectory away from Bloomsbury accompanies his *rise* in fortunes. Like his real life co-inhabitant, Mr Furnival belongs to Lincoln's Inn, but unlike Trollope's father, the fictional barrister lives in wealthy Marylebone, having long left Bloomsbury behind:

> But he had not been long a resident in Harley Street, having left the less fashionable neighbourhood of Russell Square only two or three years before that period. On his marriage he had located himself in a small house in Keppel Street, and had there remained till professional success ... enabled him to move further west. ... he had struggled long and hard before ... success had come to him, and during the earliest years of his married life had found the work of keeping the wolf from the door to be almost more than enough for his energies. (1862 Vol. 2: 74)

Remembering the novelist's recollections of his father's struggles with his 'cormorant' (1883 Vol. 1: 4) of a landlord, it is not difficult to recognise in Mr Furnival's material and social successes a fictionalisation of those Thomas

Trollope, haunted by the 'wolf' (1862 Vol. 2: 74) at the door, had doubtless dreamed of but failed to make good. Trollope Sr's much-lamented fall from Keppel Street is reprocessed to become Furnival's successful step up in the world, to Harley Street. The novel can be seen to adopt a normative socio-spatial indexing, in its use in the above passage of the lexicon of residential 'fashionability', but its later narrative re-use of Bloomsbury meanwhile puts a strange spin on such straightforward hierarchies. Drawing the previous address in Keppel Street into a comic sub-plot involving the barrister's wife's jealousy about her husband's relations with Lady Mason, the novel finds an affective value for the old Bloomsbury address that runs counter to the dominant codes of metropolitan social geography which equated a 'move further west' (1862 Vol. 2: 74) unproblematically with success and happiness.

If the emotional centre of the book concerns Lady Mason's guilt about having lied to everyone, a related narrative strand concerns her lawyer's complicity with her suppression of the truth, and the consequences of this complicity for his own marriage. Mr Furnival's conflicted feelings about his client's plight are intense, and at various points within the plot the narrator hints that the barrister's engagements with Lady Mason might be motivated by a quite excessive affection for her. Certainly, Mr. Furnival's wife, Kitty, senses that the normal bounds of professional relations have not been correctly observed, and wrongly guesses the two are having an affair. The barrister's wife's suspicion erupts at one climactic point that draws our attention to the couple's earlier residential move away from Keppel Street, when she temporarily leaves Harley Street in protest at her husband's apparent marital misbehaviour, and returns to Bloomsbury. In what James Kincaid has pointed out is one of a number of 'recurrent scenes of domestic harmony and disruption' (1977: 80) in *Orley Farm*, Sophia Furnival recruits her old confidant, Miss Biggs, to find her lodgings in the unglamorous part of London from which they both originated. For a few days the female friends live near each other around Red Lion Square, not far from Keppel Street, before Mrs Furnival realises her error, returns to her husband and Harley Street, and gives up Miss Biggs and Bloomsbury for good.

When she makes the temporary move eastwards, Mrs Furnival announces to her husband her flight from genteel married domesticity to 'very dull' (1862 Vol. 2: 70) lodgings in a letter which pointedly reminds the reader of the early days of their marriage together in a street nearby, and does so in the rose-tinted language of nostalgia:

> Oh, Tom, I wonder whether you ever think of the old days when we used to be so
> happy in Keppel Street! There wasn't anybody then that you cared to see, except

me;– I do believe that. And you'd always come home then, and I never thought bad of it though you wouldn't have a word to speak to me for hours. (1862 Vol. 2: 67)

While their fashionable house in Harley Street is tainted by her suspicions about her husband's infidelity, Mrs Furnival thus pines for the days when they lived in lowly Bloomsbury, an attitude that would have appeared comically wrongheaded to contemporary readers. In the early 1860s, Bloomsbury was acknowledged to be in social decline, and had become tagged in cultural discourse as an embarrassing place for married lawyers and other upper-middle-class professionals to inhabit (see Ingleby 2012). In this light, Mrs Furnival's nostalgia for a place other barristers' wives were agitating to leave strikes one as remarkably ironic, verging on perverse.

On the one hand, the letter's rhetoric of nostalgia contributes to the characterisation of Mrs Furnival: when the aggrieved wife responds to her friend's anxiety that her Bloomsbury lodgings are 'very dull' with the barbed surmise that they 'can't possibly be more dull than Harley Street' (1862 Vol. 2: 70), Mrs Furnival's resistance to the city's dominant spatial ideologies expresses her intransigent class inferiority (carried also in the cockneyisms that litter her prose) and her strategic gamesmanship to win back her husband's attention. On the other hand, in our knowledge of Trollope's autobiographical relation to the Bloomsbury site, the nostalgia about the absent Keppel Street seems meaningfully excessive, just as the narratorial fascination with Orley Farm had. Both the novel's Bloomsbury townhouse and its farmhouse invoke an uncanny sense of authorial doubling or *déjà vu* through the way the loss or threatened loss each is associated with in the plot mirrors the Trollope family's spatial relinquishments at the beginning of the author's life.

Mrs Furnival's musings on Bloomsbury are echoed and commented upon within a few pages by the narrator, confirming the reader's suspicion that the nostalgic impulse they embody might have an extra-narrative autobiographical function in addition to the explicit one that relates to the novel's plot and characterisation. In a voice that sounds very close to the 'Trollope' of the author's *Autobiography*, the narrator dwells upon the strange manner in which the past and its places can become tinged with utopian possibility, when viewed from a position of comparative security and success in the present:

Oh, those happy days in Keppel Street ... Those were to us, and now are to others, and always will be to many, the happy days of life. How bright was love, and how full of poetry! Flashes of wit glanced here and there, and how they came home and warmed the cockles of the heart. And the unfrequent bottle! Methinks that wine has utterly

lost its flavour since those days. … 'Ah me! I wonder whether you ever think of the old
days when we used to be so happy in Keppel Street?' (1862 Vol. 2: 68)

In that toast to those 'happy days in Keppel Street' we note not only the shrill
tones of an aggrieved fictional barrister's wife but also the sublimated voice of the
real spouse and author's mother. One does not have to listen hard to imagine a
dialogue between the two retrospective voices. Trollope's dim juvenile awareness
of the catastrophe for his parents of losing that key London address, which would
have meant so much for the family's precarious social identity, complements
the regrets of a character whose husband's career has been more successful than
Thomas Trollope's, but whose life has nonetheless somehow 'lost its flavour'. In
an alternative fate in which her husband's career had taken off, Frances Trollope
might too have only ever had a chance to exercise her literary skills in the craft
of strategic letter-writing instead of the production of fiction. A comparison of
novel and life confirms the relativity of loss: even though the Furnival family's
ascendancy contrasts so markedly with the trajectory of the downwardly mobile
Trollopes, in fact each loses *and* gains from their departures from Bloomsbury.
Returning to 'Orley Farm', through the residential coincidence it constitutes we
can trace something like authorial self-analysis. While the Trollopes, like the
Masons, lose their family home, the fundamental tragedy of *Orley Farm* is the
social cost and reputational penalty the mother suffers as a result of working so
hard to cover up her crime and retain the property. It is telling that the narrator
finally articulates her sense of loss in terms of a kind of failure of work: 'For
twenty years [Lady Mason] had striven with a labour that had been all but
unendurable; and now she had failed, and everyone knew her for what she was'
(1862 Vol. 2: 311). While the loss of the farmhouse emblematises something
lacking in Trollope's father's professional ability, the selfsame move heralds not
the end but the beginning of a period of hard yet rewarding work for his wife,
whose literary career would set the example for her sons. In his appropriation of
autobiographical sites within his fiction, Trollope stresses an affective continuity
between them. In this fictional restaging of houses and neighbourhoods lost or
on the verge of being lost, however, a kind of reflexivity about the loss Trollope's
family sustained at the beginning of *An Autobiography* emerges. In apprehending
the correspondences between Trollope's novels and life, readers encounter
the trace of a decidedly homesick self; at the same time, the author's nostalgic
impulse is tempered by the stories of the other 'occupants' of the space.

In Lady Mason relinquishing her house after such a bitter wrangling, and
in Mrs Furnival returning to Harley Street after her temporary reversion to
Bloomsbury, the novel might be seen to recapitulate those spatial losses that

formed the primal scene of Trollope's autobiography. Yet, the fictional stories that are written into autobiographical space in novels such as *Orley Farm* do not only tread deterministically the same single path of the author's autobiography but instead pick up the loose threads of lives unled, ambitions and fears unfulfilled, possibilities untested. Rewriting these remembered sites into the open, dialogic world of fiction renders them, we infer, less solipsistic in the authorial imagination, enlivening them with comedy and sensation, ameliorating their claustrophobia or loneliness. Re-imagining a site of childhood within fiction is only superficially a conservative act of shoring up, because it simultaneously breaks open the Bachelardian shell to the risks and opportunities of shared space.

What can we do with these houses from our pasts, these sites that have imprinted themselves on our psyches to which we no longer have access? When writers covertly appropriate for their fiction such places, the act might at first seem like a vain attempt at nostalgic repossession; from a different angle, however, rewriting the remembered site productively destabilises it within the authorial imagination. For Boym, our recourse to spatial retrospection is a screen to block out and distract us from thinking about time. But in novels such as Trollope's *Orley Farm*, where nostalgia is unsettled by fiction's structural plurality, multiply occupied imagined space becomes a way for authors to relinquish their ownership over their pasts, an act that coincidentally serves to undermine the past's hold over the author.

References

Armstrong, I. 2000. *The Radical Aesthetic*. Oxford: Blackwell.

Bachelard, G. 1994. *The Poetics of Space* [1958], translated by M. Jolas. Boston: Beacon Press.

Bakhtin, M. 1981. *The Dialogic Imagination* [1975], edited and translated by M. Holquist. Austin and London: University of Texas Press.

Boym, S. 2001. *The Future of Nostalgia*. New York: Basic.

Dames, N. 2001. *Amnesiac Selves: Nostalgia, Forgetting, and British Fiction, 1810–1870*. Oxford: Oxford University Press.

Hardy, T. 1887. *The Woodlanders*. London: Macmillan.

Ingleby, M. 2012. Braddon, Bulwer, and the bachelorization of legal Bloomsbury. *Nineteenth Century Gender Studies* [Online], 8(2). Available at: http://www.ncgsjournal.com/issue82/ingleby.htm [accessed: 22 October 2014].

Kincaid, J. 1977. *The Novels of Anthony Trollope*. Oxford: Oxford University Press.

King, M.F. 1980. The place of Lucius Mason in Trollope's studies of perversity. *South Atlantic Bulletin*, 45(4), 43–54.

Langbauer, L. 2011. The hobbledehoy in Trollope, in *The Cambridge Companion to Anthony Trollope*, edited by C. Dever and L. Niles. Cambridge: Cambridge University Press, 113–27.

Lefebvre, H. 2001. *The Production of Space* [1974], translated by D. Nicholson-Smith. Oxford: Blackwell.

Marcus, L. 1994. *Auto/biographical Discourses: Theory, Criticism, Practice*. Manchester: Manchester University Press.

Pionke, A.D. 2010. Navigating the terrible meshes of the law: Legal realism in Anthony Trollope's *Orley Farm* and *The Eustace Diamonds*. *ELH*, 77(1), 129–57.

Trollope, A. 1862. *Orley Farm*. 2 Vols. London: Chapman & Hall.

Trollope, A. 1864. *The Small House at Allington*. 2 Vols. London: Smith, Elder & Co.

Trollope, A. 1883. *An Autobiography*. 2 Vols. London: Blackwoods.

Wall, S. 1988. *Trollope and Character*. London: Faber & Faber.

Chapter 2

Lost Cities and Found Lives:
The 'Geographical Emotions' of Bryher and Walter Benjamin

Andrew Thacker

In his poem, 'In Transit', W. H. Auden crystallised one way in which our identities are bound up with space and place:

> Somewhere are places where we have really been, dear spaces
> Of our deeds and faces, scenes we remember
> As unchanging because there we changed ... (1991: 539)

Auden's poem, which concerns a return journey to Europe from America, points to the role of remembered spaces in the construction of our identities: we tend to recall places as unchanging locations against which we predicate our own development. In her writer's memoirs, *The Heart to Artemis* (1962), the British writer and critic Bryher wrote passionately, to use Auden's phrase, about the 'dear spaces' of Berlin in the late 1920s and early 1930s, a time of artistic experiment that coincided with key changes in her own sense of self. The categories of experiment and development thus coalesce for Bryher in her recollections of scenes from the city, for in the spaces of Berlin she was changed.

At one fascinating point in the memoir Bryher writes about why she is a Freudian rather than a Jungian, arguing that she was attracted by Freud's method of focussing upon some small 'apparently incongruous incident' since it 'could suddenly, like a miner's headlamp, light up the dark pit of the brain' (1962: 258). This is a somewhat familiar trope for the process of psychoanalysis, alongside those of an excavation into our unconscious, or an archaeology of our mind. They are all, of course, spatial metaphors of depth, seeing our lives as locations of memory that we tunnel into to discover patterns and significances: to write about our selves is thus to explore these spatial depths, treating our personal history in a metaphorically spatial fashion. But what happens when we try to think of space in a material or geographical sense rather than merely metaphorically, considering the role that particular material geographies play in the constitution of the 'dark pit' of the writer's brain? Or, more precisely, how are these two conceptions of spatiality combined in our personal lives and in the works we study as life writing? Early on in *The Heart to Artemis* Bryher notes: 'All my life I have suffered from "geographical emotions". Places are almost as real to me as people' (1962: 26). Bryher's deep connection to geography had been demonstrated earlier when Annie Winnifred Ellerman adopted the name 'Bryher' for her first novel, *Development* (1920), the name deriving from one of the Scilly Isles, off the coast of Cornwall, that she had frequently visited as a child. She later changed her name legally to indicate a full break from her parents: To rename oneself in such a way as to mark a distance from one's parents is one thing, but to identify one's new name with a place rather than a person indicates the strength of Bryher's affective attachment to geography.[1]

This chapter, then, considers the importance of space and place for the writing of the self, focussing upon two works that take Berlin as the material geography that infuses and shapes the inner narrative of the self: Bryher's *The Heart to Artemis* and Walter Benjamin's *Berlin Childhood Around 1900* (1950).[2] Both write of Berlin from a position of geographical distance (Bryher as an outsider, Benjamin as an exile) that parallels the temporal distance of many autobiographical narratives: one writes an autobiography (or biography) from the present looking back, and this temporal lag creates a certain *distance* that produces the effect of a retrospective judgement or air of objective portraiture. The spatial disjuncture of exile creates a different sense of distance, one that is both literal (the person is writing about a place, for example, that they no longer inhabit) and figurative (they write, as with Bryher, as outsiders). Both writers are fascinated, as Auden suggests, with how we register changes in the self by means of geographical locations preserved as unchanging in our memories. This chapter first considers Bryher's depiction of Berlin in *The Heart to Artemis*, then discusses Benjamin's picture of his Berlin childhood, before bringing the two together in a quite different city, Paris.

---

[1]　　　　Interestingly, Bryher also wrote a geography primer, *Picture Geography for Children* (1925).

[2]　　　　Benjamin composed *Berlin Childhood* between 1932 and 1938; the book version was first published posthumously in 1950.

Bryher

Here, as a starting point, is a description of the impact of Berlin upon Bryher, located in her book after a discussion of psychoanalysis:

> And outside was Berlin. It was the time of the Bauhaus and experiments in modern architecture. The schools were locked in a struggle between light and darkness. I loved the new functional furniture, the horizontal windows and the abolition of what I thought of as messy decoration. I saw the documentary film of a rocket; people laughed, I was interested. I understood very little of what was happening politically in Germany. Berlin was an international city but in any period of great artistic expression, and we had one in the twenties, there are always centres that draw people to them to form a kingdom of their own. 'It's got to be new', we chanted because old forms were saturated with the war memories that both former soldiers and civilians wanted to forget. We were too savage, too contemptuous, but would you have had us be prudent? We did not realise at the time that it was not the concepts themselves that were at fault but the way that they had been used. Perhaps because my own unconscious was in the process of release, the unconscious passions of the city struck me with the more force. The war losses had been the same in all countries but there had not been the total upset of all values as in Germany and Austria. I saw hunger, brutality and greed but there was also the sudden compassionate gesture, a will to help or the pre-battle awareness of the single rose, the transient beauty of some girl's face. (1962: 259)

In many ways this is a fascinating paragraph: there is a fine cultural history demonstrating how modernism was experienced as an exciting commitment to the new ('It's got to be new'); there is also a strong sense of being part of an international avant-garde movement that took as its starting point the changes wrought by the First World War; finally, and tellingly, we glimpse an international, expatriate coterie whose understanding of Berlin was primarily aesthetic rather than political – the sentence about understanding very little of the politics of Germany is clearly the result of retrospective hindsight. However, what is also of interest is the structural form of the paragraph, as signalled in its opening: 'And outside was Berlin'. The paragraph seems to take us away from the inner life of Bryher, as experienced through analytic practice, and into the external space of the city. But by the end of the paragraph the 'outside' has become cathected onto the 'inside', such that the 'unconscious passions of the city' are linked to those of Bryher's inner 'release'. Cathected seems correct here because it is somewhat ambiguous which comes first: Is the release of psychic inhibitions prompted by the modernist passions she experiences in the city? Or is she only able to see the city in this way because her unconscious is being released?

The first interpretation is, arguably, the more interesting, partly because it emphasises those moments when external space intrudes upon, and actively shapes, internal psychic space. At the end of this chapter Bryher tries to sum up what Berlin meant to her. Returning to Switzerland via Vienna she visits Freud in Vienna for the last time. For Bryher, 'in spite of being the birthplace of analysis and of many of my friends', Vienna was 'too southern for me', a statement again combining geography with emotional attachment: In other places she alludes to how her 'northernness' was more suited to cities such as Berlin (1962: 254). Bryher concludes the chapter in the following way: 'I could not help thinking sometimes of my lost city. A moment, a memory, would come back and I could not help murmuring, it was childish but I meant it, "Why, Berlin, must I love you so?" It had gone, I thought, for ever' (1962: 270). There is an interesting temporal confusion here since Bryher shifts her narrative from a retrospective account of visiting Freud in Vienna in 1933 to her memories of Berlin in the years after she left the city (she last visited Berlin in 1932 and did not return to Germany until 1960). Berlin becomes here a lost object, functioning in her psychic life somewhat like the loss of a loved one whose presence persists due to the prompts of memory. The awareness that this is a 'childish' experience indicates Bryher's realisation of the intensity of her feelings for Berlin: unlike a person the city has not really died and thus cannot really be mourned as a lost object. What has been lost, we might say, is the experience of how the modernist city of Berlin intensified the release of her unconscious; what this chapter of *The Heart of Artemis* attempts is a process of recovery, both of the spaces of the city and of Bryher's attendant 'geographical emotions'. In writing about her inner self, Bryher is recalling the exterior space of her 'lost city' (1962: 270), a city whose cultural geography in the late 1920s was partly responsible for how she 'found', we might say, her own self.

The Heart to Artemis is a book that straddles different forms of life writing, starting out as a fairly conventional autobiography tracing how the English-born Annie Winifred Ellerman, daughter of the one-time richest man in Britain, John Ellerman, escaped from the Victorian conventions of her upbringing to forge her identity amidst the avant-garde artists of modernist Europe in the 1920s and 30s.[3]

---

[3]   Until relatively recently Bryher's writings have received scant attention and she has mainly been known for her relationship with H.D. and as a patron of various modernist artists, presses, and magazines (such as Robert McAlmon and Contact Press, and the magazines *Close-Up* and *Life and Letters Today*); two of her early novels, *Development* and *Two Selves*, have been reprinted (Bryher 2000). For two excellent accounts of Bryher in Berlin see Camboni (2008) and McCabe (2011). McCabe is currently writing a biography of Bryher.

However, as the book progresses its more experimental qualities begin to emerge. Tellingly, at one point Bryher writes: 'I should like this book to be read neither as mere autobiography nor period piece but as an attempt to show how external events and unconscious drives help or hinder development' (1962: 206). The autobiographical genre of the book is shaped by two major features: First, Bryher reads her own past, particularly that of her 'repressed' childhood, through the lens of psychoanalysis; second, subtitled 'A Writer's Memoirs', the book presents her engagement with literary modernism as a parallel route into a sense of self – it is dedicated to Stéphane Mallarmé, for instance, and the opening sentence situates her own birth through the device of another modernist literary frame: 'When I was born in September, 1894, Dorothy Richardson's Miriam was a secretary' (1962: 7).

Much of the earlier part of the book charts Bryher's extensive travels as a child, exploring a different set of geographical emotions. Bryher visits France, Switzerland and Italy as a kind of late Victorian 'Grand Tour', but then also visits Egypt and Algeria (Chapter Three memorably starts: 'Nobody ever gets over their first camel'). In her later memoir, covering her life in London during World War Two, *Days of Mars* (1972), Bryher commented that her childhood hero had been the Victorian explorer, Sir Richard Burton: 'It was inevitable that, in the modern phrase, I should identify myself with him. He had had a supremely happy childhood wandering about Europe; so had I' (1972: 67). It is these happy travels that form the backdrop to her novel, *Development*, a thinly disguised autobiography of a young girl named Nancy, whose psychic development is delineated by means of her external journeys:

> Travelling has much in common with adventure, and all these days of surely an epic childhood seemed immortal to Nancy, even the hours spent moving from place to place. Her imagination, sensitive to all impressions of the loveliness and the legends ready to her hand, found time to ponder as the train jerked on, to assimilate what crowded street and ruined building had heaped there in profusion, effacing all that had held no importance from her memory, in preparation for the new atmosphere of another city. (2000: 66)

Bryher viewed her travels when young as a key factor in her embrace of modernist experimentation and in her rejection of conventional femininity and sexuality, although these topics are not explicitly discussed in the memoir. Travel, therefore, produced a sense of exile that was potentially liberating for Bryher, as it was for many other modernists. She thus noted of the international modernist expatriates of the Parisian Left-Bank in the 1920s: 'We were all exiles. We remain so to-day. It is our destiny' (1962: 207); this might also be read as a comment upon her own gender identity, as noted in *Development* where Nancy hopes forlornly that one day she will turn into a boy (Bryher 2000: 24).

However, unlike so many of these other Left-Bank writers and artists, Paris does not really liberate Bryher, partly because of her unhappy memories of the city from childhood visits. She describes herself as an 'observer' of the Left-Bank coteries and that although 'I was utterly in sympathy with the rebellion of the group ... their solutions did not solve my particular problem' (1962: 217). She does not drink (which perhaps didn't help crawling around cafes with the likes of Hemingway and Joyce) and although she recognised the 'exhilaration' of Paris at this time, she cannot identify with the 'enchantment' experienced by other expatriate modernists. Bryher, rather sadly, considers herself a 'Puritan in Montparnasse', while the Paris streets, familiar from childhood visits, start to make her feel uneasy, reminding her of the 'restrictions of childhood' (1962: 209). For Bryher, therefore, the geographical emotions produced by Paris are resoundingly negative.

Berlin, however, was a different city:

> I fell in love with Berlin at once to my own amazement. There is a time when if development is to continue, childhood associations must be put temporarily aside and I had known France too long and too well. In the sharp bite of the air of the North I could watch the first patterns evolve of the post-war decade. (1962: 249)

Berlin thus represents a *development* – a key word for Bryher – from childhood to a different sense of self, one that is intrinsically linked to the new modernist art of cinema she found in the city; she thus notes that in Berlin 'I have never encountered before or since so vital a response to experimental art' (1962: 240). Living at Territet in Switzerland Bryher began to visit Berlin for long periods of time from 1927 onwards, primarily to help gather material for the classic little magazine devoted to cinema, *Close-Up*, which was also edited by her then husband of convenience, Kenneth Macpherson (see Marcus 2007; McCabe 2012). In Berlin she travelled to Babelsberg, site of the famous UFA film studios, and soon met the important director G.W. Pabst. Since the 1910s the film industry had flourished in Germany (a high-point was reached in 1922 when 474 feature-films were made; see Roters 1983: 175), while the establishment of the 'Expressionist' style in film, associated with directors such as F.W. Murnau and Fritz Lang, established Berlin's reputation as a centre for cinematic modernism.

Berlin's embrace of the new modernist art of the cinema, however, was but one example of the exhilarating modernity of the city in the early twentieth century. By the time that British and American writers began to arrive in Berlin in the 1920s, the city had already witnessed the spiritual utopianism of the Expressionist artists associated with the pre-war groups around *Die Brücke* and *Der Blaue Reiter*. These were followed by the anti-art of German Dada, led by Richard Hulsenbeck, and then the impact of émigré artists and writers from Russia such as El Lissitzky, Kazimir Malevich and Vladimir Nabokov. Some of these Russian artists brought with them not only a modernist commitment to abstraction in the visual arts but also the utopian energy of the 1917 Bolshevik Revolution: El Lissitzky, for example, was to talk of 'the brave new world we were building'.[4] As well as functioning as a meeting place for many significant avant-garde groups the physical fabric of Berlin also embodied the newly modern city. Berlin had only become the capital of Germany in 1870 and over the next forty years it expanded rapidly to become the fourth largest city in the world, with a population in 1900 of over 2.5 million. Praising the modernity of Berlin in 1892 Mark Twain compared it to another 'new' city in America, Chicago:

> [Berlin] is a new city; the newest I have ever seen. Chicago would seem venerable beside it. The next feature that strikes one is the spaciousness, the roominess of the city. There is no other city, in any country, whose streets are so generally wide. Berlin is not merely a city of wide streets, it is the city of wide streets. As a wide-street city it has never had its equal, in any age of the world. 'Unter den Linden' is three streets in one. (2009: 203)

The restructuring of the spaces of Berlin in the late nineteenth century produced the conditions for a range of representations of the city that veered from the phobic to the utopian in a range of diverse critics, writers and artists. Berlin was thus the place in which some of the most fascinating and durable theorisations of the experience of the city first emerged, in classic works by the likes of Georg Simmel and Siegfried Kracauer. It was also where other German thinkers defined quite negatively the effect that the new open spaces of modern urban life, the 'roominess' noted by Twain, had upon human experience. One important example was the diagnosis by a Berlin psychologist, Carl Otto Westphal, of *Platzangst*, more commonly known now as agoraphobia. Westphal coined the term in 1871 and, as Anthony Vidler (2000) has shown, the discourse of spatial phobias spread across German cities in the late nineteenth century. Berlin, then, is a city with a long history of theorising the psychology of urban experience and 'geographical emotions'.

For Bryher, however, the emotional geography of Berlin comprised a number of interconnected strands: urban modernity, cinematic modernism,

---

4   Conversation quoted in Josephson (1962: 210).

and a profound encounter with psychoanalysis. Bryher's first psychoanalyst was Hanns Sachs, who she met at a party of the film director Pabst in 1927, and she later underwent initial training to become an analyst.[5] Sachs had been an adviser to the first attempt to make a psychoanalytic film, *Secrets of a Soul*, directed by Pabst and released in 1926, demonstrating the intellectual affinities between film and psychoanalysis as modernist phenomena. Sachs also contributed some articles to *Close Up*, whose 'project' as a film magazine, argues Laura Marcus, 'was substantially informed by psychoanalytic thought and theory' (1998: 240).

For Bryher, then, the experience of German film coalesced with the investigation into the secrets of her own soul via her analysis with Sachs. Her descriptions of Berlin are dominated by a discourse in which the passions of the city are identified with the release of her own unconscious, while also being influenced by the aesthetics of cinema:

> At first, however, Berlin was all excitement and promise. It was a place of violent contrasts, a baby elephant at the Zoo tossed the fallen yellow leaves about its enclosure with the petulant trunk movements of an awkward child. We went to see *Hoppla, wir leben* where shots taken on an actual battlefield were suddenly flashed on to an immense screen behind the actor's heads. The impact of the scene brought many of the audience out of their seats. We sheltered from the cold November winds inside small cafés whose red plush seats and marble-topped tables must have been a legacy of the nineties. I once met Heinrich Mann as we went inside the door. There was desperate poverty, life and death seemed to hang upon trifles, a missed bus, an unexpected meeting. I sometimes felt that a collective but unconscious mind had broken through its controls. We went to obscure cinemas to see experimental films. (1962: 254)

From the cinema and theatre to the city cafes, Berlin is here an Expressionist place of 'violent contrasts', enacted in the way in which this paragraph abruptly switches topic, echoing the cinematic theory of montage developed in the Russian films discussed in *Close Up* and also theorised by Benjamin in terms of an aesthetics of 'discontinuity' and 'shock' (see Marcus 2007, Donald, Friedberg and Marcus 1998, Benjamin 1973). The description of the audience leaping out of their seats during Piscator's staging of Ernst Toller's famous work of 'New Objectivity', *Hoppla, wir leben*, also points to the bodily affect of much early cinema. The extremes of the psychoanalytic experience, where a 'trifle' can become vitally important, are here mapped onto the city itself, as Bryher

---

5   For Bryher's links to psychoanalytic circles at the time see Friedman (2002).

perceives in the urban spaces her own unconscious release writ large, identifying her own personal psychic development with that of the 'collective' mind of modernist Berlin. Berlin, she writes, employing a fascinating set of spatialised images, was 'easier and *nearer to me* than any city where I had lived' and, again: 'I never had to translate my feelings in Berlin; in Latin countries I was a *wild plant escaped into a formal garden*' (1962: 254, emphasis added). In Berlin, then, Bryher finds herself and, when she leaves amidst the rising terror of the Nazi rise to power, she mourns the loss of the city whose uncontrolled passions enabled her own psychic development.

Benjamin

Walter Benjamin's biographical writings are marked by a similar dialectic of finding and losing to that discerned in Bryher. Benjamin experienced a strong attachment to the city of his childhood and seemed to draw upon something akin to Bryher's concept of 'geographical emotions' when writing about Berlin. In his two major works of life writing Benjamin's attempts to understand his own identity are intimately bound up with the geography of Berlin: thus in *Berlin Childhood around 1900* and 'A Berlin Chronicle' (1970) autobiography doubles as topography.[6] Noting the importance of the *Berlin Childhood* for Benjamin, one of his biographers claims that it demonstrates how his 'life's work ... is basically a constant reflection on his own city origins' (Brodersen 1990: 4).

Aside from Berlin, Benjamin wrote a number of fascinating texts about the cities that he visited, including essays on Moscow, Marseilles, Naples and, most famously, Paris, which became the locus of his major unfinished work, *The Arcades Project*. These are pieces of travel writing that combine Benjamin's brilliant ability to extract complex meaning from some image or fragment of the city, along with reflections upon his own subjective experience of the urban. Like many of the most interesting works of travel writing, particularly in the modernist period, they are not only representations of spaces, but also explorations into the self, forms of life writing that happen to take the form of travel narratives. Travel writing normally provides a textual map of some geographical area; but these texts, Bryher's memoir included, are often also memories of the psychic journey undergone by the traveller.

---

6   'A Berlin Chronicle' was, to some extent, the precursor of the *Berlin Childhood* book; for more on the complex textual history of *Berlin Childhood* see the 'Translator's Foreword' (Benjamin 2006: vii–xi).

This conjunction of memory and mapping is central to Benjamin's meditations upon Berlin and his attempts to chronicle his life by means of recalling the spaces of the city. Benjamin worked on *Berlin Childhood* between 1932 and 1938, producing at least four different manuscripts of the text, publishing several in German newspapers such as the *Frankfurter Zeitung* during the period, while 'Berlin Chronicle' was started in 1932. Significantly, both texts were started while in exile ('Berlin Chronicle' in Ibiza; *Berlin Childhood* in Poveromo, Italy; see Benjamin 1994: 399), demonstrating a poignant sense of how travel abroad prompted a voyage within, and of how in finding a shape for his life Benjamin 'lost' a city. Benjamin thus starts *Berlin Childhood* as follows:

> In 1932, when I was abroad, it began to be clear to me that I would soon have to bid a long, perhaps lasting farewell to the city of my birth.
>
> Several times in my inner life, I had already experienced the process of inoculation as something salutary. In this situation, too, I resolved to follow suit, and I deliberately called to mind those images which, in exile, are most apt to waken homesickness: images of childhood. My assumption was that the feeling of longing would no more gain mastery over my sprit than a vaccine does over a healthy body. I sought to limit its effect through insight into the irretrievability – not the contingent biographical but the necessary social irretrievability – of the past. (2006: 37)

Benjamin's narrative is thus conditioned – or driven – by the spatial distance brought about by exile. Benjamin is not writing this memoir to remember his childhood, therefore, but to actively forget the city that, while contemplating a life of permanent exile, exerts upon him a distressing nostalgia. Indeed, as he writes here, the past is to be regarded as necessarily irretrievable because the social circumstances of any period are part of the historical past. In a sense, therefore, Benjamin's 'inoculation' is directed simultaneously backwards (rejecting the pull of childhood nostalgia) and forwards (steeling himself for a life in exile). As Peter Szondi comments, in his introduction to this volume (Benjamin 2006: 18–19), Benjamin here differs from Proust, whose search for 'lost time' was a great influence on Benjamin. While Proust searches into the past to escape from time (and to seek a moment when past and present ultimately coincide), Benjamin, argues Szondi, employs a dialectical approach, looking forward when exploring the past, seeking to discover in childhood what Benjamin called 'traces of what was to come' (Benjamin 2006: 79). What we might call the forward directed focus of Benjamin's memories is also found in a comment on the phenomenon of *déjà vu* which he included (phrased slightly differently) both in 'A Berlin Chronicle' and in *Berlin Childhood*. *Déjà vu* was, he thought, somewhat misnamed as it describes an experience of sound not sight: 'Shouldn't we rather speak of events which affect us like an echo – one awakened by a sound that seems to have issued from somewhere in the darkness of past life?' (2006: 129; and compare Benjamin 1986: 59) Such events are 'like a muff that someone has forgotten in our room', indicating that a stranger has been present, and which point 'us to that invisible stranger – the future – which forgot them at our place' (Benjamin 2006: 130). Benjamin, in contrast to Auden's notion of unchanging spaces, suggests that places exist in our memories as pregnant with a future that we will one day reach back to activate. In one corner of the Zoological Garden, for instance, Benjamin feels 'traces of what was to come' in his life, noting that just as there are meant to be plants that 'convey the power to see into the future, so there are places that possess such a virtue'; in this particular 'prophetic corner' of the Garden, Benjamin notes, in a fascinating inversion of temporality, 'it seems as if all that lies in store for us has become the past' (2006: 79).

Berlin Childhood thus challenges the idea that a memoir should be concerned primarily with time, unfolding in linear fashion, suggesting instead that spatiality is also a key structural feature in the writing of a life. As Brodersen argues, Benjamin's memoir is organised not by date or history but by locations, always precisely noted: sections are thus named after places such as the loggias of courtyards, a market hall, the Tiergarten park, the Victory Column in Königsplatz, or particular streets, such as 'Blumeshof 12' or 'At the Corner of Steglitzer and Genthiner'. Brodersen thus describes the book as 'the topography of a metropolis as a world of life and experience' (1996: 5). This mixture of topography and autobiography is 'certainly not the stuff of normal memoirs. This is a particular kind of recollection, in the original sense of the German word *Erinnerung*: observations of the interior – of one's own self and its surroundings, of the city as world and landscape, of time as space' (Brodersen 1996: 5). Observations of the interior, for Benjamin, are thus simultaneously observations of exterior spaces.

In this intertwining of urban topography with memoir Benjamin, however, not only rejects the way traditional biography is motivated by temporality, he also downplays the role of narrative, to produce a text that relies, like much lyric poetry, upon *images*. In his introduction Benjamin notes that conventional biographical features, such as information on family and friends, 'altogether recede in the present undertaking' because he has 'made an effort to get hold of the *images* in which the experience of the big city is precipitated in a child of the middle class'; it is these images of a 'metropolitan childhood', he notes, that 'are capable, at their core, of preforming later historical experience' (2006: 37–

8). This focus on images is part of the 'small form' or aphoristic style Benjamin pioneered in *One Way Street* (1928) and also distinguishes the text from the more narrative-driven predecessor to *Berlin Childhood*, 'A Berlin Chronicle'. Some of the same incidents occur in both texts, although the 'Chronicle' tends to focus on the older Benjamin's exploits in the city, such as the literary cafes he visited. Even here, however, Benjamin was aware that the form he was seeking was more spatial than temporal in design. Thus in the 'Chronicle' he notes that even these extensive 'reminiscences' do not amount to an autobiography: 'For autobiography has to do with time, with sequence and what makes up the continuous flow of life. Here I am talking of a space, of moments and discontinuities' (Benjamin 1986: 28). In the 'Chronicle' Benjamin contemplates writing a life by means of that most spatial and imagistic of texts, a map:

> I have long, indeed for years, played with the idea of setting out the sphere of life – bios – graphically on a map … I have evolved a system of signs, and on the gray background of such maps they would make a colourful show if I clearly marked in the houses of my friends and girl friends, the assembly halls of various collectives, from the 'debating chambers' of the Youth Movement to the gathering places of the Communist youth, the hotel and brothel rooms that I knew for one night, the decisive benches in the Tiergarten, the ways to different schools and the graves that I saw filled, the sites of prestigious cafes whose long-forgotten names daily crossed our lips, the tennis courts where empty apartment blocks stand today, and the halls emblazoned with gold and stucco that the terrors of dancing classes make almost the equal of gymnasiums. (1986: 5)

Many of these bio-maps appear in Benjamin's two texts, but we can see in this extract how the 'Chronicle', even as the author is resisting the lure of the 'continuous flow of life' (1986: 28), tends towards it in the listing of places of biographical significance. It is only in the later *Berlin Childhood* that the formal structure of the text shifts decisively towards the spatial image and the temporally discontinuous. This is achieved mainly by a closer attention to those 'images of my metropolitan childhood' (2006: 38) which result in the narrative reminiscences of the 'Chronicle' being transformed in *Berlin Childhood* into a textual space which concentrates upon particular locations: the Tiergarten with its bridges, islands and imperial columns; the zoological gardens on the edge of the park; or the various bourgeois homes of Benjamin's family and relatives in Berlin's Old West. Benjamin's structuring of the text by images also points to the influence of modernist cinema and perhaps the theory of montage pioneered by Eisenstein; here we can note the similarity with Bryher, although Benjamin's text is perhaps the more radical of the two in terms of employing a montage-like form. Many episodes, in keeping with Benjamin's wider materialist philosophy of history as demonstrated in his masterwork, *The Arcades Project*, also concern objects perceived in the street or in the home: the 'The Moon', 'Telephone', 'The Sewing Box', or the bed in which the young Benjamin lies ill.

There is no narrative logic to the order in which these images of places and things occur, in keeping with Benjamin's discontinuous approach to his memories. There are, however, moments that seem to display a spatial logic, as when the interior of his grandmother's house in 'Blumeshof 12', with its 'almost immemorial feeling of bourgeois security' (Benjamin 2006: 87–8) is followed by two sections on exterior spaces: 'Winter Evening', concerning some 'dark, unknown' streets where Benjamin was taken by his mother while shopping; and 'Crooked Street' (Krumme Strasse), where he was taken, unwillingly, to the swimming pool. These streets represent excitement, as well as unease and anxiety, and are juxtaposed to the cosy security of the bourgeois interior of his grandparents' house; these images, as Benjamin argued, also 'preform later historical experience' (38), by dialectically linking the interior space of the bourgeois home to the commodity culture that sustained it in the exterior world. Benjamin dislikes the noise of the swimming pool, located in the 'gloomiest nook' of the street, but is enthralled by the nearby shops selling bric-à-brac, a pawnbroker's, and by a store selling writing materials that also contained inexpensive Nick Carter detective books and more 'risqué publications' hidden towards the back (94). This shop presents a set of feelings, akin to a 'magic spell', for the young Benjamin that he can bring home to his bedroom and which compensate for the 'hateful roar' of the swimming pool (96). Like Bryher, then, it is the geographical emotions produced by the spaces of Berlin that are of most significance to Benjamin.

Bryher/Benjamin

This chapter has explored how two writers engaged with the material spaces of Berlin in their life writing, trying to understand the relation in Bryher and Benjamin between finding something and losing something, between discerning the shape of one's life and becoming exiled from a city. Reading *The Heart to Artemis* and *Berlin Childhood* together thus offers a fertile way in which to think the interior spaces of life writing, one marked above all by the way in which external geographies of the city shape the interiority of the self. Bryher, the wealthy English lesbian in moral revolt at her upbringing, and Benjamin, the

Jewish Marxist intellectual in exile from his beloved city, seemed, prima facie, an unlikely pairing and the different ways in which they approached the writing of their lives and the experience of the same city appeared an interesting exercise in comparison. However, Bryher and Benjamin also found one another, not in Berlin, but in another city, Paris, through the mutual friendship of Adrienne Monnier (owner of the bookshop La Maison des Amis des Livres) and Sylvia Beach (owner of the nearby English language bookshop Shakespeare and Company).[7] In his letters Benjamin describes visiting Beach's bookshop in Rue de l'Odéon early in 1934 and his growing friendship with Monnier (1994: 436, 519). In September 1939, after the German invasion of Poland, Benjamin, along with many other Germans, was interned and detained in a camp near Nevers; it was Monnier and some others who succeeded in lobbying the French government to have Benjamin released. In December 1939 he wrote to Max Horkheimer that he had received a letter from the National Refugee Service, presumably concerning his official status, and that he believed 'it is Mrs Bryher who made the effort to solicit it for me through some of her friends' (1994: 621). Bryher, he noted, was 'editor-in-chief' of *Life and Letters Today* and has 'been following my work for quite some time and was quite worried about my internment' (1994: 621).

In December 1937 Benjamin wrote to Bryher about an article, 'Paris 1900', which she had published in the magazine *Life and Letters Today* and which was revised to form part of *The Heart to Artemis*: 'I was converted by the text', wrote Benjamin.[8] Concerning Bryher's first visit to Paris as a young girl, it centred upon her trip to the Paris Exhibition of that year. Benjamin, of course, had been working for many years on Paris and the Arcades, and it is amusing to find him praising Bryher's comparison of the grand arch of the Exhibition to the curly hair ornament favoured by women at the time: 'For the world exhibition portal ... you have found the redeeming word: You have identified the comb that crowns the curly head of Paris!' (1937).

In his letter Benjamin also praises Bryher's depiction of childhood, writing that she 'brings to bear the grace of childhood by outlining its most sombre backdrop' and demonstrates 'the aggression of children's free play (in fantasy)', something that he too has often pondered. Benjamin closes his letter by stating that he wishes, 'to read this beautiful prose text in its entirety one day' and hopes 'a little exchange can develop', before turning to his own text of childhood:

---

7   For more on these friendships see McCabe 2011; Camboni 2008.

8   I am very grateful to Birgit Van Puymbroeck for transcribing this letter and to Vike Martina Plock for translating it.

> When, in 1932, I justified to myself, unconsciously at first, that my exile was looming,
> I undertook, equally unconsciously, a kind of inoculation that was supposed to make
> me immune against homesickness for the city, in which I spent my childhood years.
> Back then I wrote under the title 'Berliner Kindheit um 1900' a series of short sketches.
> Most of them have appeared in print. I'll happily send you some! (1937)

Whether Bryher read Benjamin's sketches is not recorded, but clearly her text resonated strongly with Benjamin. It is interesting to note that in 'Paris 1900' Bryher rephrases her concept of 'geographical emotions', with the version in *Life and Letters Today* reading: 'All my life I have suffered from "geographical emotions". *Cities are so much easier to understand than people*' (1937: 33, emphasis added). In keeping with her close engagement with psychoanalysis in the 1930s Bryher here wishes to 'understand' cities, rather than just view them as 'almost as real to me as people' (1962: 26). It is, perhaps, a sentiment that Benjamin would have enjoyed, writing *Berlin Childhood* to understand how the city formed him, inoculating himself against the 'geographical emotions' of both nostalgia and exile.

Bryher's memoir of the war years, *The Days of Mars*, poignantly recalls her last meeting with Benjamin, along with Adrienne Monnier and Sylvia Beach, in April 1940 in Paris (1972: 22). By this time Bryher had become the Swiss contact for a group of friends, mainly drawn from psychoanalytic circles, who used their combined wealth to help Jews and political refugees escape from Nazi Germany by providing documents for exit visas. Bryher mentions helping some 105 people escape persecution in this way, adding that only a couple of these individuals failed eventually to escape (1962: 278): One of these was Benjamin, who took his own life with an overdose of morphine at the French-Spanish border in September 1940, believing (mistakenly) that his escape route to America via Spain was blocked. It seems an apt, yet melancholy, place to end: with the lost life of Walter Benjamin, who tried to inoculate himself against his exile from Berlin, the final part of this journey of exile being helped by Bryher who, we might say, found herself in this same city.

References

Auden, W.H. 1991. *Collected Poems*, edited E. Mendelson. London: Faber.

Benjamin, W. 1937. Unpublished letter to Bryher [19th December, Paris]. *Bryher Papers*, Beinecke Library. Box 3, Folder 111.

Benjamin, W. 1973. *Illuminations*. London: Fontana.

Benjamin, W. 1986. A Berlin Chronicle, in *Reflections: Essays, Aphorisms, Autobiographical Writings*, translated by E. Jephcott. New York: Schocken Books, 3–60.

Benjamin, W. 1994. *The Correspondence of Walter Benjamin 1910–1940*, edited by G. Scholem and T.W. Adorno, translated by M. R. Jacobson and E. M. Jacobson. Chicago and London: University of Chicago Press.

Benjamin, W. 2006. *Berlin Childhood Around 1900*, translated by H. Eiland. Cambridge, Massachusetts: Belknap Press of Harvard University Press.

Brodersen, M. 1996. *Walter Benjamin: A Biography*, edited by M. Dervis, translated by M. R. Green and I. Ligers. London: Verso.

Bryher. 1937. Paris 1900. *Life and Letters Today*, 16(8), 33–4.

Bryher. 1962. *The Heart to Artemis: A Writer's Memoirs*. London: Collins.

Bryher. 1972. *The Days of Mars: A Memoir, 1940–46*. London: Calder and Boyars.

Bryher. 2000. *Development* in *Bryher: Two Novels*. Madison: University of Wisconsin Press.

Camboni, M. 2008. 'Why, Berlin, must I love you so?': Bryher in Berlin, 1927–1932. *HD's Web e-newsletter*, Vol. 3 [Online]. Available at: http://www.imagists.org/hd/hdsweb/december2008.pdf [accessed 7 October 2014].

Friedman, S. S. (ed.) 2002. *Analyzing Freud: Letters of H.D., Bryher, and their Circle*. New York: New Directions.

Josephson, M. 1962. *Life Among the Surrealists: A Memoir*. New York: Holt Rinehart and Winston.

Marcus, L. 1998. Cinema and psychoanalysis: Introduction, in *Close Up 1927–1933: Cinema and Modernism*, edited by J. Donald, A. Friedberg and L. Marcus. London: Cassell, 240–46.

Marcus, L. 2007. *The Tenth Muse: Writing about Cinema in the Modernist Period*. Oxford: Oxford University Press.

McCabe, S. 2011. Bryher and Berlin: Modernism's geographical emotions. *The Berlin Journal*, 21(2), 8–13.

McCabe, S. 2012. Close Up & wars they saw: From visual erotics to a transferential politics of film. *The Space Between*, 8(1), 11–35.

Roters, E. 1983. *Berlin, 1910–33*. New York: Rizzoli International.

Twain, M. 2009. The Chicago of Europe [1892], in *The Chicago of Europe, and Other Travel Stories*. New York: Sterling Publishing Co., 191–203.

Vidler, A. 2000. *Warped Space, Art, Architecture, and Anxiety in Modern Culture*. Massachusetts: MIT Press.

Chapter 3

Hilary Mantel and the Space of Life Writing

Neil Vickers

In this chapter, I consider the significance of houses in Hilary Mantel's memoir, *Giving Up the Ghost* (2003). Every chapter but one of Mantel's book is set in a different house, and each house corresponds to a distinct epoch in Mantel's life, with marked differences in her outlook on the world. I shall focus on the styles of thinking that Mantel describes in just two of the chapters and on how these were associated with distinct states of her body. She says that when she lived in her grandmother's house (described in Chapter 2, 'Now Geoffrey, Don't Torment Her'), all her perceptions were 'synaesthesic' (2003: 23); during this period of her life, she also expected to become a boy. When, aged 5, she moved to her parents' first and only home of their own, she realised that her parents were unhappily married, and her hopes of becoming a boy were dashed. In the chapter describing this shift ('The Secret Garden') her relationships with her environment and her femininity were experienced supernaturally, with both involving a struggle with ghosts. *Giving Up the Ghost* contains a subtle, multi-layered mythology of space and place. In Mantel's memoir, spaces have certain supernatural properties against which places – districts, houses, gardens: spaces requisitioned for human habitation of some sort – offer at best partial shelter. *Places are subject to invasion by spaces.* Men move through spaces confidently, apparently heedless of their dangers. Whether this is the result of some secret Faustian pact or sheer stupidity is a question that is left hanging. More than once, the memoir suggests a link between the dangers of spaces and those of men. At the same time, women seem more aware of the dangers of open spaces and in some cases this expresses itself as a preference for the home. It should be emphasised from the outset that *Giving Up the Ghost* is a feminist book and that its highly idiosyncratic notions of space and place are essential features of its mythological groundwork. When the memoir first appeared, the novelist Elizabeth Lowry praised its 'visceral apprehension of the essential wrongness of things, which cannot be reasoned away' (2004: 25). The claim I wish to make is that space and place are the most fundamental metaphors Mantel calls upon to give expression to this wrongness.

According to Frédéric Regard (2003, 2004, 2007), English life writing is distinguished from life writing in other European languages by its unusual dependence on geographical knowledge. English authors, Regard argues, know *who* they are when they know *where* they are. In a recent collection (2007), Regard explores some of the ways in which imperialism might have fostered an appetite for self-knowledge through what he calls elsewhere 'the spatialisation of the subject' (2003: 91). Colonialism, he suggests, created contact zones between colonists and indigenous peoples in which each became the other's Other. Writing about those places involved writing about different kinds of inter-subjectivity – linguistic, religious, cognitive, moral and hermeneutic differences (among many others) – in which awareness of 'oneself as another', to use Paul Ricoeur's phrase, became the truest source of self-awareness (Regard 2007, Ricoeur 1992). Although the Irish War of Independence of 1919–21 and its culture are conspicuous features of Mantel's childhood, her memoir is not directly concerned with colonialism. It is, however, the case that her developing awareness as a young girl of her family and its conflicts is described in terms of her changing relationship with the spaces around her.

Behind Regard's speculation lies a recognisably French set of preoccupations based on a distinctively French approach to space as a concept. It may be helpful to spell out what I take the central features of the French tradition to be. Three stand out. First, it is rigorously anti-naturalist: when explaining our relationship with space, French theorists never give primacy to objectively-given structures in nature. Accordingly, they do not base their findings in physics or in any scientific discipline. This is in marked contrast with Anglo-American writers who are overwhelmingly naturalist. Second, the French tradition is a phenomenological tradition. It assumes that the only valid object of investigation is what space might mean from a first-person point of view. Space is always conceived of as a vehicle for human intentionality. Indeed, its interest lies, first and foremost, in the light it sheds on human intentionality. Third, the French tradition has been very influenced by psychoanalysis, and for that reason emphasises unconscious aspects of human dealings with space and the power of motivated irrationality. All of these characteristics make it well-suited to the purposes of literary criticism.

Particularly relevant to the present discussion is Gaston Bachelard's *Poetics of Space* which, though by no means the first intervention, is arguably *the* central reference in French writing on this topic. For Bachelard, all spaces are imbued with the psychic qualities their inhabitants project into them. However objectively we claim to organise a space, in reality we are seeking to house our own fantasies. This can be seen most clearly in human habitations. We dream our houses into existence, Bachelard says. We create alcoves and corners to huddle in. There might be parts of a house that have special significance for us. We associate certain rooms with certain people and certain biographical events. Because houses perform this mirroring function, 'there is ground for taking the house as a *tool for analysis* of the human soul ... Not only our memories, but the things we have forgotten are "housed". Our soul is an abode. And by remembering "houses" and "rooms" we learn to "abide" within ourselves' (Bachelard 1962: xxxviii). One of the joys of Mantel's memoir is the way she uses the different parts of her grandparents' house and the area surrounding it as a kind of broken mirror reflecting aspects of herself as a child.

Bachelard's book is the starting point for Foucault's famous lecture on 'other spaces' or 'heterotopias' (delivered in Tunis 1967 but published in full only in 1984). Foucault praised Bachelard's designation of space as a vehicle for irrational human prejudice and fantasy but regretted that he focused too much on 'interior' (i.e. domestic, intimate) space. Foucault claimed that external space has been a source of anxiety in Europe since at least the time of Galileo. The great medieval philosophers who nourished themselves on the pure milk of Aristotelian cosmology thought that everything had a place in space. Once Galileo declared that space was infinite, Aristotelianism became a dead letter. If the universe was potentially infinite, could anything be said to have a place of its own at all? From a religious point of view, the infinity that Galileo opened up was ambiguous. For if, on the one hand, infinite space was a sublime idea that readily and easily took on numinous connotations, it also, on the other, threatened the Christian world with a great vacancy in which the numinous was conspicuous only by its absence. This ambiguity is explicitly taken up in several of Pascal's *Pensées* (first published in 1669):

> I see those frightful spaces of the universe which surround me, and I find myself tied to one corner of this vast expanse, without knowing why I am put in this place rather than in another, nor why the short time which is given me to live is assigned to me at this point rather than at another of the whole eternity which was before me or which shall come after me. I see nothing but infinites on all sides, which surround me as an atom, and as a shadow which endures only for an instant and returns no more. All I know is that I must soon die, but what I know least is this very death which I cannot escape. (1958: 55)

Or again:

> When I consider the short duration of my life, swallowed up in the eternity before and after, the little space which I fill, and even can see, engulfed in the infinite immensity of spaces of which I am ignorant, and which know me not, I am frightened, and am

astonished at being here rather than there; for there is no reason why here rather than there, why now rather than then. Who has put me here? By whose order and direction have this place and time been allotted to me? *Memoria hospitis unius diei prætereuntis.* (61)

Or again:

The eternal silence of these infinite spaces frightens me. (61)

Although Foucault never mentions Pascal, the latter's reckoning with infinite space surely lies behind this strand of his argument. Nor can he have been unaware that it was explored at length in one of the most important and influential works of historiographic literary criticism to have appeared in France in the relatively recent past, Lucien Goldmann's *The Hidden God* (1955).

In the first half of his lecture, Foucault suggests that the transformations of the public sphere which took place in nineteenth-century Europe were the continuation of a centuries' long effort to tame the very idea of this infinite space. Towns and cities ceased to be independent points in space and came to be defined dynamically, through underlying networks of institutions. Indeed, the state *was* these networks. In this way, towns became objective, and in part (but only in part) 'de-sanctified'. Modern heterotopias were a consequence of these endeavours. A heterotopia is a place where a society's counter-ideals find expression. Foucault draws up a list of heterotopias in 1960s France which include psychiatric clinics, old people's homes, cemeteries (heterotopic in a society that assigns little meaning to death because the church no longer commands much allegiance), museums and libraries (monuments of, and to, alien cultures), fairgrounds, brothels, military barracks and prisons. Heterotopias are necessary because the ideals they deviate from are delusional. Foucault also claimed that heterotopias mark a boundary between sacred and profane spaces because very often the sacred is assumed to be hidden in them, sometimes in the shape of the spectral. In the original French version of his lecture Foucault used the metaphor of haunting to highlight the anxiety underpinning these efforts. Unfortunately the English translation all but eliminates the spectral from Foucault's text. Both the threateningness of external space and the spectral forms in which it is concentrated are central preoccupations of *Giving Up the Ghost*.

The theory of the heterotopia was the chief inspiration for Marc Augé's notion of the 'non-place' (*non-lieu*). Augé starts from the completely Foucauldian premise that space is a source of anxiety that humans seek to neutralise by desacralising. He presents industrial modernity as an epoch in which the rhythms of the industrial working day suppress an experience of time that is fundamentally liturgical and ritualistic. Here in miniature is the conflict between the place and the non-place. Places are 'relational, historical and concerned with identity' and always batten off some version of ritual or liturgical temporality. Spaces which are concerned with none of these things Augé calls non-places. Non-places, like places, 'never exist in pure form' (1992: 78) but they are chiefly characterised by their lack of relatedness to a sacred temporality. He claims that modernity is increasingly characterised by 'non-places': unconnected zones filled with unconnected objects. For Augé the primary function of the non-place is to suppress the recognition of human relationship in favour of individualism, transience and political domination. (Non-recognition of others is a way of allowing the economic *status quo* to do its work.) The world of non-places is

> a world where people are born in the clinic and die in hospital, where transit points and temporary abodes are proliferating ... (hotel chains and squats, holiday clubs and refugee camps, shantytowns threatened with demolition or doomed to festering longevity) ... where the habitué of supermarkets, slot machines and credit cards communicates wordlessly, through gestures ... a world thus surrendered to solitary individuality, to the fleeting, the temporary and ephemeral. (Augé 1995: 77–8)

And as I shall show towards the end of this chapter, the closing chapter of *Giving Up the Ghost*, with its succession of houses in the affluent suburbs of London's M4 corridor, has its own bleakly comic and politically astute tale to tell about the non-places that Mantel's upwardly-mobile post-war generation has made its own.

The Space of Early Childhood

Near the beginning of the memoir, Mantel talks of the 'overwhelming sensory power' (2003: 23) of her early memories: 'my early world was synaesthesic', she writes, 'and I am haunted by the ghosts of my own sense impressions, which re-emerge when I try to write, and shiver between the lines' (24, 23). She recalls learning to walk from her grandmother's house to the house next door, owned and inhabited by her great-aunt, Annie Connor. To reach her destination, young Hilary had to pass a rusty iron ring: 'Grandad says it is where they tied the monkey up but I don't think they ever really had one; all the same, he lurks in my mind, a small grey monkey with piteous eyes and a long active tail' (28). When she masters the journey, she compares the sound of the piano in the house next door with the sound of her grandmother's piano. The piano in her great-aunt's house makes a 'bronchial, damaged' (29) sound. Whenever it is played, young Hilary stands next to it 'and feels the instrument resonating like a cat purring' (29). The purring in turn reminds her of a cat belonging to Mrs Clayton, a neighbour whose husband had recently died. Mrs Clayton was so distressed by her bereavement that she had to be admitted to a psychiatric hospital. The climactic memory in this sequence occurs when young Hilary sits on the stairs eating a marzipan sweet; she becomes convinced that she has swallowed a house-fly and that she will soon die. 'After a while', Mantel writes,

> I am walking about in the room again. My resolve to die completely alone has faltered. I suppose it will take an hour or so, or I might live till evening. My head is still hanging. What's the matter? I am asked. I don't feel I can say. My original intention was not to raise the alarm; also, I feel there is shame in such a death. I would rather just fall over, and that's about it. I feel queasy now. Something is tugging at my attention. Perhaps it is a sense of absurdity. The dry rasping in my throat persists, but now I don't know if it is the original obstruction lodged there, or the memory of it, the imprint, which is not going to fade from my breathing flesh. For many years the word 'marzipan' affects me with its deathly hiss, the buzz in its syllables, a sepulchral fizz. (33)

Perhaps the most important thing to notice here is that there seems to be a principle of sympathy at work in the child's mind linking animate and inanimate objects. And what this principle communicates to the adult reader, if not always to the child, are presentiments of death. The monkey had to be tied up for unspecified reasons and has mysteriously disappeared. The bronchial piano is consubstantial with Mrs Clayton's cat and the hinterland of pain of which he is the uncomprehending emblem. And the fizzing fly like its mysterious verbal ministers – the word 'marzipan', for instance – is an unambiguous harbinger of death. Young Hilary seems to inhabit a space in which the characteristics of one thing – a piano, a cat, a dead husband, a word – mysteriously migrate into others. Space is not empty; it is kaleidoscopic. It sets before her senses a succession of beautiful, shifting, symmetrical configurations (monkey/girl; piano/cat; fly/marzipan). The sudden changes in the overall pattern were often overwhelming for the little girl. Consider, by way of illustration, the following passage in which she describes her friendship with Evelyn, a girl her own age:

> Evelyn's house – the Aldous's house – is darker than ours and has a more dumpling smell. Not being Catholics, they don't have a piano, but as they are at the end of the

common yard, they have a more tidy and well-arranged plot, with flower beds. Outside our house my grandad has grubbed out a bed for nasturtiums, and trained them up a wall. He calls them storshions ... When I try to put names to their imperial colours, to the scarlet and striated amber, my chest seems dangerously to swell ... Evelyn's dad, Arthur, grows geraniums. Their flowers are scarlet dots, their stems are bent and nodular. When Arthur comes in from work in his bib and brace, his sleeves are rolled up above his elbows, and I see the inside of his arms, the sinews and knotty veins. I think his arms are the stems of plants, that he is not human, perhaps an ogre. (43–4)

It is worth noting that this way of looking at the world was at its zenith when Mantel was obsessed with the tale of King Arthur and the Knights of the Round Table (Arthur being Evelyn's father's name). It is characteristic of Mantel's narrative method in *Giving Up the Ghost* to introduce a character by describing the setting in which she first got to know them and for the setting then to be allowed to take on an exciting but sinister life of its own. What Mantel calls her synaesthesic perception could equally be described as a capacity to disperse her emotional experience into different sensory fields.

Mantel's relationship with space was closely connected with her early intuitions about gender. Although she knew she was a girl, she identified completely with the male body. All of the games she played involved imagining herself in male roles, as a priest or a knight errant, for instance. And most strikingly of all, she managed to convince herself that when she reached the age of four she would turn into a boy (40). It is hard to say what lay behind this assumption. Part of it seems to have been identification with her grandfather, George. George included his granddaughter in everything he did and he seems to have been the person she loved most in the world. Moreover, some of the privileges of being a man seem to have appealed to Hilary. All of the men in her life travelled. Her father, Henry, commuted every day from Hadfield to Manchester: 'When he comes in from work he carries on his coat the complex city smell of smog, ink, tobacco. He has a travelling chess set ... ' (39). Her grandfather, George, was a railway signalman in Hadfield and had served in the British army in Palestine: 'In the desert, my grandfather rode a camel. He commanded it with certain words in Egyptian, known only to camels, now imparted to me' (35–6). Her Irish-immigrant grandmother had several brothers who would 'come from Hollingsworth and places even further. They give the impression, to me, of wandering the roads' (34). Women, on the other hand, stayed at home. Mantel's grandmother 'never went out' (49). 'When someone came to the door, and she didn't know who it was, she hid on the stairs' (49). Mantel's mother's penchant for movement is a sign of her unpredictable, unreliable nature. The earliest memory Mantel reports is of herself sitting up in her pram, watching her mother step back from her in order to take her photograph: 'I hold out my arms because I don't want her to go' (27). This scene in turn looks ahead to a later period in Mantel's life, when she was seven or eight and sick with anxiety that her mother will 'run, and take her chance on another life, a better life elsewhere: some princess place, where her real family lives' (81).

Space and the Female Body, Aged 7 to 11

If Mantel's early infantile body moved through kaleidoscopic space, it was because the patterns she was so adept at finding helped her to process her emotional experience somewhat at her leisure. All of this changed when her parents took her on a holiday to Blackpool. We might characterise the years between the ages of 7 and 11 as ones in which Mantel's body became the register of unspeakable family secrets. These, as I shall now show, came to her through her perceptions of space.

In Blackpool, Mantel first registered that her parents were unhappily married:

> Standing on the pier at Blackpool, I look down at the inky waves swirling. Again, the noise of nature, deeply conversational, too quick to catch; again the rushing movement, blue, deep, and far below. I look up at my mother and father. They are standing close together, talking over my head. A thought comes to me, so swift and strange it feels like the first thought that I have ever had. It strikes with piercing intensity, like a needle in the eye. The thought is this: that I stop them being happy. I, me and only me. That my father will throw me down on the rocks, down into the sea. That perhaps he will not do it, but some impulse in his heart thinks he ought. For what am I, but a disposable, replaceable child? And without me, they would have a chance in life. (53)

The child's sudden apprehension of the conflict between her parents comes to her as a vertiginous experience of space. The reader assumes that young Hilary is perceiving two things at once. The noise of nature, we think, is shot through with the noise of her parents. Each amplifies the other. The noise of nature is deeply conversational because it is *their* noise. And the fact that it is too quick to catch is a sign that the little girl senses both her parents' immersion in a set of realities that she cannot begin to understand and her own pain on making that discovery. The portents of death that had previously presented themselves to the child in the symbolic form of the monkey ring, Annie Connor's piano, or Mrs Clayton's cat were easier to endure because young Hilary was able to turn them over in her mind at her own pace and because the connection between them all remained somewhat obscure to her. On Blackpool pier, objects move at overwhelming speed. The 'rushing movement' of the waves, the 'swift thought' that strikes with piercing intensity, the perception of being hurled onto the rocks and into the sea suggest that space is much more dangerous than she had previously supposed. All of the outdoor scenes in the book up to this point have entailed painful exposure. But Blackpool pier opens up a prospect much worse than this. The sequel is just as significant:

> The next thing is that I am in bed with a fever raging. My lungs are full to bursting. The water boils, frets, spumes. I am limp in the power of the current that tugs beneath the waves. To open my eyes I have to force off my eyelids the weight of water. I am trying to die and I am trying to live. I open my eyes and I see my mother looking down at me. She is sitting swivelled towards me, her anxious face peering down. She has made a fence of Mrs Scott's dining chairs, their backs to my bed, and behind this barrier she sits, watching me. Her wrists, crossed, rest on the backs of the chairs; her lady's hands droop. For a minute or two I swim up from under the water clawing ... I feel myself taken by the current, tugged away. I am changed now. Not in that fever but in one of the series, one of those that follow it, my weight of hair is cut off. What remains is like feathers, I think, like fluff. I lose my baby fat. For another twenty-five years I will be frail. (53–4)

The imagined punishment is executed on the little girl's body. The space of the pier is exchanged for the space of the sea. Its 'weight' will remain with the little girl, overwhelming her 'weight': she becomes limp, her senses fail her. An attempt is made to circumscribe the space around her through the fence of chairs, but the vastness of the sea and the choking sensations it gives rise to are internalised through a series of fevers. This internalisation is crucial for through it the body becomes the container of the vastness of space and all its sinister contents. Before she went to Blackpool, young Hilary was able to take pleasure in her body, even if it hadn't yet turned into the one she thought she ought to have. After Blackpool, her body became the focus of all her sufferings. Through it, she became foreign to herself. And there was worse to come. Shortly after this holiday, young Hilary discovers, among other things, that she is destined to remain a girl: 'I realise – and carry the dull knowledge inside me, heavy in my chest – that I am never going to be a boy now. I don't exactly know why. I sense that things have slid too far, from some ideal starting point' (57). It is tempting to conjecture that her desire to be a boy was based on her love for her grandfather. What she discovered on Blackpool pier was that this identification could not diminish her helplessness in the face of two parents who couldn't get on.

Despite the events at Blackpool, Mantel's parents went on to have two more children in quick succession. They moved with Hilary and the first of her two brothers into their own house, a short distance from her grandparents. Shortly after the move, Mantel's mother invited Jack, a lodger-cum-lover to come and live with the family in the new house. Mantel is vague about dates but her father continued to live in the house for a period of at least four years, looking after the children when he was not at work and trying to avoid Jack and Mantel's mother. No one explained why her parents separated or why Jack moved in. His arrival is experienced in terms of the scene on Blackpool pier and its aftermath:

> This is the worst time of my life: days of despair. I am on the pier at Blackpool, with the screaming gulls and the wind, looking down into the boiling sea. Words swirl over my head, words of loathing and contempt. A great hand lifts me; it is the hand of the law. And here is my punishment, coming now, coming now; I feel the rush of air against my face. The law picks me up into the wind, the law lets me go; I fall through space, and on the rocks my head smashes open like an egg. The sea drinks my yellow blood. (84–5)

In Blackpool itself, it was her father who wanted to dash her against the rocks for the sake of his own and his wife's happiness. The punishment that is meted out in this memory of Blackpool is impersonal, abstract, incomprehensible, but above all final. There are no named others. There is a very moving scene in which her grandfather George takes his tools back to his own house, the switch signifying a wider breakdown in family relationships. Hilary's Irish grandmother and great-aunt stop going to the shops and attending Mass because they feel ashamed of what Hilary's mother has done and cannot face being questioned about it (95). The space around the family becomes contaminated:

> What happens now? We are talked about in the street. Some rules have been broken. A darkness closes about our house. The air becomes jaundiced and clotted, and hangs in gaseous clouds over the rooms. I see them so thickly that I think I am going to bump my head on them. (86)

Internal spaces suffered still greater taint. Mantel recalls that when she was seven years of age, she 'carried a simple space for God inside me: a jagged space surrounded by light, a waiting space cut out of my solar plexus' (105). One of the first things Jack did on moving into the new house was to hack at the undergrowth in the garden, so that there was a plain view 'from the Glass Place at the back of the kitchen to the crumbling back fence' (95). This single act exposes Hilary to a vision which 'wrapped a strangling hand around my life' (106). It was a vision of a creature associated with 'formless, borderless evil' (107) and Mantel imagines it infiltrating her womb. 'Within the space of a thought, it is inside me, and has set up a sick resonance within my bones and in all the cavities of my body' (107).

What happens to Hilary's body afflicts the house. Jack's passion for home improvements places the entire household in thrall to demonic forces:

> the spirits gather thickly in the half-finished house, falling from their places in the glass-fronted cupboards to the right of the fireplace, waking and stretching from their sooty slumbers behind the demolished range. They discharge from the burnt walls in puffs, they are scraped into slivers as the old wallpaper peels away, and lie curled on the floors, mocking the bristle brush. Our daily life is hushed, driven into corners. We move in a rush between the house's safe areas, and the ones less safe, where, as you enter a room, you get the impression that someone is waiting for you. The dogs, who are no longer puppies, squeal with fear in the night. My mother comes down to them, shivering in her nightdress, and sees their hackles raised, their thin forms shrinking against the dawn light. One night, I hear my mother and Jack, discussing. I am lurking in the cold Glass Place, coming in from the lavatory. 'Well', she says, 'so? So what do you think it is?' Her voice rises, in an equal blend of challenge, fear and scorn. '*Ghosts?*' She has spoken my thoughts: which I thought were unspeakable. The hairs rise on the back of my neck. (96)

Young Hilary became a very sickly child, plagued with fevers, pains, colics, difficulties breathing, and sensory distortions of various kinds, some of them brought about at her own behest. At the end of the four-year period everybody except her father went to live in a new house in a village not far from Hadfield. She never saw her father again. While Jack and her mother did not marry, young Hilary had to change her name from Thompson, her original name, to Mantel in order to maintain the fiction that Jack Mantel was her father. The girls with whom she went to school pestered her for an explanation but she was required to maintain the strictest secrecy. At the same time, the family presented itself to the outside world as an ordinary Catholic family.

The Space of Early Womanhood

Adolescence was a trial. She continued to be sickly. Jack resented her and the atmosphere in the home was charged with hostility. But Hilary proved an adept pupil at school and went to London to study law. After two years, she transferred to Sheffield to be near her boyfriend who afterwards became her husband. There she reported 'a pain which I could not explain; it seemed to wander about my body, nibbling here, stabbing there, flitting every time I tried to put my finger on it' (149). Many years later she established that these pains were caused by endometriosis, a notoriously difficult condition to diagnose, but as her doctors could find no physical cause for them at the time, they concluded that they were probably psychosomatic. Her GP put her on tricyclic antidepressants; her pains continued. She was then sent to see a psychiatrist, Dr G thought she was a hysteric. He said her ailments stemmed from the fact that she was a law student. The law, he told her, was too intellectually demanding a subject for a woman, especially one as conscientious as Mantel. He advised her to give up her studies and to get a job in a dress shop, like her mother (170). Dr G prescribed Valium; but instead of tranquillizing her, Mantel found that the drug made her furious: she wanted to burn down buildings. Dr G thought she was sliding rapidly into psychosis and he put her on antipsychotics to which she had an akathisic, psychotic, adverse reaction which resulted in her being admitted as a psychiatric inpatient. It took several weeks for her doctors to see that her psychosis was iatrogenic. She resolved to endure her pains and to steer clear of psychiatrists forever.

The reader can hardly fail to notice the strong overlap between Mantel's experiences as a young woman in the psychiatric facility and the events on Blackpool pier:

> Akathisia is the worst thing I have ever experienced, the worst single, defined episode of my entire life – if I discount my meeting in the secret garden. No physical pain has ever matched that morning's uprush of killing fear, the hammering heart. You are impelled to move, to pace in a small room. You force yourself down into a chair, only to jump out of it. You choke, pressure rises inside your skull. Your hands pull at your clothing and tear your arms. Your breathing becomes ragged. Your voice is like a bird's cry and your hands flutter like wings. You want to hurl yourself against the windows and the walls. Every fibre of your being is possessed by panic. Every moment endures for an age and yet you are transfixed by the present moment, stabbed by it; there is no sense of time passing, therefore no prospect of deliverance. (175–6)

The resemblance lies not only in the repetition of certain words and images but also in the manner in which they are connected with one another in both passages. The 'morning's uprush of killing fear' in Sheffield recalls the 'rushing movement' (52) of the sea lapping against Blackpool pier. The choking and the sense of pressure rising in Mantel's skull replicate her experience as a girl in the boarding house when her lungs were 'full to bursting' and she felt 'limp in the power of the current that tugs beneath the waves' (53). Even the chair she tries to sit down on invites comparison with the 'fence of ... chairs' (53) her mother made on that fateful holiday; like its predecessors, it offers only an appearance of safety. Perhaps most striking of all is the reference to the 'bird's cry' which recalls the 'screaming gulls' (84–5) on Blackpool pier. In Sheffield, she wanted to hurl herself against the windows and the walls. On Blackpool pier, she thought her body was going to be dashed against the rocks. Finally, the theme of no deliverance is common to all these post-Blackpool childhood experiences – not least in the garden of 20 Brosscroft where she has her vision of 'formless, borderless evil' (107) (described in this extract as 'my meeting in the secret garden'). It is tempting to characterise this epoch in the history of Mantel's body as one in which her perceptions, distorted by medication, mimicked and intensified the terrifying perceptions of space that blighted her early childhood.

But Mantel did get better. She graduated with an *aegrotat* degree and trained as a social worker specialising in the care of the elderly. And despite living with agonising physical pain, she began work on her first novel, *A Place of Greater Safety*, which was eventually published in 1992.

20 Brosscroft was a heterotopia. It was a place dedicated to a counter-ideal, adultery. It was also a place in which the boundaries between the sacred and the profane were shifting and uncertain. Most striking of all, the lesson it seems to teach is that the sacred conceals or at any rate is not as powerful as the demonic. The demons that young Hilary believed Jack had unleashed were real, not figurative. They ruin her health and almost ruin her life. All their menace derived from and was multiplied by the power of infinite space all about her. There can be few memoirs that do as much justice to the many-sidedness of Foucault's account of spatiality in the modern world.

The concluding chapter which deals with her life after her diagnosis of endometriosis describes a succession of non-places. At first she and her husband lived in a small flat 'in a no man's land along an arterial road, somewhere outside Slough' (227–8). Then they moved to a 'ramshackle flat converted from a former mother and baby home, which had been run by nuns' (228). Then they moved to a newly-built 'executive home' (230) in Surrey. The neighbours were 'grounded infotec folk ... bright philistines ... willing to defer gratification ... who seemed to have sprung straight from a pot in Homebase' (230). Here is a world where the 'habitué of supermarkets, slot machines and credit cards communicates wordlessly, through gestures … a world thus surrendered to solitary individuality, to the fleeting, the temporary and ephemeral' (Augé 1995: 77–8).

It is also a world that Mantel made her own in her non-historical fiction. But there is a difference. In Mantel's writing, non-places almost invariably turn out to conceal heterotopias. This can be seen not only in *Giving Up the Ghost* but also in *Every Day is Mother's Day* (1985) and *Vacant Possession* (1986) where social workers work on behalf of the state in slums under the watchful eye of a spirit medium, Evelyn Axon. In Mantel's funniest and, to my mind, best, novel, *Beyond Black* (2003), the world of 'Psychic Fayres', in places like Slough, is a jaded simulacrum of the realm in which the heroine, Alison Harte, actually operates. That is a realm in which battle must constantly be waged against evil spirits out to destroy lives. Satan indeed features in the novel as the character 'Nick'. But he looks like a common-or-garden thug, and so do his crew.

Frédéric Regard has observed the frequency with which the act of writing seems to drive English autobiographers to present themselves to their readers as human heterotopias (2003: 92). The act of writing is all about constructing rival spaces at variance with the dominant geographical order. This observation certainly works as a way of characterising Mantel's goals as a life writer. Near the end of *Giving Up the Ghost*, she writes:

> I have been so mauled by medical procedures, so sabotaged and made over, so thin and
> so fat, that sometimes I feel that each morning it is necessary to write myself into being
> … to take charge of the story of my childhood and my childlessness; and in order to
> locate myself, if not within a body, then in the narrow space between one letter and
> the next. (2003: 216)

As she put it in an interview shortly after the book came out: 'I don't know where I am, or who I am, or which bit of me is real. Because certainly, at 27, I lost the real me, I lost my body to go and live in this strange body and I'm waiting always for the next thing' (Dening 2003: 76).

And yet she never lost the real 'them'. For there is another Mantel who tries to come to terms with her past by giving the characters in her heterotopia a stability they did not have when she needed them to have it. The memoir ends with an address to the dead in 20 Brosscroft:

> I will always look after you, I want to say, however long you have been gone. I will
> always feed you and try to keep you entertained; and you must do the same for me.
> This is your daughter Ilary speaking, and this is her book. (2003: 246)

Mantel wants to redeem her heterotopia by making the demonic less powerful.

References

Augé, M. 1995. *Non-Places: Introduction to an Anthropology of Super-Modernity* [1992], translated by J. Howe. London: Verso.

Bachelard, G. 1962. *The Poetics of Space* [1958], translated by M. Jolas. Boston: Beacon Press.

Dening, P. 2003. Miss Neverwell: an interview with Hilary Mantel. *Irish Times: Magazine Supplement*. 12 April, 76.

Foucault, M. 1986. Of other spaces [1967 and 1984], translated by J. Miskowiec. *diacritics: a review of contemporary criticism*, 16(1), 22–7.

Goldmann, L. 1964. *The Hidden God: A Study of Tragic Vision in the Pensées of Pascal and the Tragedies of Racine* [1955], translated by P. Thody. London: Routledge.

Lowry, E. 2004. The trouble is I'm dead. *London Review of Books,* 27(10), 25–6.

Mantel, H. 1985. *Every Day is Mother's Day*. London: Chatto & Windus.

Mantel, H. 1986. *Vacant Possession*. London: Chatto & Windus.

Mantel, H. 1992. *A Place of Greater Safety*. London: Viking.

Mantel, H. 2003. *Giving Up the Ghost*. London: Fourth Estate.

Mantel, H. 2005. *Beyond Black*. London: Fourth Estate.

Pascal, B. 1958. *Les Pensées* [1669], translated by W.F. Trotter. New York: E. P. Dutton.

Regard, F. 2003. Topologies of the self: Space and life-writing. *Partial Answers: Journal of Literature and the History of Ideas,* 1(1), 89–102.

Regard, F. 2004. Replacing the self in Cardinal Newman's Apologia. *Biography*, 27(4), 721–36.

Regard, F. 2007. *De Drake à Chatwin: Rhétoriques de la découverte*. Paris: Editions de l'ENS.

Ricoeur, P. 1992. *Oneself as Another*, translated by K. Blamey. Chicago: University of Chicago Press.

II
TRAVERSING SPACES
AND TEXTS

Chapter 4

Literary Configurations of the Peripatetic

Helga Schwalm

While travel narratives, from pilgrimages to tales of extreme mountaineering, form a traditional part of life writing, the spatial/topographical turn has freshly inspired the theory and criticism with regard to life writings linking biography and topography. Whether simply tagged 'environment' or 'nature writing' (Jolly 2001: 640–44), 'autobiogeography' (Wolf-Meyer and Heckman 2002), 'psychogeobiography' (Gregory-Guider 2005), or 'eco-autobiography' (Perreten 2003), such texts represent a specific mode of autobiographical writing that composes a 'relationship between the natural setting and the self', frequently with the objective of discovering 'a new self in nature' (Perreten 2003: 1). Wordsworth and Henry Thoreau's *Walden* are frequently cited paradigms. Apart from the specific Romantic tradition, topographical life writing in general locates life courses and self-representations in specific places; it undertakes to place the autobiographical subject in terms of topographical itineraries and figurations and thus brings into play space and/or topography as a pivotal moment of biographical identity, potentially disturbing autobiography's traditional anchorage in time (Schwalm 2014).

Taking up the critical interest in topographical life writing, this chapter undertakes to explore a specific dimension pertaining to 'mapping the self' (Regard 2003): the 'peripatetic', which in this context designates a specific nexus of life writing, space, poetic reflection and walking. Starting with Thomas de Quincey's engagement with William Wordsworth and moving on to Laurie Lee and beyond into Robert Macfarlane's contemporary writing, the focus of this chapter will be on how walking in relation to (literary) topographies and itineraries comes to serve as a poetic code and configuration in peripatetic biographical texts, functioning as an intertextual matrix that generates particular modes of culturally recognisable, predetermined physical and mental experience. I shall argue that such peripatetic mappings of the biographical subject are self-consciously aesthetic and intertextual, retracing the self via paths of others; and yet twentieth-century peripatetic texts also come to stage their subjects in the face of topographies whose biographical significance lies in their (seeming) absence of cultural meaning.

The etymology of the peripatetic suggests a reference to antiquity, more precisely to Aristotelian philosophy. The *Online Stanford Encyclopedia of Philosophy* provides the following definition:

> Those affiliated with Aristotle's school later came to be called Peripatetics, probably because of the existence of an ambulatory (peripatos) on the school's property adjacent to the exercise ground. Members of the Lyceum conducted research into a wide range of subjects, all of which were of interest to Aristotle himself: botany, biology, logic, music, mathematics, astronomy, medicine, cosmology, physics, the history of philosophy, metaphysics, psychology, ethics, theology, rhetoric, political history, government and political theory ... and the arts. In all these areas, the Lyceum collected manuscripts, thereby, according to some ancient accounts, assembling the first great library of antiquity. (Shields 2008)

The somewhat loose name 'peripatetics', then, was applied to the Aristotelian disciples with reference to the architecture of its prime site, more precisely to its cloister, which they would walk up and down during lessons. Prior to Aristotle, the practice of *peripatein* features in the Platonic dialogues. As Angelika Wellmann has lucidly argued in her Derridian reading of Plato's *Phaedrus*, the peripatetic is based on and enhances the prioritisation of live, dialogic speech over (dead, lifeless) writing: through the acting out of live philosophical conversation the 'writing of the soul' is written into the 'memory of literature' (1991: 15).[1] The movement of the body, thus Wellman's reading of Plato, figures as the true act of production of this writing.

Although its ancient origins do not offer any exact definition in terms of a specific mode of thought, three semantic attributes of the peripatetic are implied through its etymology that are relevant for this chapter: the peripatetic entwines 'live' philosophical reflection, didactics/dialogue, and the physical effort of moving along by foot. It is precisely this threefold figure conflating reflection, dialogue and bipedal exercise that appears at the heart of poetic self-reflexivity towards the end of the long eighteenth century – in the Romanticism(s) of Rousseau, Wordsworth and Coleridge, but also in the radical writing of Thedwell, for instance. Not only does it evolve as a basic figure ('Grundfigur') and as a poetic code ('poetischer Code') (Wellmann 1991: 9) of literature, but it also features prominently in literary auto/biography. Wordsworth's *Prelude*, of course, is the prime example.

While the peripatetic implies by way of its etymology a dimension of 'liveness', of immediacy of (physical) experience and groundedness, peripatetic

---

[1]   The translations of all quotations from this text are my own.

subjects pursue intertextual lines and itineraries locating their vital physical presence in a topography that is invested with cultural/literary meaning. In this sense, peripatetic autobiographers 'stroll along the textual paths of their predecessors' (Wellmann 1991: 9); subjectivity is constituted by way of a topographical experience that is intertextual from the start. Such highly intertextual, literary practices of topographical-peripatetic life writing may, perhaps, be conceptionalised as specific biographical forms of 'geopoetics', to borrow a term coined by Kenneth White (1987) and disseminated by scholars in the field of contemporary East European literatures. Geopoetics signifies a focus on the production of territories and landscapes in literature, the textual construction and semantic charging of specific topographies (Marszalek and Sasse 2010: 9).

The connection of the peripatetic and 'autobiographical geopoetics' in English literature evidently goes back to Wordsworth and his fellow lake poets. Wordsworth projects the classical figure of peripatetic reflection onto a genuinely Romantic experience of landscape, which generates a literature that is deeply autobiographical, subjective, and self-conscious. Much important work has been done in this field (Langan 1995 and others), hence a few somewhat cursory remarks should suffice here in order to mark the starting point of peripatetic autobiography.

Wordsworth, of course, was a life-long formidable walker (while Coleridge's period of avid walking was constrained to one decade); walking to him was 'a mode of being' rather than a simple 'mode of traveling' (Solnit 2000: 104). Many of his poems, but above all his *Prelude*, testify to Wordsworth's autobiographical self-fashioning as walker: 'Happy in this, that I with nature walked' (1995: 322). Thomas de Quincey humorously summed up his idol's pedestrian achievements in his biographical sketches of the Lake Poets:

> Wordsworth was, upon the whole, not a well-made man. His legs were pointedly condemned by all female connoisseurs in legs ... not that they were bad in any way which *would* force itself upon your notice – there was no absolute deformity about them; and undoubtedly they had been serviceable legs beyond the average standard of human requisition; for I calculate, upon good data, that with these identical legs Wordsworth must have traversed a distance of 175 to 180,000 English miles – a mode of exertion which, to him, stood in the stead of alcohol and all other stimulants whatsoever to the animal spirits; to which, indeed, he was indebted for a life of unclouded happiness, and we for much of what is most excellent in his writings. But, useful as they have proved themselves, the Wordsworthian legs were certainly not ornamental. (2003a: 55)

Again and again, Wordsworth evokes the biographical and poetic significance of walking the 'public road': it revealed to him 'passions of mankind' and 'depth of human souls' (1995: 479) – both in relation to himself as poetic subject and to the vagrant subjects he observes. In terms of his topographies, the poet notoriously employs and rewrites various and diverse pretexts: the pastoral and the georgic, poetic melancholy, and, in *The Prelude*, the Petrarchan model of autobiographical epiphany, where the ascent of a mountain culminates in a moment of (self-)recognition. Moreover, Wordsworth writes, travels and walks in the wake of eighteenth-century picturesque travel narratives, which 'discovered' in aesthetic terms the landscapes of the North-West – Wales, The Lake District, Scotland, along with the mountainous terrain of the Alps – and at the same time framed them, as it were, by intertextual and intermedial means.

In the context of Wordsworthian autobiography, then, walking, especially mountain walking, constitutes the crucial mode of experience and reflection that – at least in autobiographical retrospect – generates certain 'spots of time', transforming a particular moment and location in life into a kind of spatio-temporal nexus of biographical and poetic meaning. Pertinent examples would be Wordsworth's account of his arrival on the summit of Mount Snowdon (1995: 512–15) or his 'crossing' of the Alps (231–49). Thus in the Snowdon instance, 'With forehead bent/Earthward, as if in opposition set/Against an enemy', the speaker 'panted up/With eager pace' to experience 'a light upon the turf/ [Falling] like a flash' (513). The physical-topographical experience of struggling uphill gives way to a vision that blends real (mountains) and metaphorical topography ('sea', 'ocean'), visibly shifting topographical perception to a more imaginative mode: 'on the shore/I found myself of a huge sea of mist,/Which meek and silent rested at my feet./A Hundred hills their dusky backs upheaved/ All over this still ocean, and beyond,/Far beyond, the vapours shot themselves/ In headlands, tongues, and promontory shapes,/Into the sea, the real sea' (512). Subsequently, after his return, the sublime 'lonely mountain' scene revisits the autobiographer: 'The perfect image of a mighty mind,/Of one that feeds upon infinity,/That is exalted by an under-presence' (514). Wordsworth's reflections famously culminate in his analogy ('a genuine counterpart and brother' [514]) between (the impact of) nature's sublime power and the 'glorious faculty' (515) of the poetic imagination.

Elsewhere in Wordsworth, walking also serves to both ground the poetic self in, and separate it from, economic reality. 'The Old Cumberland Beggar', for example, merges poetic self-reflection and a critique of the new rural poverty through a juxtaposition of different modes of walking and seeing (Schwalm 2010). Indeed, both politics and poetics are never far from 'Romantic vagrancy'

(Langan 1995); while the socio-economic context of the poet-autobiographer's itinerary or destination may be concealed, as in 'Tintern Abbey', it may be lined up explicitly with political zeal, as in the case of Wordsworth's journey through France and across the Alps in *The Prelude*. With regard to the economic dimension of walking, Anne Wallace has argued that in the wake of the enclosures, the new Romantic walking fashion placed the walker in the 'ideological space vacated by the farmer', with 'excursive walking as a cultivating labour capable of renovating both the individual and its society by recollecting and expressing past value' (1994: 11).

If Wallace's argument begs questions concerning the historical timing as critics have argued (see, for example, Jarvis 2000), it also invites reconsideration as to the complex significance of walking as physical exercise beyond substituting the farmer's labour. Devoid of economic purpose, it guarantees an immediate, concrete physical experience of space that, while undercutting the gentleman's steady spatial perspective and high viewpoint linked to the privilege of economic disinterest (Barrell 1972: 7–8 and 1992: 42–3), reiterates the aesthetic experience of perpetually shifting points of view and perspectives that is the very hallmark of the picturesque with its aesthetic ideal of 'prospect' and (latent) nostalgia for 'an old order of rural paternalism' (Bermingham 1986: 70).

In any case, there appears to be a specific English/British side to the cultural function of the peripatetic as it emerges in Britain in the wake of the agrarian, industrial, and transport revolutions. For the German 'Wanderlust', Althaus (1999) has alternatively suggested a double Romantic conceptualisation of walking: as a basic anthropological need and at the same time a national impulse – part of a larger cultural and political project. Citing Rousseau's (Emile's) recommendation of walking, Althaus contends that walking serves to inscribe a bourgeois habitus – a position and attitude of independence, uprightness, enlightenment and rationality in observing the social and natural environment – into the bourgeois body. A bourgeois and masculine habitus along with melancholy introspection in nature may be singled out as principal driving factors in the formation of new cultural patterns (Althaus 1999: 32–7). Whereas this 'habitus' as delineated by Althaus may apply to both the German and English/British culture of walking, there also appear to be significant differences.[2] With

---

2   The final factor in Althaus's account, which is the politically unifying function of a mountain view, bringing together what does not yet belong together and compensating for what has not been achieved in political terms ('Naturerlebnis als Politikersatz') (1999: 41), would seem specifically German and not to apply to English Romanticism. Also, with the English Romantics (and Dorothea Wordsworth in particular) in mind, gender may not seem to work in quite such an unequivocal way as suggested by Althaus's conception of a decidedly masculine wanderlust.

regard to the latter, it needs to be emphasised that not only does walking replace or substitute the farmer's labour, but it engages in the aesthetics and politics of space: the aesthetic ideal of the picturesque and the geographical and socio-economic reality of the parliamentary enclosures strongly inform the Romantic geopoetics of walking. Rewriting picturesque topographies in the peripatetic mode (while echoing the picturesque pictorial framing and thus medial detachment of landscape experience), the poet and autobiographer traverses the environment in the sense of Michel de Certeau's walking as a spatial practice (1984) and thus grounds his poetological and biographical reflections by way of the immediate physical sensation afforded by walking. In short, it guarantees an immediate, concrete physical experience of one's (life) course.[3]

Next to Wordsworth, perhaps none of the Romantics bring configurations of biographical space-time into play in quite such a sophisticated fashion as Thomas de Quincey. Certainly, de Quincey shares Wordsworth's 'topographical turn' of autobiographical self-reflection and the intertextual embedding of his autobiographical project in his work. As autobiographer and biographical essayist on Wordsworth and the Lake Poets, he engages not only his biographical subjects but also himself in a complex semantic web of what may be termed biographical peripatetic topographies in the service of a perpetually deferred autobiographical identity.

At the centre of de Quincey's *Confessions of an English Opium Eater* (1821), walking the city as a vagrant is constructed as the context and emblem of an original loss and pain ('my heaviest affliction' [1997: 173]) that will eventually lead de Quincey to become an opium eater. In particular, it is the loss of his young prostitute saviour, substitute sister ('I loved her as affectionately as if she had been my sister' [165]) and fellow 'houseless wanderer' (173) in London, Ann, which he claims as his key experience of traumatic loss and displacement within an urban topography. On his wanderings through the 'mighty labyrinths

---

On the German cultural history of the peripatetic and its functional change in the eighteenth and nineteenth centuries also see Albrecht (1999), who parallels the two cultural heydays of walking around 1800 and 1900 with the historical moments of rise and crisis of the middle class/middle-class culture ('Bürgertum') (1999: 3–12, esp. 8). The first parallel between the rise of the middle class and walking does not seem to correspond to the time scale of English cultural history with its earlier formation of the middle class.

[3]   This notion lives on in popular accounts of the meaning of walking: 'Conceived of as a conversation between the body and the world', an unnamed internet writer on walking stipulates, 'walking becomes a reciprocal and simultaneous act of both interpretation and manipulation; an embodied and active way of shaping and being shaped that operates on a scale and at a pace embedded in something seemingly more authentic and real' (*Walking as Knowing as Making* 2005).

of London' he continues to search for her – 'Whither had she gone?' –, but 'all in vain' (173). In de Quincey's 'psychogeography' (Coverley 2006), the topography of central London is thus turned into a complex of circular itineraries and lost directions.

The revised *Confessions* of 1856 also stage the young de Quincey as a rural walker. Prior to his London existence, having eloped from school on foot, he literally walks in Wordsworth's footsteps (in Wales) and simultaneously feels drawn towards the Lake District as Wordsworth's home, with the poet his 'deep deep magnet' (1997: 76). The text evokes the autobiographical crisis to a significant degree as a crisis of topography.

At this critical point of his life, the choice is one of 'mapping' his future life, of deciding whither he was bound. Indeed, the question of '*whither*' occurs more than once in the course of his narrative (1997: 17 and 74, italics in the original). Furthermore, *what* the young, impecunious runaway experiences in the mode of the peripatetic is a truly Wordsworthian topography:

> I saw held up aloft before my eyes that matchless spectacle 'New, and yet as old/As the foundations of the heavens and earth', an elaborate and pompous sunset hanging over the mountains of North Wales. The clouds passed slowly through several arrangements, and in the last of these I read the very scene which six months before I had read in a most exquisite poem of Wordsworth's. (1997: 95)

This is not a simple case of real-literary analogy as de Quincey elaborates, explicitly citing Wordsworth to articulate his visual experience reminiscent of his Romantic predecessor and idol: 'The scene in the poem ('Ruth'), that had been originally mimicked by the poet from the sky, was here re-mimicked and rehearsed to the life, as it seemed, by the sky from the poet. Was I then, in July 1802, really quoting from Wordsworth? Yes reader ... ' (1997: 96). His reference, de Quincey suggests, is not a subsequent intertextual marking but (possibly) a kind of intertextual experience synchronous with the experience of landscape itself.

Wordsworth's topographical writing clearly functions as a code of experience and self-representation that is self-consciously (inter)textual. In excess of his literal wandering in North Wales and London, transgressing his actual experience of pedestrian travel, the auto/biographer de Quincey also again and again employs a highly intertextual topographical rhetoric. He projects a self that is not at home in the landscape, or topography, of his biography, but is doubled, dispersed, and displaced (see Schwalm 2009). Identity confusion features as a confusion of self and other projected onto his narrative's topography. As his sister sets out to find her absconding brother, she believes she is following her brother, whereas she has unwittingly long overtaken him. She thus becomes a textual figure of transgression and excess as the counterpart of an absent self:

> Sunset saw the pursuers crossing the Mersey ... and so much did my chasers, that pursued when no man fled, accomplish before sleeping. On the next day, long and long before the time when I, in my humble pedestrian character, reached Chester, my sister's party had reached Ambleside ... But it happened that my pursuers, not having time to sift such intelligence as they received, were misled into an excursus of full two hundred miles more, by chasing an imagery 'me'. (1997: 114)

Not only is de Quincey's autobiographical logic as rambling and digressive as his physical movement through the landscapes of Wales and London, but in the rhetorical web of this key episode, pursuer and pursued, subject and object are inverted and confused. Travel, topography, and identity confusion go hand in hand. De Quincey's account thus generates a complex terrain of textual lines and figures far exceeding any recognisable biographical plot. His reiterations, textual revisions and rewritings evoke his sense of being '*not* one' but a 'system of links' (2003b: 13), as do the digressive structure of his autobiographical narratives and the proliferation of images and leitmotifs like the worm and the wandering Jew. The vagrancy of a solitary self is de Quincey's key image and structural principle articulating the displacement of identity. Wherever he is or goes, de Quincey is '*outside*, a solitary point of consciousness surrounded by infinite reaches of space and time', and unlike Wordsworth, de Quincey is unable to 'experience an immanent spiritual principle in nature' (Miller 1965: 23–4). The peripatetic quality of his experience resides in the transgression of the boundaries of the self.

Moving beyond de Quincey into the later nineteenth century, a less cursory trajectory would obviously need to explore prominent stations such as Stevenson's topographical pilgrimage of crisis and epiphany, charged with self-irony, across the Cévennes (1879) as well as the amusing explorations of the alpine *Playground of Europe* by Leslie Stephen (1910). Just as Stephen's construction of the *English* intellectual in the peripatetic mode would need to be pursued, a more comprehensive view would also display the new imperial geopoetics of Victorian life writing. However, this chapter leaves these gaps unfilled in order to leap ahead to a modern peripatetic autobiographer: Laurie Lee, who occupies a key position in rethinking the autobiographical meaning of topographical experience in the twentieth century.

How, then, does Laurie Lee reconfigure the autobiographical peripatetic? While the Wordsworthian peripatetic generates a subjectivity that is both poetic and 'grounded' in his environment, and while de Quincey openly plays with the textuality of topographical experience, employing topography as a biography generator as well as a metaphor of displacement, Laurie Lee undertakes to self-consciously place himself in a *new* topography devoid of memory, devoid of cultural meaning. He does so after his childhood reminiscences in *Cider With Rosie* (1959), where he famously reinvents a deeply stationary, parochial English countryside (interwoven with a tribute to his mother). In contrast, the autobiographical sequel *As I Walked Out One Summer Morning* (1969), which I want to focus on, eventually positions the young poet and autobiographer in the face of a topography that strikes him as semantically empty. The time is just before the outbreak of the Spanish Civil War; Laurie Lee, too, travels on foot, fully aware of the cultural tradition of leave-taking and setting out in the peripatetic mode:

> I was propelled, of course, by the traditional forces that had sent many generations along this road – by the small tight valley closing in around one, stifling the breath with its mossy mouth, the cottage walls narrowing, like the arms of an iron maiden, the local girls whispering, 'Marry, and settle down' ... And now I was on my journey, in a pair of thick boots and with a hazel stick in my hand. Naturally, I was going to London, which lay a hundred miles to the east; and it seemed equally obvious that I should go on foot. But first, as I had never yet seen the sea, I thought I'd walk to the coast and find it. (1993: 223)

The choice of routes to take is one that signifies freedom, and yet, as he walks, he is 'taunted by echoes of home' (223). Once the young Laurie Lee is past the initial overwhelming feeling of 'wretchedness' in the face of vagrant homelessness 'soaking alone in [a] nameless field' (224) under the English sky, sensing the lack of direction in the face of his own liberty ('The day's silence said, Go where you will. It's all yours' [223]), he begins to enjoy the seeing of new things as he moves along on foot 'in a landscape not yet bulldozed for speed' (225). Thus at this point, the peripatetic is linked to a nostalgic view of premodern England, reminiscent of English landscape painting: 'Just a spire in the grass: my first view of Salisbury' (225).

The autobiographer's walk takes him via the South Coast, which disappoints his expectations derived from Hardy, to London. He survives by resorting to busking. Indeed, like Wordsworth in poems such as 'The Old Cumberland Beggar', Laurie Lee places himself within a larger context of an economic practice of vagrancy and yet stands apart: 'I was not the only one on the road; I soon noticed there were many others. ... Some, of course, were professional tramps, but the majority belonged to that host of unemployed who wandered aimlessly about England at the time' (231). As he leaves London, having exhausted his opportunities there, Lee echoes the conflation of biographical and topographical choices of de Quincey: 'So where should I go? ... France? Italy? Greece?' However, unlike de Quincey's recognition (or vision) of Wordsworthian landscapes, Lee 'knew nothing at all about any of them, they were just names with vaguely operatic flavours'. And further: 'I knew no languages either, so felt I could arrive new-born wherever I chose to go' (254).

Although Lee's peripatetic vagrancy is charged with ambiguity, suggesting socio-economic practice as well as poetic reflection, topography promises a new kind of biographical experience once he has left England. The autobiographer's epiphanic insight occurs in the Spanish mountains; as he wakes up in the Galician mountains, having slept rough, he experiences this unwritten dimension of life:

> I lay on my belly, the warm earth against me, and forgot the cold dew and the wolves of
> the night. I felt it was for this I had come: to wake at dawn on a hillside and look out
> on a world for which I had no words; to start at the beginning, speechless and without
> plan, in a place that still had no memories for me. (260)

The foreign mountainous scenery represents what is unwritten by himself and others, outside and beyond ready autobiographical meaning. Laurie Lee's personal biographical geopoetics, then, rests on an unwritten, culturally blank territory (blank for an Englishman at least). The Spanish hillside conveys a biographical and cultural blank sheet, devoid of personal or cultural memory. At this moment of quasi-epiphany, topography functions as a biography generator in the literal sense: it neither engenders reiteration or crisis (as in conversion narratives), nor intertextual doubling, but a sense of autonomy, of fresh self-fashioning. Rejecting the intertextually charged geopoetics of Romanticism, Laurie Lee's Spanish mountains offer to him the prospect of life as self-projection. Of course, the world will catch up with Laurie Lee, enmeshing him in the reality of the Civil War, but the autobiographical memory of a moment of seemingly 'pre-textual experience' constitutes the centre of Lee's text. As he perceives the Spanish topography as an emblem of life yet unwritten, not previously spelt out by himself or others, he does so in the belief that walking is his radically individual 'Lebensform' (Boomers 2004), his 'mode of existence'.

Autobiographers such as de Quincey and Laurie Lee, then, pursue biographical and poetic itineraries that are both self-consciously grounded in, and written into, specific topographies and at the same time amount to figurations of displacement or escape from biographical pretexts. It is at this point, perhaps, that the critically acclaimed 'New Nature Writing' (Cowley 2008) of Robert Macfarlane may enter the picture, searching for the unwritten, wild places of England and beyond. Again, Macfarlane's writing is openly intertextual and yet endeavours to map a new, personal itinerary on the edge of more familiar biographical geopoetics in the Romantic tradition, of more conventional landscape poetics and popular tastes. In his topographical trilogy, he weaves autobiographical moments into his cultural history of mountaineering (2003); in a second step he proceeds to 'map' (2007: 17) his search for *The Wild Places* (2007) of England. Increasingly, Macfarlane's perception and interest narrows in scale to the hitherto neglected minute pockets of wilderness in his immediate vicinity. What these wild spots offer is a sense of defamiliarisation, 'making a stale world afresh, surprising and wondrous again, to discover astonishment on the terrain of the familiar' (2007: 230). This is an experience that MacFarlane (referring to Stephen Graham's *The Gentle Art of Tramping* of 1923) explicitly ascribes to the 'subversive power of pedestrianism' (230), singling out the English countryside's hawk and the hare as perfect emblems of his enterprise: 'they were the perfect pair of familiars for my map-making. The hawk turning its sentinel circles in the air, looking down onto the land. The hare knowing the land peerlessly at ground level, able to move faster over it than anything else earthbound' (302). Crucially, Macfarlane evokes and moves beyond the sublime experience of an uninhabitable und inhospitable nature that strikes him as 'comfortless', 'entirely, gradelessly indifferent' (157). His winter ascent of Ben Hope affords no Worthsworthian epiphany, 'no companionship with the land', nor 'any imputation of meaning' (157). In the end, however, it is the nameless 'little places' of wilderness invested with private autobiographical meaning, 'special by personal acquaintance' (236), that the narrative turns to as places confronting the writer with an experience of otherness, of being 'not us', 'uncompromisingly different', pertaining to a 'world operating in patterns and purposes that you do not share' (307). Figuration, not elevation, triggers a sense of the sublime of topography. This is the point where Macfarlane's eco-writing attains a deeply ethical note that is emphatically on the opposite end of any pathetic fallacy. He confines himself to delineating the minute features of his environment as he encounters it on his walks; at another point, he evokes the strangeness of what he sees by way of an unsettling comparison that rhetorically echoes nature's spectacle. Like a secret signature, the rabbit prints in the snow are rendered 'legible' through the face of Munch's screamer: 'the two rear feet are placed laterally to make elongated eyes, and between and behind them fall the forefeet in a slightly offset paired line, forming nose and oval mouth. Thousands of these faces peered at me from the snow' (Macfarlane 2012: 8). In the face of the uncanny signature of the other, intertextuality/intermediality is called upon for the purposes of autobiographical sense making.

To conclude: Not only is auto/biographical memory supported by the peripatetic experience of places/landscapes, as Gregory-Guider argues in his study of psychogeoautobiography (2005), but biographical experience itself is inextricably linked to topographies that actually function as biography generators. In the texts that I have discussed these topographies increasingly do not seem places to inhabit, as Regard (2003) has proposed with references to mapping the self, but spaces to traverse, leaving behind the restraints of 'locatedness' in favour of a network of decentring itineraries. In any case, walking generates experiences that are both physical and already textual; the dialogic element of the ancient peripatetic appears to be, perhaps, translated into the dialogue of self and text. In this sense, the peripatetic mode engages with biographical (geo)poetics. The walker's slow pedestrian motion and physical experience of topography is inscribed into an intertextual terrain that is charged with cultural/literary meaning – as the site of epiphanic significance, of a paradoxical signature of the unwritten, or a secret code of the natural world perceived as radical other.

References

Albrecht, W. 1999. Kultur und Physiologie des Wanderns, in *Wanderzwang – Wanderlust: Formen der Raum- und Sozialerfahrung zwischen Aufklärung und Frühindustrialisierung*, edited by W. Albrecht and H.-J. Kertscher. Tübingen: Niemeyer, 3–12.

Althaus, H.-J. 1999. Bürgerliche Wanderlust, in *Wanderzwang – Wanderlust: Formen der Raum- und Sozialerfahrung zwischen Aufklärung und Frühindustrialisierung,* edited by W. Albrecht and H.-J. Kertscher. Tübingen: Niemeyer, 25–43.

Barrell, J. 1972. *The Idea of Landscape and the Sense of Place 1730–1840: An Approach to the Poetry of John Clare.* Cambridge: Cambridge University Press.

Barrell, J. 1992. The public prospect and the private view: The politics of taste in eighteenth-century Britain, in *The Birth of Pandora and the Division of Knowledge.* London and Basingstoke: Macmillan, 41–63.

Bermingham, A. 1986. *Landscape and Ideology: The English Rustic Tradition, 1740–1860.* Berkeley: University of California Press.

Boomers, S. 2004. *Reisen als Lebensform. Isabelle Eberhardt, Reinhold Messner und Bruce Chatwin*. Frankfurt: Campus.

Certeau, M. de. 1984. *The Practice of Everyday Life* [1980], translated by S. Rendall. Los Angeles: University of California Press.

Coverley, M. 2006. *Psychogeography*. London: Pocket Essentials.

De Quincey, T. 1997. *Confessions of an English Opium Eater* [1821 and 1856]. London: Penguin Popular Classics.

De Quincey, T. 2003a. Lake reminiscences, No. I. – William Wordsworth [1839], in *The Works of Thomas de Quincey,* Vol. 11, edited by J. North. London: Pickering and Chatto, 40–65.

De Quincey, T. 2003b. Autobiographical sketches [1853], in *The Works of Thomas De Quincey* Vol. 19, edited by D. Roberts. London: Pickering and Chatto.

Cowley, J. (ed.) 2008. *Granta 102. The New Nature Writing.* London: Granta Publications.

Gregory-Guider, C.C. 2005. *Autobiogeography and the Art of Peripatetic Memorialization in Works by W.G. Sebald, Patrick Midiano, Iain Sinclair, Jonathan Raban, and William Least Heat Moon*. University of Sussex (microfilm).

Jarvis, R. 2000. *Romantic Poetry and Pedestrian Travel*. Basingstoke: Macmillan.

Jolly, M. (ed.) 2001. *Encyclopaedia of Life Writing*. London: Fitzroy Dearborn.

Langan, C. 1995. *Romantic Vagrancy. Wordsworth and the Simulation of Freedom*. Cambridge: Cambridge University Press.

Lee, L. 1993. *As I Walked Out One Midsummer Morning* [1969]. London: Penguin.

Macfarlane, R. 2003. *Mountains of the Mind: A Study of a Fascination*. London: Granta Books.

Macfarlane, R. 2007. *The Wild Places*. London, Granta Books.

Macfarlane, R. 2012. *The Old Ways: A Journey on Foot*. London: Penguin.

Marszalek, M. and Sasse, S. (eds.) 2010. *Geopoetiken: Geographische Entwürfe in den mittel- und osteuropäischen Literaturen*. Berlin: Kulturverlag Kadmos.

Miller, H. 1965. *The Disappearance of God*. New York: Schocken Books.

Perreten, P. 2003. Eco-autobiography: portrait of place/self-portrait. *Autobiography Studies,* 18(1), 1–22.

Regard, F. (ed.) 2003. *Mapping the Self: Space, Identity, Discourse in British Auto/biography*. Saint-Étienne: Publications de l' Université de Saint-Étienne.

Schwalm, H. 2009. Circularity and subjectivity in autobiography: Conversion, closure, hermeneutics, and beyond. *Symbolism: An International Annual of Critical Aesthetics,* 9, 41–66.

Schwalm, H. 2010. The Lake Poets/Authors: Topography, authorship and romantic subjectivities, in *Gender and Creation: Surveying Gendered Myths of Creativity, Authority and Authorship*, edited by A.-J. Zwierlein. Heidelberg: Winter, 131–48.

Schwalm, H. 2014. Autobiography. *The Living Handbook of Narratology* [Online], edited by P. Hühn et al. Available at: http://www.lhn.uni-hamburg.de/article/autobiography [accessed: 27 July 2014].

Shields, C. 2008. Aristotle. *Stanford Encyclopedia of Philosophy*. [Online]. Available at: http://plato.stanford.edu/entries/aristotle [accessed: 27 July 2014].

Solnit, R. 2000. *Wanderlust. A History of Walking*. Chicago: University of Chicago Press.

Stephens, L. 1874. *The Playground of Europe* [1871]. London: Longmans.

Stevenson, R.L. 1907. *Travels with a Donkey in the Cévennes* [1879]. London: Chatto & Windus.

Wallace, A. 1994. *Walking, Literature, and English Culture: The Origins and Uses of the Peripatetic in the Nineteenth Century*. Oxford: Oxford University Press.

Wellmann, A. 1991. *Der Spaziergang. Stationen eines poetischen Codes*. Würzburg: Königshausen und Neumann.

White, K. 1987. *L'esprit Nomade*. Paris: Grasset.

Wolf-Meyer, M. and Heckman, D. (eds.) 2002. Autobiogeography: Considering space and identity. *Reconstruction: Studies in Contemporary Culture* [online], 2(3). Available at: http://reconstruction.eserver.org/Issues/023/TOC.htm [accessed: 27 July 2014].

Wordsworth, W. 1995. *The Prelude. The Four Texts (1798, 1799, 1805, 1850)*, edited by J. Wordsworth. London: Penguin.

Walking as Knowing as Making: A Peripatetic Investigation of Space. 2005. [Online]. Available at: http://www.walkinginplace.org/converge/intro.htm [accessed: 27 July 2014].

Chapter 5

'The mystery-magic of foreignness': Mr Isherwood Changes Places

Eveline Kilian

Just as the real world can be geographically mapped and spatially configured, the literary text must be considered as a space in its own right that operates according to its own rules of spatial organisation. Furthermore, the relationship between world and text can be specified in spatial terms: Due to the spatial limitation of the text, the work of art is 'a finite model of an infinite universe', so that the recreation of the extra-textual world in the text requires an act of 'translation' (Lotman 1977: 210), in other words a transposition that also entails a transformation. In the realm of life writing, this act transforms the autobiographical subject into a 'purely semiotic presence' (Regard 2003: 17), a move that opens up new possibilities of self-fashioning. In terms of meaning production, Paul Ricoeur (1991) has highlighted the struggle between discordance and concordance, between the heterogeneity and contingency of events and the unified composition of the narrative in the textual creation of the self. Ricoeur and Lotman, in accordance with traditional theories of autobiography (e.g. Dilthey 1989, Gusdorf 1980, Olney 1972, Pascal 1960), stress the primacy of coherence so that the shaping vision of the narrative provides a strategy of containment against the fragmentation and potential dissolution of the self. The subject of this chapter, Christopher Isherwood, does not conform to this model. His autobiographical texts refuse closure and present a subject that is elusive, deliberately ambiguous in its referentiality to the author and under permanent (re)construction. Isherwood uses textual spaces to lose and reinvent himself, a process, I will argue, that is closely linked to his movement through geographical spaces and his construction of specific places as catalysts of displacement.

The Elusive Autobiographical Subject

It is difficult, not to say impossible, to distinguish between Isherwood's autobiographical and fictional writings, since the dramatisation of self is central to all his works (see Schwerdt 1989). We know, for example, that his Berlin stories are autobiographical fictions. The four central narratives of *Goodbye to Berlin*, which focus on individual characters, are framed by two texts significantly marked as personal reminiscences: 'A Berlin Diary (Autumn 1930)' and 'A Berlin Diary (Winter 1932–3)', and yet Isherwood stresses the fictional character of the book. He not only admits to 'the weeding out of superfluous details' (1978: 161) but also to having changed the characters beyond recognition, as in the case of the real-life original of Sally Bowles, Jean Ross. His memory of her has faded completely and been superseded not only by Sally Bowles in his eponymous Berlin story but also by the actresses who played Sally on stage and on screen:[1] 'Art has transfigured life and other people's art has transfigured Christopher's art', as Isherwood comments on this process of continual modification (1978: 51). Although he does not say so explicitly, referring to himself in the third person signals that he himself has also undergone such transformations over time, mainly in his own literary texts in which he reworked memories of his past self into more idealised self-projections (as the term 'transfigured' suggests).

Lions and Shadows, published in 1938, shares its title with one of Isherwood's early, discarded attempts at novel writing, a coming-of-age story he describes as 'a day-dream about my Youth' (1996: 46). While he called the hero of this youthful attempt Leonard Merrows, the protagonist of the published version bears his own name. Yet, its preface begins with a disclaimer: 'I had better start by saying what this book is not: it is not ... an autobiography' (5). Instead, he advises the reader to '[r]ead it as a novel' (5).[2] However, in later years he repeatedly refers to it as an autobiographical work (Isherwood 1980: 7, 1966: 91, Wickes 2001: 43).

Lions and Shadows ends with Christopher Isherwood's departure for Berlin in 1929, and this is where *Christopher and His Kind* (1976), which covers the years 1929 to 1939, begins. Although it is considered his autobiography proper,

---

[1]   Isherwood's *Goodbye to Berlin* spawned a number of adaptations, for example John van Druten's play *I am a Camera* (1951), which was subsequently turned into a film directed by Henry Cornelius (1955). Van Druten's play also formed the basis of Joe Masteroff's musical *Cabaret* (1966), which was made into a hugely successful film directed by Bob Fosse in 1972 with Liza Minnelli as Sally Bowles.

[2]   One of the reasons for this, we might surmise, lies in the projected development of the first-person narrator as a writer: The book describes 'the first stages in ... the education of a novelist' (Isherwood 1996: 5) and at the same time provides evidence of the achievement of this goal.

we need to be cautious, since the book confronts its readers with at least three different personae or selves in the book: the I, the writer of the autobiography; 'Christopher', the author's younger self; and 'Christopher Isherwood', the narrator of the Berlin stories (e.g. Isherwood 1978: 38). His 'true' self is again elusive and fugitive. The autobiographical subject weaves itself in and out of texts of varying fictional status thus forcefully calling into question the very idea of a 'true' self.

The term autofiction comes to mind to describe this kind of writing. It emerged in the 1970s, at first in the French context, to define the work of authors who contested the notion of transparent referentiality in autobiography and self-reflexively addressed the fact that the self is never in full possession of itself, that it is always and ineluctably decentred, both ontologically and linguistically (see Gratton 2001, Beggar 2014). It denotes a merging of autobiography and fiction and often refers to texts in which there is a nominal identity between author and protagonist but which overtly use fictionalising strategies in the portrayal of the protagonist's life (see Jones 2000).[3] Isherwood's work not only betrays an awareness of the instability of the subject but uses it as the very basis for the creation of a malleable linguistic self that reemerges differently in each textual space it inhabits. The series of works that bring forth 'Christopher Isherwood' present us with a kind of palimpsest, a number of superimposed texts that produce an infinite regress or mise-en-abîme which constantly defers the truth about the autobiographical subject. This textual network confronts us with two contradictory moves. Intermittently, Isherwood suggests a kind of asymptotic approach to his 'true' self, a coming closer and closer to it with each version, for example when he claims that *Christopher and His Kind* is more 'frank and factual' (1978: 9) than his previous autobiographical attempt, *Lions and Shadows*. This promise is repeatedly frustrated, however, by the recurring displacements and refashionings of the subject that emerges as a perpetual shape-shifter.

It is significant that the autobiographical subject evolves by attaching itself to different geographical places, to foreign, un-English spaces, which decentre the subject even more by immersing it in a foreign language and providing it with a new discursive universe into which to project itself. The confrontation with the foreign effects a degree of self-alienation, a dislocation of the self from the self, a discovery of the Other in oneself, and this process suggests a spatial dimension, as Bernhard Waldenfels has pointed out: the foreign is commonly conceptualised

---

3   More recently, Max Saunders has revitalised the term autobiografiction, which dates back to 1906 and which he uses to describe 'the profusion of modern literature's experiments with life-writing' between the 1870s and the 1930s (2010: 8).

as an elsewhere that is approached through movement and modulation of distance (1997: 10–26, 186–95). In Isherwood's works, the autobiographical subject is involved in two interconnected processes of spatialisation: a kind of restless textual wandering that effects a successive restructuring of the self in different books and that is paralleled by a geographical trajectory, by movements from place to place, whose aim is not so much to arrive somewhere but to get away from something, or more specifically to propel the self out of itself, to escape from a self that the subject seeks to leave behind. The self Isherwood seeks to shed bears the imprint of his upbringing, his family, a specific set of values and code of conduct characteristic of the English upper-middle class. His travels abroad remove him further and further from his place of origin, a spatial distancing that also gradually enables him to voice his own homosexuality and initiate a cautious movement out of the closet. The following sections will be dedicated to these movements, mainly focusing on *Lions and Shadows*, the Berlin stories and *Christopher and His Kind*.

England

Lions and Shadows addresses the issues of class and sexuality to varying degrees as well as firmly establishing Isherwood's ambitions as a writer. By the end of the book he has had several manuscripts rejected and his first novel, *All the Conspirators*, published. The first-person narrator displays a chameleon-like quality in that he proves insecure but easily adaptable to all kinds of social situations and extremely prone to imitating his friends. His 'suggestibility' (1996: 162) facilitates the many self-fashionings that also find expression in the literary endeavours he outlines in *Lions and Shadows*. They gradually become an important site for the projection and exploration of his alter egos and provide a model for his subsequent writings.

The text covers his public school years and his studies at Cambridge as well as a brief spell as a medical student at King's College London and his life in London up to his departure for the Continent in 1929. It is to close friends and places that the narrator allocates the role of pulling him out of himself, the former because he can emulate their attitudes and ways, the latter because they take him away from his parental environment. The most influential model is his schoolmate Chalmers (modelled on the real-life novelist and poet Edward Upward) who implicitly sets the pattern. During a pre-university stay in France, Chalmers distances himself from all things English by immersing himself in the French language:

At Rouen he imagined himself as having escaped into a world in which it was possible to speak openly and unaffectedly of all those subjects which in England must be introduced by an apology or guarded with a sneer – poetry, metaphysics, romantic love. Like all shy people, he enjoyed a freedom from his inhibitions in speaking a foreign language. (1996: 20)

At this point, Isherwood is still too much enveloped in his 'Englishness' to follow suit – he describes himself as 'very pink and young and English', suspicious of and yet fascinated by 'a Continent complete with poisonous drains, roast frogs, bed-bugs and vice' (17) –, but he later replicates Chalmers's approach during his Berlin years when he embraces German as a defamiliarising force and succumbs to the fascination of the foreign: 'For him, the entire German language ... was irradiated with Sex. For him, the difference between a table and ein Tisch was that a table was the dining-table in his mother's house and ein Tisch was ein Tisch in the Cosy Corner'[4] (Isherwood 1978: 23).

At Cambridge, the stage is set for Isherwood's battle against the spectre of his hated background. The two friends hone their spirit of opposition by pitting their own rebellious selves against the college authorities. Under the guidance of Chalmers, Isherwood begins to lose some of his 'puritan priggishness' (1996: 45). But it is mostly on account of his class affiliation that Chalmers, the 'natural anarchist' and 'born romantic revolutionary' (112), challenges him and forces him, the 'upper-middle-class Puritan' (13), to reflect his treacherous collusion with what his friend calls 'the college "Poshocracy"' (34). It is a mark of Chalmers's influence on him that his initial fascination with Cambridge, his joy of being there and the intellectual stimulation it affords him, eventually give way to contempt. His years at university end with his deliberately failing the Tripos exam: an act of open defiance, a piece of pseudo-revolutionary heroism chiefly staged to impress Chalmers, which results in his being sent down from Cambridge.

He adopts Chalmers's reading of Cambridge as the epitome of all they despise in the older generation and their own social class. Therefore rejecting the 'Other Side' first and foremost means exorcising that side from his own self and in doing so transforming the self. Cambridge is only one step in a long process that involves a number of spatial relocations and repeated sheddings of skins. The text contrasts the protagonist's naïve and erroneous assumption that a change of place will automatically effect a 'purification' of the self with the reality of a more

---

4   The Cosy Corner was a gay bar he frequented in Berlin, in Kreuzberg near Hallesches Tor.

complex force field that belies any such simple equation. Instead of rejecting his old affiliations once and for all, his loyalties shift constantly and his class-hatred alternates with fears of being a social outcast and with longing for the comforts of conformity (1996: 152). He is so deeply implicated and entangled in the despised system that he will not be able to free himself so easily from its grip and must be prepared for obstacles and failures.

Back in London, his next attempt at liberating himself is triggered by his awareness of how much he still adheres to his stilted 'Kensington manners' (1996: 93), which stand out from the free and easy exchange between parents and children he encounters at the Chelsea home of the violinist M. Cheuret, for whom he works as a private secretary: 'it was difficult to realize, even, that we were all inhabiting the same city. This was another world' (1996: 86). This experience, as well as his reunion with his old schoolmate Hugh Weston, the fictionalised version of W.H. Auden, who impresses and disturbs him with his utter lack of sexual inhibition (1996: 120–21), spur his desire to leave home, again on the assumption that this would enable him to leave his old self behind: 'It was hopeless. As long as I remained at home, I could never expect to escape from my familiar tiresome, despicable self. Very well, then: I would leave home. I would start all over again, among new people who didn't know me' (1996: 122).

In a flight of fancy, he imagines travelling the world: He would go to Mexico, Paris, a mining village in Wales; alternatively, he sees himself as the leader of a revolution in Albania, or a member of the Spanish Foreign Legion in Lisbon (1996: 122). With retrospective self-irony that already prefigures the next failure, Isherwood describes the actual outcome of his plan as 'the mildest and most respectable of domestic adventures' (1996: 123). His far-flung projects take him no further from his mother's house in North Kensington than to a derelict little street in a bohemian 'art-slum' (1996: 126) in South Kensington, where he takes over the room of a friend. What is more, his self-stylisation as a London bohemian is not entirely successful, and betrays a marked discrepancy between expectation and reality:

> Yes, it was a nice snug little setting for my cosy independent bachelor life; or at any rate for the pleasing impression of that life which I wished to convey to my visiting friends. ... Mine was the rigid tidiness of the celibate: that pathetically neat room, as I now picture it, seems to cry out for the disorderly human traces of cohabitation. ... But the room, as long as I occupied it, remained virgin, unravished. (1996: 137)

The space he has created is much more a reflection of his old self than evidence of his transformation. He cannot live up to his own vision of bohemian life due to his lack of sexual exploits and his class consciousness, and this shows in his room, which looks 'all sort of respectable – like a public park' (1996: 137), as one of his friends remarks. After a number of complications in his boarding-house, he returns back home: 'The New Life had ignominiously failed' (1996: 161). This frustrating cycle is mirrored by the journey to Scotland he subsequently undertakes with a friend. As much as the excursion suits his 'escapist temperament', it will invariably end with a return to his old life, with a movement back to his 'nursery prison of minor obligations, duties, habits, ties' (1996: 163, 166), a vision that reveals his anxiety about the past always catching up with him.

This is the prevailing impression towards the end of *Lions and Shadows*, when Isherwood realises that 'I hadn't advanced an inch, really, since those Cambridge days' (1996: 187). Consequently a new attempt at relocation is needed, and this time, in order to finally break his circular movements and recurring failures, a more radical one: 'I must leave England altogether – the break with the old life must be complete, this time … I'd go to Berlin' (1996: 188). His choice of destination is not accidental. For one thing it is motivated by Hugh Weston, who embodies what Christopher wants to become and who has already been in Berlin for several months; and secondly, Weimar Berlin had acquired a reputation of exceptionality and sexual freedom (Fryer 1993: 70–71, Page 2000: 8–9), of a city where outsiders, as Peter Gay has argued, for a brief spell, had become the insiders (1968: xiv), in short: for Christopher and his friends Berlin was 'buggers' territory' (Isherwood 1978: 42). So in March 1929 he embarks on 'yet another stage of my journey' (1996: 191). The motif employed here, of the journey with different stages, seems to imply a different concept of change, away from a reliance on instantaneous rupture to successive spatial repositionings and gradual modifications of the self.

Berlin

According to *Christopher and His Kind*, the major issue during Isherwood's Berlin years was losing his inhibitions about his homosexuality and freely indulging in his homosexual desires. As far as his textual alter egos are concerned, he is for a long time elusive about his sexual preferences, however, and experiments with different ways of approaching the subject in his earlier works. Both first-person narrators of his Berlin books, the thinly fictionalised William Bradshaw in *Mr Norris Changes Trains*, who bears the author's two middle names, and the Christopher Isherwood of *Goodbye to Berlin*, are merely witnesses to the homosexual encounters between other characters. Although fear of public exposure[5] probably also played a part in this decision, Isherwood foregrounds aesthetic reasons: his intention to establish a sense of distance and objectivity (Isherwood 1978: 141–2, Webster 1971: 64) and to create a narrator who is merely recording – 'a camera with its shutters open' (Isherwood 1987: 9) – without being under scrutiny himself. What is quite obviously at stake here is his particular self-conception as 'Isherwood the Artist' (1996: 60) and literary chronicler of life. Nevertheless, using his own name for the narrator while at the same time not really wanting to be a character in the story (Geherin 2001: 74–5) points to his concern with how to shape the self through the medium of literature. In fact, his writing acts as the privileged site for his self-transformations, because it leaves the author in complete control and even allows him to simply erase part of his old self:

> In writing *Goodbye to Berlin*, I destroyed a certain portion of my real past. I did this deliberately, because I preferred the simplified, more creditable, more exciting fictitious past which I'd created to take its place ... And so, gradually, the real past had disappeared, along with the real Christopher Isherwood twenty years ago. Only the Christopher Isherwood of the stories remained. (1963: vii–viii)

Christopher and His Kind, which has been called a revisionist autobiography (Terkel 2001: 168), heralds a new Christopher Isherwood, a claim backed up by statements like: '"Christopher Isherwood" in the early books wasn't *me* at all' (Scobie 2001: 185). Needless to say, we are presented with a different rather than a 'truer' version of the author's self; after all, he confesses to having burnt the diaries of his Berlin years and more than once remarks on the scarcity of original sources from which to work. Much less controversial than its truth value, however, is this new self's firm spatial embedding and connection to a particular place.

Christopher and His Kind bluntly confronts the reader with the following statement: 'To Christopher, Berlin meant Boys' (1978: 9). The capitalisation of Boys, among other things, indicates that Berlin stands for a kind of breakthrough in Isherwood's self-fashioning. On the first pages, he stresses the importance of Berlin as a place of initiation with W.H. Auden introducing him to the gay life of the city. This is implicitly contrasted with the restraints and inhibitions of his

---

5   The reasons he gives in *Christopher and His Kind* for his reticence about the narrator's sexuality in *Mr Norris Changes Trains* are that 'he feared to create a scandal', that he did not want to embarrass his mother and that he didn't want to take the risk of having his uncle's allowance cut off (1978: 141). It is perhaps also noteworthy that he was privy to E.M. Forster's repeated hesitations to publish his novel *Maurice* for similar reasons of discretion (see Zeikowitz 2008: 24, 75).

previous life and dramatised as a plunge into delirious freedom in a rhetorical flourish simultaneously undercut by the ironic distancing of the first-person narrator from his younger incarnation (addressed in the third person): 'Now he burned ... to unchain his desires and hurl reason and sanity into prison' (10). In Berlin, his existence seems to resolve itself into a set of simple oppositions: His life in England was insincere, because he outwardly conformed to the expected standards of respectability, whereas in Germany he can shed his allegiance to these norms and be truthful to his inner self (13). England and its values are epitomised by his mother Kathleen whom he aggressively and defiantly confronts with his promiscuous homosexuality as if to exorcise the power she holds over him. Although it is his declared wish 'to find a place where I can be what I am' (17), his actions and reflections are just as much about repudiating and obsessively dissociating himself from what he claims to have left behind: 'Before long, he would be rejecting her England' (126).

Englishness is invariably connected to a certain class consciousness and the value judgments of his mother, who actually seems to have approved of his boyfriends as long as they were 'gentlemen, not working-class; Englishmen, not undesirable aliens' (217). Even his forays into the gay subculture of Berlin and his relations with the working-class youths he picked up at the Cosy Corner are not entirely dissociated from his maternal heritage: 'Christopher was suffering from an inhibition, then not unusual among upper-class homosexuals; he couldn't relax sexually with a member of his own class or nation. He needed a working-class foreigner' (10). Similarly, his insistence that his lover Heinz 'proclaim himself an unashamed proletarian' (106) by entering 'domestic servant' as profession on his passport application in 1933, solely serves his own spirit of resistance. In retrospect, he self-critically analyses his various attempts at 'slumming' (46) and his idealising of the working class as a case of inverted snobbery (1971: 188) and even classifies his attitude as a form of sexual colonialism (1978: 31–2).

As I already suggested earlier in this chapter, language plays a crucial part in Isherwood's self-transformation. Being surrounded by a foreign language affords him a sense of liberation, quite independent of his own command of that language. Once he has acquired a certain knowledge of German, he can speak freely about his sexual desires, because these German words 'had no association with his life in England' (1978: 30) – and it should perhaps be noted that German was the language his mother Kathleen hated, which in turn made him profess his love for it (1971: 3–4). But even when he is not yet able to speak German on his arrival in Berlin, the narrator experiences a sense of freedom by simply hearing it all around him. It transports him into a state of suspension in which he can give free rein to his imagination. This becomes clear with respect to his first German lover,

Bubi, whom he casts as 'The German Boy', as the essence of Germanness that he can take possession of: Bubi was the first candidate 'to claim the leading role in Christopher's love-myth ... By embracing Bubi, Christopher could hold in his arms the whole mystery-magic of foreignness, Germanness. By means of Bubi, he could fall in love with and possess the entire nation' (1978: 11). This projection only works as long as his fantasy obliterates the real Bubi, however. Consequently, when he meets Bubi again three years later and his German has become much more fluent, the spell is broken: 'the collapse of their language-barrier had buried the magic image of The German Boy. Bubi seemed an entirely different person' (1978: 15).

This example is significant, because it again demonstrates that Isherwood's self-constructions are indifferent to the idea of 'truth' and actually rely on a principle of derealisation. He seeks constellations that allow him to loosen his moorings in the past and provide an unencumbered space for new self-projections. The fact that the older Isherwood exposes this tendency in his younger self should not be taken for a mark of greater honesty and frankness but for yet another posture of literary self-exploration and creation. As Avrom Fleishman has pointedly stated in his study *Figures of Autobiography*: 'The intention to "tell the truth about oneself", like other imaginative projects, is a fictional premise which may issue in highly rewarding constructions of the self' (1983: 10).

Unsurprisingly, Isherwood's infatuation with Berlin leads him to imagine this space of unbelonging as his true destination and to emphasise 'how completely at home one can be as a foreigner' (1978: 24). This fantasy is only short-lived, however. His vision of the city as his new homeland, no doubt almost exclusively based on its reputation of sexual licentiousness, is soon rivalled by another aspect of the capital that he can no longer ignore: the Berlin of increasing Nazi terror. The rampant anti-semitism that causes most of his Jewish friends to leave Germany as well as the regular raids on the boy bars and on the Hirschfeld Institute in May 1933 force him to reconsider his position: 'This wasn't his homeland ... No, indeed it wasn't' (1978: 98).

Further Travels and America

Consequently, in 1933 he has reached another impasse that leads to his decision to leave Germany: 'This ended Christopher's grand journey of home rejection and defiance of Nearly Everybody. What followed this was no longer defiant; just a succession of moves on a chessboard, compelled by a stronger opponent' (1978: 145). Between 1933 and 1937 Christopher and his German boyfriend

Heinz travel restlessly in Europe, only returning to Germany for short and risky visits. The lack of agency and choice alluded to is due to considerations for Heinz' safety and the haphazard granting of tourist permits or emergency short-term visas by one country or another. Heinz is finally arrested in Germany for draft-evasion and put on trial. This is the end of their relationship – and the loss of 'that part of myself which only existed in his company' (1978: 215).

Although the passage quoted above implies an end to his crusade of defiance, this is contradicted by other statements which suggest a continuation of the same pattern of movement and spatial distancing from England fuelled by the same spirit of rejection, for example his comment on his departure from London in March 1934 to rejoin Heinz in Amsterdam: 'Thus he symbolically rejected Kathleen's England. But this short journey was to be only the first phase of his rejection. To remain in Amsterdam would be like lingering undramatically backstage after making your final exit. No, Heinz and he must go much farther away' (1978: 132). In 1929 he had thought it necessary to leave England for another European country; now he feels it is time to leave Europe altogether. This idea tentatively shapes itself in his mind in 1934, when they travel to the Canary Islands and 'Christopher would be able to think of himself as having escaped from Europe; politically the islands belonged to Spain but geographically they are part of Africa' (1978: 133).

And indeed, the distance he will put between himself and England in order to become 'another' will become ever greater. The travels he subsequently embarks on with Auden in 1938 take them to China and then to America. In New York, the 'German pattern' repeats itself when he is introduced to a young and sexy boy, whom the narrator calls 'Vernon' and whom he immediately turns into a fantasy: 'Christopher reacted to Vernon much as he had reacted to Bubi, on his first Berlin visit. Both were infatuations based on a fantasy; only, this time, Christopher was looking for The American, not The German, Boy' (1978: 234).

Back in London, he imagines replacing Berlin with New York as his potential 'home': 'Vernon ... was a citizen of the New World which Christopher had begun to hope might be the homeland he had failed to find in Germany' (1978: 239). After his return to America the following year, his faith is badly shaken, however, and he finds himself almost frightened by his status as a foreigner:

> At the end of Christopher's brief visit in 1938, he had felt absolutely confident of one
> thing, at least. If he did decide to settle in America – and, by America, he meant New
> York – he would be able to make himself at home there. ... But now New York, on that
> bitter winter morning, appeared totally, shockingly transformed from the place he had

waved goodbye to, the previous July. Christopher experienced a sudden panicky loss of confidence. (1978: 251)

His life story at the end of 1939 concludes very much like *Lions and Shadows* ten years earlier: with an open prospect. Except that at the very end of *Christopher and His Kind*, this aesthetically pleasing structural parallel is counterposed by the narrator's closing statement assuring the reader that the protagonist of his story will spend more than half of his life in the States and find his ideal companion there. Even at this stage, his self-construction is still determined by his opposition to England and his mother, as he explains in *Kathleen and Frank*, his biography of his parents: 'His [Christopher's] final ritual act of breaking free from her was to become a citizen of the United States, thus separating himself from Mother and Motherland at one stroke' (1971: 362).

Conclusion: Textual and Geographical Spaces

The discussion of Isherwood's autobiographical writings has shown him to be a subject who primarily wants to get away from himself. In temporal terms, this movement translates into a rejection of the past; with respect to space, it means putting as much distance as possible between himself and England. Psychologically, both England and the past are connected to the oppressive influence of his mother. In his writings, several processes combine in pursuing his aim of perpetually displacing the autobiographical subject: the textual movements and scattering of the self as well as the protagonist's geographical journeys.

For Isherwood, the literary text becomes the space in which he effects the gradual effacement of his old self by creating a series of mutations and variations of 'Christopher Isherwood'. He turns the inevitable decentring produced by any narrative projection of the self into the guiding principle of his texts thus creating a centrifugal dispersal of the autobiographical subject that cannot be contained and defies coherence. Isherwood uses his textual authority to write and rewrite his own self in successive versions. His autobiographical self is a largely imaginary one, and its different textual versions erase what remains of original memories and sources. He uses two narrative strategies of spatialisation in particular that enmesh the subject in a web of textual cross-references, rereadings and reassessments and increasingly derealise and obliterate his ties with any extra-textual reality: a high degree of intertextuality interweaving diaries, letters and quotations from his previous works, which are set off against each other, as well as a splitting of the autobiographical subject into different personae in a single text, effectively destroying the notion of a unified self.

These textual polishings and reconstructions not only put an unbridgeable distance between the subject and his former lived experience but also imply a repeated and intentional fictionalising of the self. Isherwood's own reflections on the diminishing difference between his fiction and non-fiction (see Smith and Smith 2001: 137) at one point led him to contemplate a project called *The Autobiography of My Books*, which he intended to be concerned with the merging of autobiography and fiction, with the fictionality of autobiography and the autobiographical nature of his fictional works (Isherwood 1971: 362). Although he finally discarded this plan, it nevertheless clearly demonstrates that he considered his life writing first and foremost as a literary project committed to aesthetic criteria and contributing to his reputation as a writer rather than as a faithful reconstruction of his life.

The second part of my argument takes us from Isherwood's textual strategies of spatialising the self to the use of geographical spaces in his self-projections. Leaving his old self behind invariably involves physical movement and travel. It is remarkable, however, that his various destinations are much less instrumental in any search for identity than they are in the stripping of his past affiliations. This peculiarity sheds an instructive light on the mutual construction of self and space. Henri Lefebvre has made a strong case for the social production of space structuring the relations of production and reproduction in a society, which include economic, class and sexual relations. These comprise spatial practices which in turn engender specific subjects who inhabit 'a space in which they must either recognize themselves or lose themselves' (Lefebvre 1991: 35). Isherwood's example makes us aware of a hierarchy of spatial imprints. The shaping force of what he summarises as 'England', notably his early life in an upper-middle class home, exerted the deepest formative influence on him; it proved to be much more permanent than the effect his exposure to any other kind of environment could have. In terms of Gaston Bachelard's phenomenological framework, it constitutes his 'original shell' (1994: 4) that accompanies him wherever he goes, and his travels abroad largely serve the purpose to undo this early moulding of the self so that in his writings places like Germany or America are staged as spaces of disidentification.

The obstacles he encounters when attempting to transform the self through spatial relocation inform the various models he devises and experiments with in the course of his life to describe the interdependence of places and selves. The first one, which repeatedly fails, posits a radical change of self effected by a new geographical and linguistic environment: 'I would start all over again, among new people who didn't know me' (Isherwood 1996: 122). The second one, which is suggested by the endings of *Lions and Shadows* and *Christopher and His Kind*, projects a journey of the self through various stages accompanying his physical movements. His vision of the relationship between these different selves ranges from a more conciliatory, integrative view acknowledging the persistence of early influences in his later life (e.g. in *Kathleen and Frank*) to the virtual killing off of a former self, as the present-day narrator in *Down There on a Visit* suggests with respect to one of his younger alter egos: 'The Christopher who sat in that taxi is, practically speaking, dead' (1985: 7). And the third model assumes the coexistence of different, independent and spatially coded selves, as he explains in an interview: 'I wanted to be "German Christopher" instead of "English Christopher" ... I still believe ... that you are a different person in different places'. These selves can even interact and challenge each other: 'while I'm in England, my American half ... comes out; but while I'm here [in America], my English half comes out' (Terkel 2001: 167). Such statements confirm Isherwood's 'ambiguous position as an outsider, a non-joiner' (1978: 81) and portray him as a permanent foreigner suspended between places and reinventing himself in his literary worlds.

References

Bachelard, G. 1994. *The Poetics of Space* [1958], translated by M. Jolas. Boston: Beacon Press.

Beggar, Awatif. 2014. L'autofiction: un nouveau mode d'expression autobiographique. *@analyses: Revue de critique et de théorie littéraire* [Online], 9(2), 122–37. Available at: https://uottawa.scholarsportal.info/ojs/index.php/revue-analyses/article/view/1003 [accessed 8 August 2014].

Dilthey, W. 1989. Das Erleben und die Selbstbiographie [1910], in *Die Autobiographie: Zu Form und Geschichte einer literarischen Gattung*, edited by G. Niggl. Darmstadt: Wissenschaftliche Buchgesellschaft, 21–32.

Fleishman, A. 1983. *Figures of Autobiography: The Language of Self-Writing in Victorian and Modern England*. Berkeley: University of California Press.

Fryer, J. 1993. *Eye of the Camera: A Life of Christopher Isherwood*. London: Allison Busby.

Gay, P. 1968. *Weimar Culture: The Outsider as Insider*. London: Secker & Warburg.

Geherin, D.J. 2001. An Interview with Christopher Isherwood [1972], in *Conversations with Christopher Isherwood*, edited by J.J. Berg and C. Freeman. Jackson: University Press of Mississippi, 74–89.

Gratton, Johnnie. 2001. Autofiction, in *Encyclopedia of Life Writing: Autobiographical and Biographical Forms*, edited by Margaretta Jolly. Chicago and London: Fitzroy Dearborn/Routledge, 86–7.

Gusdorf, G. 1980. Conditions and Limits of Autobiography [1956], translated by J. Olney, in *Autobiography: Essays Theoretical and Critical*, edited by J. Olney. Princeton: Princeton University Press, 28–48.

Isherwood, C. 1963. About this Book [1954], in *The Berlin Stories: The Last of Mr. Norris; Goodbye to Berlin*. New York: New Directions, v–xiii.

Isherwood, C. 1966. Foreword to *All the Conspirators* [1958], in *Exhumations: Stories, Articles, Verses*. London: Methuen, 91–3.

Isherwood, C. 1971. *Kathleen and Frank*. London: Methuen/Minerva.

Isherwood, C. 1978. *Christopher and His Kind: 1929 – 1939* [1976]. London: Magnum.

Isherwood, C. 1980. *All the Conspirators* [1928]. London: Methuen/Magnum.

Isherwood, C. 1985. *Down There on a Visit* [1962]. London: Methuen.

Isherwood, C. 1987. *Goodbye to Berlin* [1939]. London: Methuen.

Isherwood, C. 1996. *Lions and Shadows: An Education in the Twenties* [1938]. London: Minerva.

Isherwood, C. 1999. *Mr Norris Changes Trains* [1935]. London: Vintage.

Jones, E.H. 2000. Autofiction: A brief history of a Neologism, in *Life Writing: Essays on Autobiography, Biography and Literature*, edited by Richard Bradford. Houndmills: Palgrave Macmillan, 174–84.

Lefebvre, H. 1991. *The Production of Space* [1974], translated by D. Nicholson-Smith. Oxford: Blackwell.

Lotman, J. 1977. *The Structure of the Artistic Text* [1971], translated by G. Lenhoff and R. Vroon. Ann Arbor: The University of Michigan.

Olney, J. 1972. *Metaphors of Self: The Meaning of Autobiography*. Princeton: Princeton University Press.

Pascal, R. 1960. *Design and Truth in Autobiography*. London: Routledge.

Regard, F. 2003. Topologies of the Self: Space and Life-Writing, in *Mapping the Self: Space, Identity, Discourse and British Auto/Biography*, edited by F. Regard. Saint-Étienne: Publications de l'Université de Saint-Étienne.

Ricoeur, P. 1991. Life in quest of narrative, in *On Paul Ricoeur: Narrative and Interpretation*, edited by D. Wood. London/New York: Routledge, 20–33.

Saunders, M. 2010. *Self Impression: Life-Writing, Autobiografiction, and the Forms of Modern Literature*. Oxford: Oxford University Press.

Schwerdt, L.M. 1989. *Isherwood's Fiction: The Self and Technique*. Houndmills and London: Macmillan.

Scobie, W.I. 2001. The youth that was 'I': A conversation in Santa Monica with Christopher Isherwood [1977], in *Conversations with Christopher Isherwood*, edited by J.J. Berg and C. Freeman. Jackson: University Press of Mississippi, 181–8.

Smith, S. and Smith, M. 2001. To help along the line: An interview with Christopher Isherwood [1975], in *Conversations with Christopher Isherwood*, edited by J.J. Berg and C. Freeman. Jackson: University Press of Mississippi, 131–40.

Terkel, S. 2001. Christopher Isherwood [1977], in *Conversations with Christopher Isherwood*, edited by J.J. Berg and C. Freeman. Jackson: University Press of Mississippi, 166–80.

Waldenfels, B. 1997. *Topographie des Fremden: Studien zur Phänomenologie des Fremden I*. Frankfurt am Main: Suhrkamp.

Webster, L. 2001. A very individualistic old liberal [1971], in *Conversations with Christopher Isherwood*, edited by J.J. Berg and C. Freeman. Jackson: University Press of Mississippi, 57–71.

Wickes, G. 2001. An interview with Christopher Isherwood [1965], in *Conversations with Christopher Isherwood*, edited by J.J. Berg and C. Freeman. Jackson: University Press of Mississippi, 24–44.

Zeikowitz, R.E. (ed.) 2008. *Letters between Forster and Isherwood on Homosexuality and Literature*. New York and Basingstoke: Palgrave Macmillan.

Chapter 6

Critical Topographies in Depression Era Lives

Martin Klepper and Alexandra Wagner

The Great Depression as a period in US history (1929 to 1941) has its very own, very distinct iconography. Indeed, the time seems less characterised by processes or events (with the exception, perhaps, of the stock market crash and the election of Roosevelt) than by pictures, such as Walker Evans's or Dorothea Lange's photographs of Dust Bowl victims, Margarete Bourke-White's images of breadlines, Aaron Douglas's, Ralph Stackpole's and Bernhard Zakheim's murals of community challenges and community life, and John Ford's or Victor Fleming's moving pictures. Moreover, although in actual fact physical mobility was on a downturn during these years (people tend to stay put during difficult times), the popular conception of the Depression looms large with 'Okies'[1] moving West, migrant workers seeking jobs, hobos and vagabonds making their way along the highways and railway lines, men and children taking to the road (as symbolised by the most persistent filmic genre of the time, the road movie) and marathon dancers competing for the longest uninterrupted motion (Dickstein 2010: 54, 66; Young 2002: 231, 121).

How did this preoccupation with space and movement register in Depression Era life writing? Are experience and representation structured along spatial rather than temporal markers? How do crisis, space and mobility interact in autobiographical texts of the time? In this chapter we will explore these questions in a tentative way with the help of Richard Wright's *Black Boy* (1945) and Jerre Mangione's *An Ethnic At Large* (1978), two texts from different times and different social spaces. We aim to understand the way in which the written self emerges from the configuration of crisis (both personal and social), mobility (migration, relocation, travel), space (locations and positioning) and the available patterns or protocols afforded by genre and popular media.

---

[1]   The expression 'Okies' refers to the Dust Bowl refugees from the Midwest migrating to California. Many, though by no means all of them, came from Oklahoma. At the time, the term had a clearly derogatory connotation.

Critical Topographies

Our term 'critical topographies' has three trajectories: firstly, life writing employs the pattern of crisis and resolution (Egan 1984: 8), especially when we are talking about the Great Depression. Life during the Depression was about getting through the crisis, and, as a result, the topographies of autobiographical texts from this time are more often than not critical topographies in their urgent quest for a safe and sustaining space. Secondly, the very name and period of the Depression is linked to a critical attitude: a time of deep doubts, fundamental questions and soul-searching acts of re-orientation. It stands to reason that Depression autobiographies are especially critical about their social, political, and ideological environment. Thirdly, critical topographies are also meant to remind the critic of autobiographical texts that spatial configurations are not simply formal structures, but also figures with an ideological message – whether pertaining to class, race, sexuality, gender or other categories of social differentiation (see Friedman 1998).

In exploring two autobiographies about life during the Depression Era, we define space as the productive tension between physical places in their concrete dimensions and the mental or social connotations of such places, both in terms of narrated and narrating spaces.[2] Spatial relations are employed as cognitive maps bringing together physical places and their social connotations with temporal expectations and anxieties: Where do I go from here? Autobiography enacts a process of (re-)mapping, of revisiting the itineraries of the past. Mobility involves movement in space, which makes space palpable, and it negotiates the transition or liminality between spaces. Mobility, whether physical or social (and most often both), results in the positioning of the speaker or, rather, triggers a necessity for re-positioning. Positioning is a social act which situates the speaker on a plane of social differentiation in respect to the categories salient in a particular society (Smith and Watson 2010: 42–9). Crisis refers to 'social dislocation, disruption, strain' (Elder 1999: 9) as well as 'the point in a story ... at which the tension reaches a maximum and a resolution is imminent' (Cuddon 1999: 195). As Mikhail Bakhtin has pointed out, crisis is intimately linked to the former terms:

> [the chronotope of the threshold] can be combined with the motif of encounter, but
> its most fundamental instance is as the chronotope of *crisis* and *break* in a life. The

---

2   We are using the terms 'narrated' and 'narrating spaces' in the same way as Chatman uses 'story-space' and 'discourse-space' (1978: 96). The narrating space is the space the narrator inhabits as he is describing the earlier spaces he remembers. For a short overview on space in narrative theory see Wagner (2014: 82–9).

word 'threshold' itself already has a metaphorical meaning in everyday usage (together with its literal meaning), and is connected with the breaking point of a life, the moment of crisis, the decision that changes a life. (1981: 248)

Finally, in invoking the term chronotope, Bakhtin reminds us of the connection between time, space (including mobility), crisis and genre. We understand genre as a schema for producing knowledge (Frow 2006: 84) by bringing together spatial, temporal, aesthetic and social parameters:

> ... spatial and temporal indicators are fused into one carefully thought-out, concrete whole. Time, as it were, thickens, takes on flesh, becomes artistically visible; likewise, space becomes charged and responsive to the movements of time, plot and history. This intersection of axes and fusion of indicators characterizes the artistic chronotope.
>
> The chronotope in literature has an intrinsic *generic* significance. It can even be said that it is precisely the chronotope that defines genre and generic distinctions ... (Bakhtin 1981: 84–5)

Even though Bakhtin stresses the significance of space in any narrative, the question arises why the cultural expressions of the Great Depression are so extraordinarily preoccupied with images and spaces? Perhaps, in the United States a sense of place is not as easily to be taken for granted as in other countries – exactly because mobility has value in and of itself. In that regard, sense of place would always be in a state of crisis. As American actor Rockwell Gray has remarked in an essay:

> Like many men and women today, hardly knowing where home is any longer, I have had to build myself a composite sense of place. This primary task of modern autobiographical memory is especially salient in America, where constant mobility exacerbates the already complicated search for a clear sense of identity. Any study of the controlling patterns of autobiography must emphasize its function in our current culture as an antidote to anonymity, disconnection and uprootedness. (1989: 57)

Wright and Mangione

Richard Wright's *Black Boy* was published in 1945 by HarperCollins. But it was only half of what Wright initially had written under the original title *American Hunger*. Because the influential Book-of-the-Month Club only wanted to select the book's first, more conciliatory part for its March 1945 selection, Wright –

expecting 'substantial sales' (Andrews and Taylor 2003: 9) – agreed to publish only the first part of his text and even wrote a new ending for that purpose (Rowly 2001: 284–90). Wright was born in Roxie, Mississippi in 1908 and grew up in the South, arriving in Chicago in 1927. In the course of the Great Depression he and his family eventually became dependent on public welfare. And it was also in Chicago that Wright realised that he wanted to become a writer.

Gerlando 'Jerre' Mangione was born in Rochester, New York in 1909 into a family and community of Sicilian immigrants. Rochester, in the words of Bernhard A. Weisberger, was at that time 'an outpost of upstate Yankee values' (2001: 7), in which being Sicilian was very much synonymous with being an outsider. In an act of singular courage, Gerlando left Rochester in 1928 against the will of his family to study in Syracuse, ninety miles east. Later, even though the Depression had hit, Mangione went to New York to lead a more or less bohemian life. Mangione wanted to become a writer, but having to earn money, his best bid was to join the Rural Resettlement Administration and then the Federal Writers' Project as PR specialist and editor. The New Deal programmes made Mangione's career – not only was he surrounded by important writers, inspiring him to write his first book (a fictionalised memoir of his childhood, *Mount Allegro*), but he also turned his experience on the job and his deep bond to Roosevelt's scheme into his second book, *The Dream and the Deal: The Federal Writers' Project, 1935–1943*. Eventually, Mangione became a literature professor at the University of Pennsylvania. *An Ethnic at Large*, his memoir of America in the Thirties and Forties, was published in 1978. Incidentally, Mangione and Wright knew each other from the Federal Writers' project and met later on several occasions.

For both, Mangione and Wright, the context of the Great Depression was instrumental in their choice of career: The intellectual climate of the time but also the opportunities afforded by the Federal Writers' Project nudged them towards writing. It is significant, however, that this context in both cases intersects with their status as outsiders. Mangione grew up at a time when Italians were not yet fully accepted as 'white', while Wright felt the full brunt of Jim Crow throughout his life. In this sense, the threshold which Bakhtin theorises as break and crisis also refers to the gateway into or boundary line against a white world: a passage or barrier which both had to negotiate in order to understand and define (or even master) the social significance of different spaces in America. For both, the act of writing also entails the effort to open, to re-define and to (symbolically and materially) appropriate spaces, which had been traditionally closed to the ethnic and racial other.

Jerre Mangione's *An Ethnic at Large*

Jerre Mangione's memoir, *An Ethnic at Large*, will appear rather familiar in its patterning of a life, because conventional motifs offer a frame for the author's experience. Mangione opens his book with a classical spatial metaphor for the immigrant experience, which structures the entire text:

> Before my parents considered me old enough to go beyond the picket fence that separated me from the children on the street, I would peer through it for hours, longing to play with them and wondering what they could be saying to one another. Although I had been born in the same city as they, I spoke not their language. English was forbidden in our home – for reasons of love. (2001: 13)

At the end of the book and at the age of thirty-five, Mangione has learned to play with the children of America, and he has mastered their language without foreclosing the love of his parents' home. The last chapter of the memoir, 'A White House Weekend', presents the author reluctant to leave Eleanor Roosevelt's Camelot, heading for his work in Philadelphia and reporting to his parents 'that I would be coming to Rochester the following weekend to give them a full report of my White House sojourn' (365). The fences have transformed into open gates.

Thus, *An Ethnic At Large* is organised along the lines of the chronotope of a typical immigrant autobiography: the journey from the ethnic community into the heart of America, the function of which is to learn 'the language' (literally and figuratively) of the new community and to learn to belong. Mangione's story is about finding and pushing open the gates. The self he constructs in the process of narrating is completed with 'the end of my apprenticeship as an American' (367), which coincides with the death of his hero, Franklin Delano Roosevelt, whose America is his America and whose wife, in Mangione's imagination, has become the alter ego of his mother: 'were they to meet they would recognise each other as sisters' (365).

The White House is the preliminary end of his journey and apprenticeship: 'I had learned how to protect myself from the bruising paradoxes of everyday American life, and how to cope with the ever-recurring sensation of being a foreigner in my own native land' (367). He has also mastered the language, published his first book and is well on his way to a professorship in English. Mingling without a fence separating him from others is the destiny of his journey as the cinematic ending of the book reveals, when he receives the news of Roosevelt's death during a concert in Philadelphia:

My companion that evening was a piquant, blue-eyed brunette from Virginia, a direct
descendant of one of the nation's founding fathers. Earlier in our relationship, she
had revealed I was the first Italian she had ever dated. Our tears intermingled as the
orchestra commemorated the audience's grief with a rendition of Beethoven's *Eroica*.
(370)

Needless to say, the Academy of Music, which is the setting for this last scene,
serves as a class marker – and an appropriate destiny for the second chronotope
structuring the text: that of the bildungsroman.

However, Mangione's metaphorical and material journey is not quite as
straightforward as these quotations and the often-invoked chronotopes suggest.
In his introduction to the memoir, Bernhard A. Weisberger reminds the reader
that the narrative has picaresque and bohemian qualities as well. The memoir
has no climax, no central turning point, unless one wants to take Jerre's sojourn
in Fascist Italy in the early thirties, located at the heart of the narrative, as the
expression and resolution of a crisis. His first twenty years had been an attempt at
getting away from the Sicilian diaspora in Rochester, which he had experienced
as suffocating, and at entering 'America'. After five years of bohemian living in
New York, he reports, however:

I found myself admiring my relatives for some of the same qualities I had once found
intolerable. There were still vestiges of my childhood resentments, but on the whole I
felt lucky to be one of them. It gave me a root feeling, a connection with a substantial
past that made the uncertain present more bearable. It was shocking to realize that
more than once I had thought of cutting myself off from such a natural source of
strength. (175)

Rockwell Gray once wrote: 'we cannot know who we are without knowing
where we have been; and recall of all those now absent places is necessary to
a full sense of dwelling in the present. To dwell is to be embedded, and to be
embedded is to belong through a history of having belonged in many places
before' (1989: 53). In Mangione's version it is really the uncertainty of the
present, which triggers a sense of nostalgia and the necessity of remembering
the now absent places.

Belonging in Manhattan is precarious at the time: 'Night and day men and
women dug into trash and garbage pails, scavenging for anything that could be
eaten or sold. There were breadlines, often lined four abreast by men who kept
their heads down ... the landscape was blighted with "Hoovervilles"' (Mangione
2001: 96). Nevertheless, Mangione states: 'I was more responsive than ever to

the Horatio Alger syndrome implanted by my public-school teachers' (175).[3] America, now symbolised by 'demonic Manhattan' (175), stands in tension to Sicily, personified by Mangione's relatives. He never expresses it explicitly, but the shock of experiencing Sicily at first hand and his continual anxiety in the Fascist country seem to have eased this tension: his ancestral homeland was not a real alternative anymore. And again, it is a visualised rendition of memory which indicates the disappointment (or disillusionment):

> Instead of the undulating hills and lush vegetation I had heard described all through my childhood, I saw sun-scorched fields and towering naked mountains and precipices, endlessly menacing, some in the shape of monsters. The mythologists who placed the gates of Hades in Sicily were certainly more reliable than the memories of my Rochester relatives. (180–81)

But even after this sobering experience with his roots, the fact that he keeps travelling underlines the persisting liminal quality of Mangione's position. Before Sicily, his frequent changes in jobs and moves between lodgings (even though clearly related to his precarious status as a would-be man of letters during the Depression), his sexual affairs, relations, friendships and occasional returns to the Sicilian cocoon had defined him as a character in search of his place. In the coda to his book, Mangione writes that he had resolved this tension 'by becoming an ethnic at large, with one foot in my Sicilian heritage, the other in the American mainstream' (369).

After his return from Sicily, while the Italian heritage appears to linger on as a vague concept, his depictions of America seem mostly assembled from other narrations, photographs and images. Depression America is described by drawing on the journalist Oscar Ameringer (96). The above-mentioned description of Manhattan with its breadlines reads like a photograph by Margaret Bourke-White. The South, yielding 'enough evidence of land and human erosion to convince us that only the government was in a position to rehabilitate the barren land and the people who could no longer eke a living from it' (222), is a place with which he never became comfortable. Washington feels unreal to him: 'Every time I returned from a field trip, its trees and grass seemed more like stage props, its people further encased in a cocoon far removed from the Depression and all the other unpleasantries of the outside world' (227–8). In addition, he condemns the 'concentration camps – American style' (319), the internment

---

3   With 'Horatio Alger syndrome' Mangione refers to the belief in American-style self-invention as opposed to his parents' belief in the family as the only trustworthy space.

camps housing tens of thousands of Japanese, German and Italian migrants, whom he visits as an employee of the Department of Justice. Were it not for the people he met and befriended (among them Eleanor Roosevelt), one would be tempted to translate his title as 'an ethnic on the run' – Mangione never seems to be really at home in any one place. It comes as little surprise that Mangione's job at the Federal Writers' Project was the publication of 48 state guides.[4]

We do not know where Mangione wrote *An Ethnic At Large*, but in his text he talks at length about the places where he wrote his first memoir, *Mount Allegro*. At one time he is invited to the farm of his friend Paul Corey at Cold-Spring-on-Hudson, then to Kenneth Burke's place in New Jersey, and once to the artists' community Yaddo in Saratoga Springs. These places differ considerably from other narrated spaces in the book. Here, Mangione can concentrate on his writing and on the conversations with other writers he meets. They are retreats from the world at large – perhaps more real to the author than places like Washington. Mangione in his memoir, and perhaps his life too, never seemed to belong spatially. His topography of America remains precarious: one has the impression that he is still searching for a place called home.

Noting that Franklin Delano Roosevelt, Mangione's hero, was especially popular with immigrants and their families, he remembers one of his speeches: 'Always the astute politician he must have had them in mind when ... he opened with the words "Fellow immigrants"' (2001: 370). Mangione, born in Rochester, positions himself as one of the immigrants, who is in the process of inscribing himself into the American text. In order to do that, it seems, he has to assume the attitude of a surveyor. He learns the language, he crosses the fences, he plays with the Americans, he even enters the White House. And yet, his map of America and his place within it remain strangely uprooted, a mental map, a network of people and functions.

Richard Wright's *Black Boy (American Hunger)*

Richard Wright's spatial experiences differ considerably from Mangione's. Wright's story does not end at the White House dinner table. And although both texts can be read against the backdrop of the chronotope of the bildungsroman, it is perhaps more important that Wright's course of life in many ways resembles

---

4   The American Guide Series was one of the major outcomes of the Federal Writers' Project within the New Deal. They contained histories of the states and descriptions of cities and towns including photographs and automobile tours.

the lives represented in slave narratives, in which mobility means finding an exit from segregation, racism and enslavement in the South. The chronotope of the slave narrative is the background for Wright's journey to Chicago:

> I headed North, full of a hazy notion that life could be lived with dignity, that the personalities of others should not be violated, that men should be able to confront other men without fear or shame, and that if men were lucky in their living on earth they might win some redeeming meaning for their having struggled and suffered here beneath the stars. (2005: 415)

Wright hopes to find freedom and fair living conditions in Chicago. Upon his arrival in 1927 he wonders whether his dreams will come true:

> My first glimpse of the flat black stretches of Chicago depressed and dismayed me, mocked all my fantasies. Chicago seemed an unreal city whose mythical houses were built of slabs of black coal wreathed in palls of grey smoke, houses whose foundations were sinking slowly into the dark prairie … What would happen to me here? Would I survive? (261)

The title of the second part of *Black Boy (American Hunger)* illustrates this ambivalence between initial hopes and actual experiences: 'The Horror and the Glory'.

As an African American having grown up in the South, Wright is highly influenced by the places and living conditions of this environment. The narrated spaces in the text and his figurative language reflect their influence and illustrate the nexus between space, mobility and crisis in this autobiographical text. In the South, Wright is in a constant state of liminality between different homes, schools and jobs. Until he is about 15 years old, he never remains in one school for longer than a year. Living in the house of his devout grandmother and aunt, he is even forbidden to read books and write. In his jobs as a paper boy, as a help in the house of a white family and in an optician's shop, he experiences the living conditions of an African American in early twentieth century segregated America. He can, for example, only use a library under the pretence of borrowing books for his white boss at the optician's shop. As an African American, some spaces are simply closed to him.

When he is finally able to move out of his grandmother's house and away from her influence over him, he feels free: 'No longer set apart for being sinful, I felt that I could breathe again, live again, that I had been released from a prison' (122). The text's dominant spatial metaphor, however, is the 'American Hunger' of his original title. Among many other things, through *American Hunger* Wright wishes to understand the 'meaning of [his] environment' (301). Writing his memoir and thus remembering the many places and spaces of his upbringing serve Wright as a means for achieving a sense of place and thus a sense of his identity. After having arrived in Chicago, he realises what being a 'Black Boy' means:

> A dim notion of what life meant to a Negro in America was coming to consciousness within me, not in terms of external events, lynchings, Jim Crowism, and the endless brutalities, but in terms of crossed-up feelings, of psyche pain. I sensed that Negro life was a sprawling land of unconscious suffering, and there were but few Negroes who knew the meaning of their lives, who could tell their story. (267)

Gray's notion of a sense of place as the basis for knowing oneself and having a sense of self explains the specific American hunger Wright is writing about. While Gray refers to today's culture of anonymity and uprootedness as the reason for the necessity of embeddedness, Wright searches for the place where he belongs because of his marginal position as an African American. The 'sprawling land of unconscious suffering' (Wright 2005: 267) illustrates the situation of many of his fellow African Americans: lacking a sense of place and position in society and therefore being unable to develop a sense of belonging.

Black Boy has been read as an autobiographical bildungsroman (Hodges 2003, Wagner 2014). The plot pattern of the bildungsroman suggests movement. This is a spiritual or mental movement from a state of unknowingness to being educated and knowing about the world and oneself. It also refers to an actual journey of the protagonist, who abandons the security of his home for an identity-forming journey during which he or she hopes to find his/her true self. That journey results in a particular topography inscribed into the text. Therefore, space and movement belong together in the bildungsroman and show that situating oneself in a certain place usually goes along with travelling and orienting oneself within that place, exploring and transgressing its boundaries. During the protagonist's educational journey, physical places and social spaces are explored, crossed and measured and thereby actively conquered (Hallet and Neumann 2009: 21). However, the traveller Wright is by far not as hopeful and optimistic as the traveller in the classic examples of the genre, and the journey itself is not undertaken as freely as Mangione's life journey, but rather resembles the pattern of the slave narrative. Still, Wright's journey through the South and finally to the North combines the search for a sense of self and self-knowledge with exploring and conquering spaces. *Black Boy* can therefore be read as a quintessentially African American version of the bildungsroman: In a movement from the South to the North and from passivity to activism the protagonist painfully learns to understand the power relations in various social spaces and has to come to terms with his own position within these spaces.

Wright's acute treatment of narrated spaces (Southern small town America as well as Chicago's breadlines and cultural meeting places), his vivid descriptions of his journey north, and his awareness that 'deep down, I knew that I could never really leave the South, for my feelings had already been formed by the South, for there had been slowly instilled into my personality and consciousness, black though I was, the culture of the South' (2005: 414) are aspects of what we call a critical topography.[5] An additional aspect is the actual crisis in Wright's life and the text's immanent critique of the living conditions of African Americans. Wright's moment of crisis – the turning point in his life narrative – is in a way a spatial crisis, a crisis that not only takes place in a particular socially and culturally marked space but also finally results in Wright being able to position himself, to situate himself as an African American in early twentieth- century US society.

This moment of crisis is a typical Depression Era situation: Wright is forced to go to a relief station to plead for bread. Even before this, the 'black boy' has lost his initial naivety about Chicago. Again and again he questions his possibilities as an African American in US society: 'Could a Negro ever live halfway like a human being in this goddamn country?' (349) The tone of these remarks becomes sharper as the narrative progresses and the questions begin to lack the tone of childish naivety that dominated the first part where the narrator mainly spoke with the voice of the child or young boy: 'Why could I not eat when I was hungry? Why did I always have to wait until others were through? I could not understand why some people had enough food and others did not' (19). Wright now asks rather fundamental questions that not only concern his own personal situation but also that of African Americans in general: 'What quality of will must a Negro possess to live and die with dignity in a country that denied his humanity' (341)?

One morning in 1932 Wright finally arrives at one of the city's relief stations, because he cannot provide enough food for the family and especially for his ill mother: 'As I walked toward the Cook County Bureau of Public Welfare to plead for bread, I knew I had come to the end of something' (299). Wright's

---

⁵   The importance and relevance of space and writing about these spaces for Wright become obvious when one compares the original last sentence of the book's first part ('This was the culture from which I sprang. This was the terror from which I fled' [2005: 257]) with the sentence with which Wright substituted this rather negative description for the publication of the first part in 1945: 'I headed North, full of a hazy notion that life could be lived with dignity' (2005: 415). Although Wright changed the tone of the sentence, he not only kept the references to movement and space but also marks the 'journey' north as fundamental part of his life story in both sentences.

journey of apprenticeship has come to a threshold, which would unexpectedly lead to a new, future life as a writer. Bakhtin's description of the threshold as being 'connected with the breaking point of a life, the moment of crisis, the decision that changes a life' (1981: 248) comes to mind again and seems to have found a perfect illustration in Richard Wright entering the Bureau of Public Welfare in Chicago.

At the relief station Wright is asked to give a brief account of his life: Telling his story and observing the other people telling each other about their situation not only impresses Wright but also changes his perception of his own situation. For the first time he feels a 'sense of direction': 'I began to feel something more powerful than I could express' (Wright 2005: 301). This is the turning point in Wright's life narrative: 'I had felt the possibility of creating a new understanding of life in the minds of people rejected by the society in which they lived' (301). At this moment, Wright decides to become a writer.

This moment of crisis forms the basis of the text's critical topography. The city of Chicago, the South, later on New York or this little public welfare office are more than simply the locations of Wright's experiences. Traversing these many loci have made him a writer – a critical writer who questions society and the space(s) he lives in. Wright describes fundamentally spatial experiences. Envisioning the task of the writer as an activity of re-mapping the country, he asks: 'Well, what had I got out of living in the city? What had I got out of living in the South? What had I got out of living in America' (383)? One hundred pages earlier, the autobiographer had felt overwhelmed by the situation during the Great Depression: 'The Depression deepened … I felt bleak. I had not done what I had come to the city to do' (299). After his encounter at the relief station, Wright knows more about himself and seems to have found his position in life and in society even though 'all I possessed were words and dim knowledge that my country had shown me no examples of how to live a human life' (383). Nevertheless, Wright ends his autobiographical account on a rather hopeful note describing how his future as a writer might look:

> I wanted to build a bridge of words between me and that world outside, that world which was so distant and elusive that it seemed unreal. I would hurl words into this darkness and wait for an echo, and if an echo sounded, no matter how faintly, I would send other words to tell, to march, to fight, to create a sense of the hunger for life that gnaws in us all, to keep alive in our hearts a sense of the inexpressibly human. (384)

These last lines of Wright's autobiography in particular do not only reference the crisis the autobiographer had been describing in the chapters before, but also express a certain future-oriented movement of its protagonist. It is not the autobiographer himself anymore who presents his life as a wanderer or walker, but after the epiphany at the relief station he sends out his writing 'to tell, to march, to fight' to cure the 'American Hunger'. And Wright's autobiographical act itself – *Black Boy* was written at a time in his life when his career as a writer was just beginning – appears like an act of mapping his future against the backdrop of his past.

Conclusion: Patterns of Depression Era Lives

Both Mangione and Wright employ patterns of the bildungsroman to supply their experience with a trace of retrospective teleology. The telos is the identification of their respective positions within the promise of America. This pattern includes the journey, which is imagined in a fundamentally different way by each writer. In Wright, the journey follows the map of a neo-slave narrative: from the South on to a social and spiritual journey in the North; in Mangione, the journey follows the script of the American Dream: the young man leaves home, seeks to make his own fortune, travels East, South and West and ends up at the table of Eleanor Roosevelt. Space is almost synonymous with crisis in Wright's memoir: the protagonist experiences his epiphany at the public welfare office, which, to him, suddenly epitomises or iconises the potential and the fate of African Americans. Economic and racial crises merge. His reflection on the breadline, which could also be a line of migrant workers or of waiting slaves, serves to indicate his vocation as the recorder of the 'sprawling land of unconscious suffering'. Crisis, space and genre come to an almost complete consonance. In Mangione's memoir, the historical crisis materialises in specific places: in the breadlines in New York, in the squalid houses in Sicily, on the miserable farms in the South. Economic crisis and his personal anxiety as a second generation Sicilian immigrant merge at times, propelling him to leave the past behind and enter white America. For both, Wright and Mangione, America as an idea and promise, both positive and negative, a place to belong and to criticise, is always a powerful presence, a sprawl of obstacles and gateways. For both, the idea of place and mobility in America becomes an increasing concern in the process of what narrative psychologists call 'selfing' and 'futuring' (see for example Kraus 2013). Like Rockwell Gray, albeit for quite different reasons (the racial and social crisis of Wright, the ethnic and economic crisis for Mangione), they have to build a composite sense of place in order to counter disconnection and uprootedness.

References

Andrews, W.L. and Taylor, D.E. 2003. Introduction, in *Richard Wright's Black Boy (American Hunger): A Casebook*, edited by W.L. Andrews and D.E. Taylor. Oxford: Oxford University Press, 3–22.

Bakhtin, M.M. 1981. *The Dialogic Imagination: Four Essays* [1975], translated by C. Emerson and M. Holquist. Austin: University of Texas Press.

Chatman, S.B. 1978. *Story and Discourse: Narrative Structure in Fiction and Film*. Ithaca: Cornell University Press.

Cuddon, J.A. 1999. *Dictionary of Literary Terms & Literary Theory*. London: Penguin.

Dickstein, M. 2010. *Dancing in the Dark: A Cultural History of the Great Depression*. New York: Norton.

Egan, S. 1984. *Patterns of Experience in Autobiography*. Chapel Hill: The University of North Carolina Press.

Elder, G. 1999. *Children of the Great Depression: Social Change in Life Experience*. Boulder: Westview Press.

Friedman, S.S. 1998. *Mappings: Feminism and the Cultural Geographies of Encounter*. Princeton: Princeton University Press.

Frow, J. 2006. *Genre*. London: Routledge.

Gray, R. 1989. Autobiographical memory and sense of place, in *Essays on the Essay: Redefining the Genre,* edited by A.J. Butrym. Athens: The University of Georgia Press, 53–70.

Hallet, W. and Neumann, B. 2009. Raum und Bewegung in der Literatur: Zur Einführung, in *Raum und Bewegung in der Literatur: Die Literaturwissenschaften und der Spatial Turn*, edited by W. Hallet and B. Neumann. Bielefeld: transcript, 11–32.

Hodges, J.O. 2013. An apprenticeship to life and art: Narrative design in Wright's *Black Boy*, in *Richard Wright's Black Boy (American Hunger): A Casebook*, edited by W.L. Andrews and D.E. Taylor. Oxford: Oxford University Press, 113–30.

Kraus, W. 2013. The quest for a third space: Heterotopic self-positioning and narrative identity, in *Rethinking Narrative Identity: Persona and Perspective,* edited by C. Holler and M. Klepper. Amsterdam: Benjamins, 69–83.

Mangione, J. 2001. *An Ethnic At Large* [1978]. Syracuse: Syracuse University Press.

Rowly, H. 2001. *Richard Wright: The Life and Times*. Chicago: University of Chicago Press.

Smith, S. and Watson, J. 2010. *Reading Autobiography: A Guide for Interpreting Life Narratives*. Minneapolis: University of Minnesota Press.

Weisberger, B. 2001. Introduction, in *An Ethnic at Large*, by J. Mangione. Syracuse: Syracuse University Press.

Wagner, A. 2014. *Wissen in der Autobiographie: Zur narrativen Konstruktion von Wissensordnungen in nordamerikanischen autobiographischen Texten*. Trier: Wissenschaftlicher Verlag Trier.

Wright, R. 2005. *Black Boy (American Hunger): A Record of Childhood and Youth (The Restored Text Established by the Library of America)* [1945]. New York: HarperCollins.

Young, W.H. 2002. *The 1930s*. Westport: Greenwood Press.

III
CONTESTED SPACES,
PRECARIOUS LIVES

Chapter 7

Postcolonial Literary Cartography: Writing the Self in Contemporary Algeria

Elizabeth H. Jones

In his 1984 essay, 'Postmodernism, or The Cultural Logic of Late Capitalism', later developed into a monograph of the same name, Fredric Jameson argues that the contemporary world is undergoing a 'mutation in the lived experience of built space' (1984: 58). Grounding his analysis primarily in the architecture and spaces of the Western world, he contends that space is increasingly characterised by a new 'depthlessness' that is not merely metaphorical, but which 'can be experienced physically and literally' (1984: 62). The profound and bewildering effect of this change is clear: Jameson tells us that 'we ourselves, the human subjects who happen into this new space, have not kept pace with that evolution; there has been a mutation in the object, unaccompanied as yet by any equivalent mutation in the subject; we do not yet possess the perceptual equipment to match this new hyperspace' (1984: 80). Unable to locate ourselves in space, according to Jameson we are similarly unable to organise the past and future into coherent experiences and there is 'an imperative to grow new organs, to expand our sensorium and our body to some new, as yet unimaginable, perhaps ultimately impossible, dimensions' (1984: 82). Jameson ends his discussion by calling for 'an aesthetic of cognitive mapping' which will 'endow the individual subject with some new heightened sense of its place in the global system' (1984: 92).

If Jameson himself does not elaborate in detail upon what 'cognitive mapping' might entail, it is clear that its primary function is to allow subjects to reorientate themselves and resist the alienation experienced in the contemporary world. Brian Jarvis picks up Jameson's argument and proposes that

> [t]he dilemma facing the critic of late capitalism may not be an absence of maps [as Jameson argues], so much as an inadequacy in our own cartographic skills. I would suggest that the maps are already there, if we are prepared to look for them. In fact,

they can be uncovered in precisely those postmodern art works Jameson spends much
of his essay denouncing. (1998: 51)

Jarvis suggests, then, that art may provide a privileged way in which to portray and
understand space, that art could represent a form of postmodern cartography.
His discussion proceeds to examine the spaces depicted in a range of recent
literary and cinematic texts. While Jameson and Jarvis's focus on postmodernism
prioritises the study of North America, its spaces and its cultural products,
other theorists' discussions of postmodern space address a wider geographical
area. James Clifford, for instance, argues that postmodernity represents 'the
new *world order* of mobility, of rootless histories' (1997: 1). Caren Kaplan
similarly stresses the world-wide disorientation prevalent in the current age and
warns against an excessive focus on the West. Emphasising the upheavals in the
contemporary experience of space, for instance, she argues that the twentieth
century saw 'unprecedented numbers of refugees as people ... fled their homes to
avoid famine, genocide, or incarceration' (1996: 5). Citizens of the margins are
clearly also prone to experiencing disorientation and alienation in contemporary
space, even if the cause and character of such feelings may be different to those
in the ultra-capitalist spaces of North America. Perhaps Jameson's call for
'cognitive mapping', and indeed Jarvis's notion of literary cartography, can be
extended to recognise the quest for sites of belonging experienced by those in
the global peripheries? Debates about postmodernism, postcolonialism and
neo-colonialism, and the relationship and rivalries between them are certainly
well-worn, and it is not the intention here to replay them. The priority is, rather,
to recognise the fundamentally spatial nature of postcolonialism and the crucial
importance that literary self-orientation may play in the lives of postcolonial
peoples. If colonialism involved the physical domination of many of the world's
spaces, postcolonialism involves 'an imaginative recovery of a "local place"'
(Karancheti 1994: 125) and, we may add, a sense of self.

Turning to consider the specific nature of life writing, as opposed to other forms
of literature, in relation to the notion of literary cartography, the work of Kaplan
is again helpful. She argues that 'traditionally, Western autobiographical writing
has participated in the literary construction of "home"; a process of generalizing
the particular, fabricating a narrative space of familiarity, and crafting a narrative
that links the individual to the universal' (1992: 130). Writing autobiography,
then, according to Kaplan, is often a practice in which the individual establishes
a sense of identity, a textual space of self-knowledge, which brings together
mental and physical senses of belonging. Kaplan's discussion moves beyond
a consideration of classic, Western autobiography, with its stringent generic

taxonomies and normative white, male, middle-class authorship.[1] Describing this as 'itself a form of colonial discourse', Kaplan instead seeks to juxtapose 'postcolonial writing and reading strategies' and 'feminist concerns' in order to question 'whether or not autobiography is recoverable as a feminist writing strategy in the context of transnational affiliations among women' (1992: 116). In other words, Kaplan aims to establish whether innovation in form and a greater diversity of authors can counter the somewhat conservative traditions of autobiography as a genre. Coining the term 'out-law genres', Kaplan refers to life-writing works that may challenge expectations in terms of form and authorship. She tells us: 'out-law genres renegotiate the relationship between personal identity and the world, between personal and social history. Here, narrative inventions are tied to a struggle for cultural survival rather than purely aesthetic experimentation or individual experience' (1992: 130). If Western subjects' autobiographical writings play a role in establishing a sense of individual belonging, then the stakes are higher yet for 'out-law subjects', whose location at the margin inherently threatens any possible sense of spatial belonging, either personal or collective.

Bringing together Kaplan's notion of out-law life writing and Jarvis's call for literary cartography, this chapter will examine two postcolonial life-writing texts in order to explore the ways in which space is articulated in the autobiographical production of some particularly disenfranchised people in an embattled cultural terrain. It will look specifically at the autobiographical writings of two Algerian women writing in French in the post-Independence period to examine the ways in which these literary texts map their relationships with space.

Algerian Women's Out-Law Life Writing

Algeria, the former jewel in the crown of the French Empire, has endured over the course of five decades not only the turmoil of transition from colonial rule to independence, but has done so via a bloody war of independence, a civil war, and a period of terrorist activism. In fact, following 130 years of French colonial rule, which entailed the enforcement of a clear ideological doctrine as part of

---

[1]   Serge Doubrovsky, a noteworthy writer of innovative life writing, refers directly to the strict traditions of Western autobiography, arguing, for example, that the expectation is that it should be written by '[a]-great-man-in-the-twilight-of-his-life-and-in-an-elegant-style'. Professing his own sense of inadequacy in relation to this he goes on to say: 'can't fill those shoes. ... I DON'T HAVE THE RIGHT TO. Not a member of the club, I'm not allowed in. MY LIFE DOESN'T INTEREST ANYONE' (1989: 256; my translation).

a 'civilising mission' (Harrison 1983: 75), as well as occupation by a million settlers of European origin, it is hardly surprising that Algeria has in recent times been the stage upon which a number of heavily weighted and conflicting ideological, cultural and political struggles have been competing for dominance. In *Maghrebian Mosaics,* Mildred Mortimer contends that

> [t]hroughout the colonial era, Algeria's contact with the French colonizer was longer, more complex, and more violent [than that of Morocco or Tunisia]. If we view the process of colonization as a wound – which many Maghrebian writers do – we must conclude that Algeria's wound was deeper and more painful than that of its North African neighbors, Morocco to the west and Tunisia to the east. (2001: 1)

Far from resulting in an untroubled state of freedom and self-determination, the attainment of independence in 1962 has been characterised by a range of cultural and political battles. From French Republican secularism to a spectrum of Islamic beliefs, from Modernity to Tradition, recent Algerian history can be characterised by renegotiation of central aspects of Algerian identity.[2] If the actual war of independence evoked such obviously spatial matters as questions of territory and sovereignty, of national and cultural affiliations, the post-Independence period has given rise to fundamental questions about who belongs in Algeria, who is involved in rule making and what behaviours can be considered acceptable across the full range of spaces from the most private to the most public. Unsurprisingly, gender and family relations have been a key battleground for those seeking to construct an Algerian identity in the wake of colonial domination.[3] This is a cultural terrain that has witnessed a radical struggle in relation to many of the most fundamental aspects of identity and community, and as such provides a challenging testing ground through which to explore the notion of literary cartography and the ways in which subjects may seek to locate themselves through literature.

The field of Algerian women's literature written in French is a very new one. The first critical study to be dedicated to it was published just 15 years ago, in 1997 (see Segarra 2010: 6). Since this time, and despite doom-laden predictions by those such as Albert Memmi of the inevitable demise of Algerian writing in the

[2]   As Maïssa Bey stated in an interview in 2011, there has been a regression in the rights of Algerian women which is frequently blamed on religion but is really due to a complex interaction of political and ideological struggles, including a backlash against French cultural values.

[3]   The *code de la famille,* for example, has been the site of numerous revisions and renegotiations since independence. Initially rejected, then passed in 1984, this law legalised polygamy and returned women to the status of minors.

former colonial language of French (Mortimer 2001: 4), this emerging literary space has flourished. As Segarra notes, in less than two decades the field has been transformed, witnessing 'a quantitative and qualitative enrichment' 2010: 7; my translation). Pertinently, within this field, life writing dominates literary production. This fact, however, has both positive and negative repercussions: Like many postcolonial subjects, Algerian women writers are frequently reduced to their biographies. In other words, whilst their work may frequently be considered to be of anthropological interest as a source of information, its literary value is underestimated. As Belinda Jack argues, it is necessary to look beyond the sociological interest of Francophone texts to see their literary, linguistic and formal merits (1996: 22). And while most Algerian women writers tend to produce one book which contains a single, clear, autobiographical message (Bey 2011), there are notable exceptions to this pattern. The two writers whose works will be addressed here have both written more than ten books, and combine both literary quality and innovation with political engagement. Further similarities include their date of birth and timeframe of writing: Maïssa Bey was born in Algeria in 1950, Malika Mokeddem in 1949. Both began publishing in the 1990s after first establishing themselves in professional careers, Bey as a teacher and Mokeddem as a doctor. Both have won literary prizes and have been translated into other languages. The writing of both can be said to be politically driven, a refusal to be silenced by the bloody events of the Algerian civil war and the 'intellocide' (Hamil 2004: 53) of the 1990s in which numerous writers and intellectuals were assassinated.

Each of these authors has written a range of texts, some of which are obviously spatial in theme: Mokeddem, for instance, has written extensively about nomadism and deserts, about sailing boats around the Mediterranean. Bey's *Bleu, Blanc, Vert* (2007) is structured around the space of the city of Algiers. Here, however, recognising that all life – and therefore all literature – is inherently spatial, this analysis will focus on two texts, *Mes Hommes* (2005), by Mokeddem, and *Entendez-vous dans les montagnes* (2002), by Bey, that are united by their status as forms of life writing. Mokeddem's text displays many of the features identified by Lejeune as characteristic of autobiography: the first person narrative establishes nominal identity between author, narrator and protagonist (2005: 33), and thereby an autobiographical pact. Whilst the narrative does not follow the typical pattern of beginning at birth and following each stage of the protagonist's life, there is at least a chronological progression motivated largely by the development of the main character. Bey's text is generically more ambiguous. No simple nominal relationship between protagonist and author is established within the main body of the text, and the story at times bears hallmarks of fictional improbability. However, as we shall see, the text is prefaced by a family photo, the title of which points unequivocally to the author herself and suggests that readers should not be deterred from receiving this as a piece of autobiographical writing. As the coming discussion will demonstrate, despite their differing textual properties, both of these texts contain significant representations of space and both comply, in different ways, with Kaplan's notion of 'out-law' autobiographies.

Maïssa Bey, *Entendez-vous dans les montagnes* (2002)

Maïssa Bey's *Entendez-vous dans les montagnes* is a short text, prefaced by a photo of an apparently happy family scene: a bespectacled, round-faced man has his arms around two similarly-dressed, smiling children. They are perched on a wall, the backdrop made up of spectacular mountain scenery. The happy family snapshot, which seems to recall idyllic early family holidays, is entitled 'the only photo of Maïssa's father, summer 1955' (2002: 10).[4] This preface at once invokes the claims to uniqueness on which autobiography has traditionally thrived whilst also pointing clearly towards the referential elements of the text. Incongruously, despite this intimate, happy family scene, however, this work constitutes no simple, autobiographical account of childhood and early family relations. On the contrary, the text addresses an anonymous encounter with an unknown man in France. As will be seen later on in the discussion, the text's complex relationship with self-referentiality is inextricably interlinked with the troubled sense of spatial belonging that it depicts.

The protagonist, named only as 'elle' (she), is presented to the reader as travelling across France, from North to South, within the nondescript space of an ordinary train. The anonymity of the location is foregrounded: on the back cover we are told that the train is travelling 'somewhere in France'. We read early on that the main character is hoping to have the train compartment to herself so she can read her book in peace, and the implication is that she is happy in the impersonal, non-engaging blandness of this functional space, perhaps a 'non-place'.[5] The protagonist's serenity is punctured, though, by the entry of a man in his sixties, shortly followed by a young woman. Upon this, we become party to the protagonist's immediate imaginative association between him and her

---

4   The translations of all quotations from this text are my own.

5   The notion of non-places was coined by Marc Augé in *Non-lieux: Introduction à une anthropologie de la surmodernité* (1992) and refers to anonymous spaces that are severed from history and community, for example chain hotels, airports or shopping malls.

father: 'my father would have been about the same age' (20). We are also made aware that the void within her memory is so profound that she has no sense of her father's smell, voice or walk and has had to content herself with trying to piece together his face from photos. The man on the train's lack of eye contact and apparent unawareness of her reinforces the sense of anonymity, however, and in this country, away from her native Algeria, she is surprised by the ability of people not to notice each other, to become 'invisible' (12). A clear parallel is established between the nature of social relationships and the space that they take place in. The flatness and lack of interaction of the French travellers is mirrored by the bleakness and uniformity of the 'warehouses' and 'houses that are almost all the same' (14) that can be seen out of the window. The environment is ordered and geometrical, and, adhering to the French train timetable, whose punctuality is alien to the protagonist, the train cuts through it with clinical, impersonal efficiency. In fact, the anonymity of this space is nothing but a façade, and it quickly crumbles to reveal the complex, sometimes painful and deeply rooted relationships between French and Algerian people. The protagonist's peace is disturbed first by a dream of her homeland, of a rocky, dusty terrain covered in forests and geraniums (15). A shift of narrative perspective reveals to us that simultaneously, prompted by the sight of her, the man in his sixties also begins to think of sunshine, of men's voices, of the army, of war and death (16). For him, this anonymous vehicle, this train 'somewhere in France', becomes the scene for an encounter with Algeria, the colonial memory that refuses to go peacefully away, and which continues to trouble and unsettle many sectors of both societies. The narrative slowly skirts around the revelation that the protagonist's father, an Algerian school teacher, was tortured and killed by French soldiers during the Algerian war. In a bizarre, perhaps fantastic, coincidence of spaces, the conversation reveals that the Frenchman in this carriage was a soldier stationed at the very barracks where these French soldiers were posted at the exact time when this happened. The unlikely denouement confirms that this Frenchman did in fact carry out the order to shoot the father – illegally – under the pretence that he was trying to escape (72).

Locating the encounter between these two characters in a train compartment highlights the importance of space for the narrative. It is neither an open public nor a private space, but it is a space of confinement, where, over the course of a long journey, the intersection of individual and wider cultural preoccupations become concentrated and are revealed. It could perhaps be called a semi-closed cell, with a vantage point on the outside world, but no possibility of reaching it. The semi-permeable membranes of the windows act not to diffuse the tensions within the compartment, but rather to seal them in and exacerbate them. When the train is attacked by thieves, the cell feels vulnerable; outside, somewhere, is an unknown threat. The movement of the train breaks down, and instead of a space of movement and observation, it becomes one of stasis and entrapment. As the status of the space changes, this impacts upon the passengers' behaviour as their anxiety pushes them into interacting, destroying the initially comfortable, anonymous coexistence between them. Rather than any train journey, anywhere in France, this compartment becomes emblematic of the superficial normality of contemporary France: apparently functional, efficient, unremarkable, but ultimately vulnerable to haunting by the unhealed trauma of the Franco-Algerian conflict. In this narrative we learn that colonial power relations live on: whereas the protagonist, a woman narratively constructed to have committed no atrocities in the war, professes no sense of belonging in either Algeria or France (28, 30–31, 33), the man, who committed atrocities during the war, is portrayed as commanding an easy sense of belonging and familiarity with both countries (36–7, 45). Space in this text, then, is highly functional in that it provides privileged insight into the political and ideological threads that structure the lives of those who move in it.

Malika Mokeddem, *Mes Hommes* (2005)

For Malika Mokeddem, in *Mes Hommes*, the primary subject matter is that of gender relations in the aftermath of Algerian independence. In this very different life writing narrative, rather than a father who was tragically lost in the anti-colonial struggle, the paternal figure is over-present and over-bearing, a willing proponent of a kind of neo-colonial gender conservatism. Perhaps in an act of filial revenge and as the ultimate gesture of resistance to the paternal authority that he has repeatedly tried to assert, the father is deliberately relegated to just one of the numerous men who have played an important role in the narrator-protagonist's life. Each chapter of this text deals with a different male figure, from the real father to substitute father figures, to romantic relationships in adulthood. If the coincidence of imagined textual and physical spaces encapsulated in an encounter in a train was revealing for Bey's protagonist, it is a rather more gritty, material, corporeal view of space and identity that sheds light on Mokeddem's intratextual avatar. Drawing upon the work of Judith Butler, Heidi J. Nast argues that gender is fundamentally a cultural performance, and 'such performances and contests around power relations take place in lived space. Spatiality constrains, enables and is constituted by forces that both stabilize dominant relations of gender and sexuality and that unsettle the relations between them' (1998: 5).

In *Mes Hommes,* an interdependent triad of body-space-identity gives us a prime example of the ways in which body and space come together in particular contexts to enact, reinforce and sometimes challenge gender relations.

Early in Mokeddem's text, it becomes clear that the domestic space of the protagonist's formative years will be depicted as neither a refuge nor an asylum, but rather as poisoned by the increasingly harsh gender conflicts that have characterised post-Independence Algeria. Any sense of clear separation between public and private spaces is shown to be illusory as public and political ideologies impact upon the protagonist's home life. The gender hierarchy that is being renegotiated and reinforced in the aftermath of French colonial rule is, in the protagonist's case, first experienced at home, then carried on in the external world, and in many instances takes on a corporeal significance. Within the home, women are of lesser importance than men: the father refers to his daughters dismissively as belonging to their mother ('your daughters'), whereas the boys of the household are 'my sons' (2005: 11).[6] And the subjugated position of women is quickly internalised by the infant protagonist and responded to in the way she moves her body in space. Yearning for a relationship with her uninterested father, she becomes a passive observer, and spends her days finding hiding places from which she can watch him come and go. Addressing him directly, the adult narrator reflects: 'I wouldn't have missed your comings and goings for anything in the world' (13). The physical restraint that is already evident at this preschool age seems to directly mirror the social, political and personal constraints in this male-female relationship, and the protagonist's corporeal self-policing steadily grows with age. As a teenager she is ever more overwhelmed and undermined by the close proximity of so many bodies in her home space: the family eat together out of the same pot and all sleep together not only in one room but on conjoined mats. We are told that 'insomnia is a way of separating myself from the family group [le corps familial] sleeping on the floor. All together. To flee this suffocation' (40). The many younger siblings are presented as noisy and unruly, and entirely at odds with the protagonist's desire to spend her time reading and studying quietly (40, 124). Over the course of time, the protagonist develops various strategies to find a space for herself. In withdrawing more and more to the off-limits 'guest room', she finds herself, quite literally, a room of her own in which to indulge her thirst for reading, a source of 'freedom' and deliverance from family life (15). However, in withdrawing her body from family space like this, she symbolically withdraws from cultural acceptance. Perhaps most damagingly, the protagonist develops anorexia (38–9), a decisive

---

6   The translations of all quotations from this text are my own.

way of suppressing her body in order to avoid participating in the shared space of mealtimes and communal life. Not eating is quite evidently about rejecting the female body, about reinforcing the corporeal invisibility previously achieved by hiding as a preschool child, about refusing her place at both the family meal table and in the wider symbolic order (42). We are told that 'this anorexia, a backup to my insomnia, was already a form of absence. It was about dicing with disaster and escaping via the alternative world [l'ailleurs] of books' (41).

The protagonist's primary justification for leaving the domestic sphere and the specific corporeal regime that it entails is provided by going to school. These daily escapes from the over-crowded family home are presented as a relief and an escape, despite involving a long walk through the desert heat. Perhaps more menacingly, however, just as in the private sphere she has learnt to conceal herself so as not to trouble her father, in public space she is pressured to do the same because her presence is unwanted and unacceptable. Boys shout at her, throw stones at her (104), even flash their bodies at her (22). Her body, moving purposefully through the town, defies the cultural message that girls must be modest, that they must make themselves invisible, in sum that in public space they should aim for 'the erasure, the abdication of the body, of the unwanted' (24). If the female body moving through public space is a target for aggressive behaviours, the protagonist also learns that 'out of place' bodily performances can be tools for resistance (see Cresswell 1996). Some years later, she delights in eating ostentatiously on her student balcony during Ramadan, and smokes in lecture theatres and at the hospital (56). She is happy to lose her virginity in private so she can never be subjected to the humiliating ritual of her sheets being publically inspected for blood on her wedding night (57). In these corporeal performances, the protagonist is presented as using her body in specific spatial contexts in order to produce transgressive behaviours and resistant cultural meanings.

In the end, it is also the body-space-identity triad that allows the protagonist to form a sense of belonging in space. It is a relationship with a French man, sharing a bed with him and eating the food he cooks for her that allows her to establish a more healthy relationship with her own body, overcoming her anorexia. When he cooks for her 'it is exotic and erotic ... We make love standing up in the aromas' (73). That the man she chooses loves sailing is clearly of importance, and the couple embark upon a long trip becoming 'travelling people' (122). For a time, the wide open spaces of the ocean contrast starkly and positively with the stifling claustrophobia of her former life in the desert, directly mirroring the welcome shift in gender relations that changing space represents. Ultimately, however, it is in reclaiming a domestic space for herself alone, specifically the space of her own bed, that symbolises her reclaiming of selfhood. Following the breakdown of her marriage she takes an axe to the marital bed, an act of physical violence in which she symbolically destroys this privileged site of corporeality and coupledom. Replacing the bed with a new one, she tells us she needed 'a nest that was free of memories' (170). The bed becomes a site of self-assertion and self-identification as she flouts the mores of both her own culture and to some extent those of French culture, in which taking pleasure in sleeping alone is rarely the norm. The rejection of her French partner and the regularisation of her legal status that marriage to him has entailed seems to make a statement about the protagonist's search for belonging: France may not be rejected entirely, remaining her country of residence, but neither does the protagonist fully settle there. Instead, it is in a provisional state of foreignness, to some extent outside of both French and Algerian societies, that the protagonist finds a space of selfhood.

Life Writing and the Search for a Place of Belonging

The life-writing texts examined here clearly differ substantially in terms of both form and content. Yet, drawing again on Kaplan's notion of the potential of 'out-law' life-writing texts, both can be said to represent forms of literary cartography. For Mokeddem the case is most straightforward. In *Mes Hommes* there is overt reference to the importance of the literary endeavour, the intratextual voice telling us that writing is 'how I built myself up. Resisted being dissolved into the tribe or washed away by the perversions of nationalism' (2005: 213). In other words, just as withdrawing into the guest room is a way in which the protagonist is able to find peace for her reading and a site in which to establish her identity, so the authorial voice designates writing books as a way in which to assert her individuality and locate her subjectivity. The potency of this contribution to the world outside her work is evident from the death threats that Mokeddem has received as a result of her writing.[7] Moreover, she asserts clearly that to continue writing is a deliberate strategy to fight against fundamentalist oppression: 'what better way to mock them [the fundamentalists] than to continue writing about men loved freely, in spite of everything' (2005: 19–20)?

In the case of Bey, the link with a notion of postcolonial cartography may at first seem more elusive. Quite clearly this text does not consist of a simple autobiographical depiction of spaces that have been experienced by the author.

---

7   In one of a number of comments upon this, Mokeddem indicates that 'the forces of darkness have caught up with me here in France' (2005: 19).

However, a return to the author's own comments in an interview reveals that the presumably fictional encounter on the train is far from divorced from her own personal identity and sense of cultural belonging. She states that 'there was the desire to take a stand against silence and amnesia and denial, to recreate moments one hasn't lived but that have forged one's awareness of the world. To achieve a sort of re-enactment – as in police work' (2006: 16). In this text, Bey does not describe the spaces of her childhood and growing up, but uses an imaginary space, both physical and textual, to project an absolutely fundamental aspect of her identity. The void left by the shooting of her father can only be narrated in a fictional text, but this does not make the work any less autobiographical. Molly Hike's reminder that writing does not merely involve transcribing onto paper a pre-existing self, but rather entails participation in the multiple discourses that establish and re-establish this self, is pertinent: 'it is by definition a revisionary activity in as much as it reinscribes a prescribed subjectivity in another register, intervening in the social construction of identity to bring a somewhat different self into being' (1991: xv).

Grounding this work in the space of a train in France is deeply symbolic: a reminder to the French that the atrocities committed on Algerian soil will continue to haunt them. Just as the protagonist's presence in France forces her fellow traveller to relive memories of his time in Algeria which are sometimes painful, so Maïssa Bey's book could be said to be remapping postcolonial Franco-Algerian relations, seeking to reinscribe the trauma of the Algerian conflict into mainland France in a way that is of immense personal and collective significance. The memory of atrocities committed in Algerian space, the text seems to warn, will not necessarily stay within these cultural boundaries, but is a constant undercurrent in French space too, becoming visible at unforeseen moments. It is in these unexpected eruptions that those damaged can begin to find acknowledgement of their own broken senses of belonging in space. If postcolonial literary cartography can be defined as a textual inscription of cultural space that seeks to renegotiate the individual's place in the world, then Bey's *Entendez-vous* certainly complies with this model.

In sum, this brief analysis of two contemporary Algerian women's autobiographical texts has argued that the links between space and identity as well as literary production are fundamental. The power struggles and the conflicting ideologies battling for dominance in contemporary Algeria play out in a spatial manner, with concrete geographical consequences for the ways in which certain individuals are able to move in space, and the ways in which their 'out of place' behaviours can be resistant. This chapter has sought to highlight the manner in which for these two authors life writing forms a bridge between physical and mental space, between self and others, in a way that can not only help the individual to better understand the world around them, but also to re-map and renegotiate the very meaning of the spaces they move through.

References

Augé, M. 1992. *Non-lieux: Introduction à une anthropologie de la surmodernité.* Paris: Editions du Seuil.

Bey, M. 2002. *Entendez-vous dans les montagnes.* Paris: Poche.

Bey, M. 2006. The rebel's daughter: Algerian novelist Maïssa Bey, in *Women's Review of Books,* 23(4), 16–17.

Bey, M. 2007. *Bleu, Blanc, Vert.* Paris: Poche.

Bey, M. 2011. On peut librement s'exprimer en Algérie, mais le pouvoir y est indifférent. [Online]. Available at: http://fatea.blog.lemonde.fr/2011/01/31/on-peut-librement-sexprimer-en-algerie-mais-le-pouvoir-y-est-indifferent-maissa-bey-ecrivain/ [accessed: 30 October 2013]

Clifford, J. 1997. *Routes: Travel and Translation in the Late Twentieth Century.* London: Harvard University Press.

Creswell, T. 1996. *In Place/Out of Place: Geography, Ideology and Transgression.* Minneapolis: University of Minnesota Press.

Doubrovsky, S. 1989. *Le livre brisé.* Paris: Grasset.

Hamil, M. 2004. Exile and its discontents: Malika Mokeddem's forbidden woman. *Research in African Literatures,* 35(1), 52–66.

Harrison, C. 1983. French attitudes to Empire and the Algerian War. *African Affairs,* 82(326), 75–95.

Hike, M. 1991. Foreword, in *Gender and Genre in Literature: Redefining Autobiography in Twentieth-Century Women's Fiction,* edited by J. Morgan and C.T. Hall. New York and London: Garland, xii–xvi.

Jack, B. 1996. *Francophone Literatures: An Introductory Survey.* Oxford and New York: Oxford University Press.

Jameson, F. 1984. Postmodernism, or the cultural logic of late Capitalism. *New Left Review,* 146(1), 53–92.

Jameson, F. 1991. *Postmodernism, or, The Cultural Logic of Late Capitalism.* London: Verso.

Jarvis, B. 1998. *Postmodern Cartographies: The Geographical Imagination in Contemporary American Culture.* London: Pluto.

Kaplan, C. 1992. Resisting autobiography: Out-law genres and transnational feminist subjects, in *De/Colonizing the Subject: The Politics of Gender in*

Women's Autobiography, edited by S. Smith and J. Watson. Minneapolis: Minnesota University, 115–38.

Kaplan, C. 1996. *Questions of Travel: Postmodern Discourses of Displacement*. Durham and London: Duke University Press.

Karancheti, I. 1994. The geographics of marginality: Place and textuality in Simone Schwarz-Bart and Anita Desai, in *Reconfigured Spheres: Feminist Explorations of Literary Space*, edited by M.R. Higonnet and J. Templeton. Amherst: University of Massachusetts Press, 125–44.

Lejeune, P. 1975. *Le Pacte autobiographique*. Paris: Seuil.

Mokeddem, M. 2005. *Mes Hommes.* Paris: Grasset.

Mortimer, M. 2001. *Maghrebian Mosaic: A Literature in Transition.* Colorado and London: Lynne Rienner.

Nast, H.J. and Pile, S. 1998. Introduction: Making places bodies, in *Places Through the Body*, edited by H. J. Nast and S. Pile. London: Routledge, 1–22.

Segarra, M. 2010. *Nouvelles romancières francophones du Maghreb*. Paris: Karthala.

Chapter 8

Inhabiting the In-Between: (Mis)placing Identity in Katherine Mansfield's Notebooks

Kathrin Tordasi

In the last years of her life, Katherine Mansfield found her thoughts going back to New Zealand, the country of her birth. The diaries she kept during that time resonate not only with her longing to return but with her determination to recreate the place she remembered. Dividing her time between France and London, Mansfield proclaims in 1916: 'Now I want to write recollections of my own country. Yes I want to write about my own country until I simply exhaust my store' (1997: 45).

The identification of New Zealand as home comes late. Like fellow expatriate Janet Frame, Mansfield needed to look at the places of her childhood from a spatial and temporal distance before she could embrace them. Since sickness prevented her from going back in person, however, that embrace remained tainted with a sense of separation and restlessness. Exiled in Europe, Mansfield revisited New Zealand only in her writing – a method she had already practiced as a teenager when she pulled London into her Wellington diaries. It is indeed striking that Mansfield often split her attention between two places: the one she was inhabiting and the one she wished to move to. As a result her stories, and especially her notebooks, capture a double sense of being cut off from and cast back to the places that shaped her. Interestingly enough, though, Mansfield uses her notebooks not just to record her personal experience but also to develop a way of writing about a particular type of identity, a sense of self that crystallises in the memory and the intersection of places. What we can read in her diary entries, her drafts and correspondence is a meticulous engagement with the interdependencies of self and space, or more precisely, liminal space, that area which combines and confuses the territories that are usually separate. What happens to the subject that is caught on the threshold, though? Reading Mansfield's diaries, Vincent O'Sullivan detects a 'sense of discompature *everywhere*' (1994: 13). Sure enough, Mansfield's notes establish her as 'a divided being' (2008: 304) and yet there is a 'being', a subject which emerges not only from the rift between spaces but from their combination.

In this chapter, I want to show how Mansfield's notebooks oscillate between placing and misplacing their writer's identity. To this end, the following analysis will illuminate both Mansfield's effort to deal with her British heritage as well as her connection with the shifting, complex New Zealand of her youth. Using examples from Mansfield's letters and notebooks, the chapter will explore a New Zealand landscape that emerges through the lens of both the coloniser and the colonial, with Mansfield as an author who has been positioned on the margin by her contemporaries and her own estimate. The aim will be to examine the connection between the representation of landscape and the narration of self, giving an idea of how a blurring of spatial transitions might influence the formation of a person's identity.

The Notebooks

During the thirty-four years of her life Mansfield produced a vast collection of notebooks, letters and other unbound pages. Containing a sometimes seamless blend of diary entries, grocery lists and story fragments, Mansfield's notes make it near impossible to decide which real-life accounts are fictionalised and which story drafts are autobiographical. These transitions complicate the categorisation of Mansfield's notebooks in terms of genre, but at the same time the blurring of distinctions can be seen as an idiosyncrasy that permeates not only Mansfield's short stories but also the manner in which her notebooks engage with questions of identity and the search for self-knowledge. Of course, Mansfield's tendency to switch between forms of expression, the gaps in her records, their non-chronological order and the possibility that there are still pieces missing from the oeuvre we have available today complicate any overview of her life writing.[1] More often than not, the histories of the self which emerge from Mansfield's notes draw from a multitude of impressions, shifting points of view, contradictions and inconsistent memories. Consequently the task of determining Mansfield's relationship with her home country and other places poses a challenge to biographers that is sometimes further complicated by the lack of first-hand knowledge of the geographies in question. The difficulties involved are illustrated, for example by the publication history of Mansfield's Urewera diary.

---

[1]   Very recently, a group of unpublished and forgotten stories were discovered in the King's College London Archives, for example (see Mansfield 2013).

In 1907, the eighteen-year old Mansfield returned from her London College to New Zealand one more time before she left the country for good. During that time, she partook in a camping trip through the Ureweras, a sparsely populated area on the North Island. Pertaining to Mansfield's visit to the town of Rotorua, John Middleton Murry's earliest (and abridged) publication of her notebooks quotes the original text as: 'She thinks Rotarua [sic] is loathsome and ugly – that little Hell' 1927: 30). Almost fifty years later, Ian A. Gordon corrects Murry's reading in *The Urewera Notebook*, transcribing the same sentence as: 'She thinks Rotorua is loathsome and likes only that little Hill' (1974: 20). With this misreading and a number of omissions (only a small percentage of the Urewera diary appears in Murry's edition), Murry creates the image of 'an unhappy young woman on her return to New Zealand, miserably trailing her way through a "loathsome" trip' (Gordon 1974: 19). In comparison, Gordon's complete transcript of the camping journal reveals that Mansfield often felt 'blissfully happy' (1974: 19) during her time in the Ureweras. Years later still, Margaret Scott's edition *The Katherine Mansfield Notebooks* changes the transcript yet again to: 'she likes only that little Hell' (Mansfield 1997: 143), assuming that 'Hell' is an expression of Mansfield's fondness for Rotorua's 'marvellous' (1997: 142) hot mud pools.

In Murry's defence, Mansfield's handwriting is very hard to decipher. In addition, one can assume that Murry's efforts at reproducing Mansfield's descriptions of New Zealand were complicated by the fact that Murry had never been to the antipodes himself. Nevertheless the point remains that his edits create the impression that Mansfield had disliked New Zealand and preferred to live in and identify with Europe, and London in particular. As further analysis will show, this stands in contrast especially to Scott's transcripts. Her unabridged edition of the notebooks introduces a Katherine Mansfield who is torn between her desire to be a part of the bohemian environment of London and her connection with the country of her birth. The question is, if we want to make sense of Mansfield's ideas on how the self is formed and where its attachments lie, do we need to organise the notebook entries, arrange them chronologically or even try to separate them into autobiography and fiction? Or is it not rather more likely that the notebooks in their raw state offer a more authentic record of a fluctuating and open-ended experience of identity?

Considering that the concept of the fluid self gained considerable prominence during Mansfield's time, it seems very likely that she used her notebooks to explore different methods of capturing a vision of the self as it accumulates. The idea of identity not only as a mode of self-awareness flowing through various stages, but also as a compilation of personalities or voices, emerges ever more clearly as her writing progresses. Around 1920, Mansfield relates how the sea view from a horse carriage inspires her to think about the different layers of her consciousness:

> ... while I watched the spray I was conscious <u>for life</u> [sic] of the white sky with a web of torn grey over it, of the slipping, sliding, slithering of the sea, of the dark woods blotted against the cape, of the flowers on the tree I was passing – and more – of a huge cavern where my selves (who were like ancient seaweed gatherers) mumbled, indifferent and intimate ... and this other self apart in the carriage grasping the cold knob of her umbrella thinking of a ship, of ropes stiffened with white paint & the wet flapping oilskins of sailors ... (1997: 209)

With this vision of a multitude of selves simultaneously available to her, Mansfield introduces a concept of identity that is not unified but rather a gathering of past and present, lived and imagined personae. In this sense, Mansfield's notebooks can be seen as an example of experimental writing which strives to capture a complex narrative of the self, a narrative that does not only shift from one self to many, but also multiplies the number of places which touch upon a person's consciousness in a single moment. Thus the depiction of a carriage might overlap with a view of the sea and inspire images of caverns and ships. Does this mean, however, that such a spreading out of selves results in a sense of endless unrest? Directly after writing about the sea cavern, Mansfield puts the question as follows: 'Shall one ever be at peace with *one*self, ever quiet and uninterrupted' (1997: 209; emphasis added)? In response to this question, Mansfield uses her notebooks to seek out fixed points. More often than not, these fixed points manifest as places: The descriptions of London, Wellington, Rotorua and others serve as touchstones for the self-reflecting I. Far from concretising her position, however, Mansfield's associations with cities, forests, lakes and so forth turn out to be rather indeterminate. This brings us back to the ambivalence that Gordon and Scott acknowledge in Mansfield's notes and raises, once again, the question of belonging.

In a letter to South African writer Sarah Gertrude Millin, Mansfield writes that in her youth New Zealand 'seemed to me a small petty world' (2008: 80). She remembers her sense of relief when she finally 'came to London' before she remarks that only at this later stage in her life, her 'thoughts go back to New Zealand – rediscovering it, finding beauty in it, re-living it' (2008: 80). Yet despite her claim that she felt estranged from the New Zealand of her teenage years, even Mansfield's early notes convey a sense of ambivalence. In 1906 she expresses her unhappiness over her return to Wellington (1997: 108) only to note a few days later that she 'feel[s] quite at home again' (149). Throughout her notes, her opinions of England alternate just as regularly. She loves London while she stays in Wellington (108), but begins to loathe the city soon after she returns to Europe (164). These shifts in opinion strengthen the impression that longing and indecision continuously shape her relationship with both New Zealand and England. Grounded in her experience as a second-generation settler, her search for a place to identify with also remains hampered by an imperialist discourse that urged New Zealanders to 'identify with British thought and British feeling' (Anonymous 1903: 129) even if they had never set foot on English soil. Despite her attraction to London life in particular, however, Mansfield's perspective of New Zealand tends to focus not only on details which a colonialist mindset would define as 'other', she also expresses an affinity with Māori culture and a native landscape that defies the invasion of English agriculture. A straightforward identification with 'British thought' (Anonymous 1903: 129) remains impossible, it seems: Even after living in England for years, Mansfield sees herself as a 'stranger' (Mansfield 1997: 166), an outsider in the country she had felt drawn to as a youth and exiled from the places that supply the material for her best stories. It comes as no surprise, then, that Mansfield speaks of herself as 'a divided being' (Mansfield 2008: 304).

How do the notebooks deal with that experience? If unity, or even continuity, remain out of reach, what kind of self – or selves – emerge from Mansfield's notes? In order to approach this question, we need to look deeper into the concept of home. If spaces serve as fixed points for the topography of the self, then perhaps the home space might function as a constant. But what if the notion of 'home' is either distorted by the fantasies of others or complicated by the manifestation of the stranger within the self?

The New Zealand Bush and 'The Wizard London'

In Mansfield's notebooks, the process of 'placing' the self creates a distinctive dynamic between pull and rejection, absorption and detachment. London, for example, both beckons to the diarist and unsettles her. At two points Mansfield's notebooks compare the city to a wizard, once when she expresses her longing to return to London in a poem, and the other time in her Urewera diary. Not surprisingly, perhaps, the wizard evokes ambiguous associations: 'When I get back to London streets/When I am there again/I shall forget that Summer's here/While I am in the rain./But I shall only feel at last/The wizard has his way/And London's ever calling me/The live long day' (1997: 86–7). On the one hand, one can read this stanza as a testament to Mansfield's enchantment with London life. On the other hand, the image of the wizard who 'has his way' also implies an air of manipulation, of the wizard exerting power and the poem's speaker giving in. The second mention of the wizard associates London even more directly with a force that intrudes upon Mansfield's enjoyment of her Urewera camping trip: 'As she brushes her hair a wave of cold air strikes her, clamps cold fingers around her heart – it is the wizard London' (1997: 145). Instead of simply calling, the city now 'strikes' and 'clamps', both verbs evoking a strong sense of assault. This might suggest that there is at least an element of involuntariness or doubt in Mansfield's desire to emigrate to Europe. Then again, the notebooks create a similar ambiguity in their depiction of New Zealand. When engaging with the New Zealand bush, for example, the text evokes either intimacy when the bush becomes 'a part of' (1997: 171) the author or distance when the young Mansfield writes about herself in the third person (for example 1997: 145). Clearly Mansfield has conflicting associations with both London and the remoter 'wild places' (1994: 144) of New Zealand; this is in part because her identifications with and through space remain rooted in a colonial context.

In her correspondence Mansfield at times called New Zealand a 'young country' (2008: 115) and a 'little land with no history' (1988: 30). Her comparison of New Zealand with a piece of 'clay' (1988: 30) echoes the pioneers' view of the British colony as a blank slate. During the settler period, the imperial propaganda that surrounded the colonisation of New Zealand operated with two assumptions. First, it was assumed that the British settlers would turn New Zealand into a copy of England, importing codes of behaviour and modes of thinking along with architecture and agriculture. Second, it was expected that the British settler and his offspring would have a strong 'desire to remain "British"' (Orr 1993: 54). This set-up predicted and promoted a process in which England would overwhelm New Zealand, assimilating both its topographical and socio-cultural matrix and overwriting it with 'English grasses, western domesticated animals, English flora ... English birds, rabbits and fertilizer' (Mahar 2005: 77). Many of these attitudes survived into Mansfield's generation. Among other pledges of allegiance, such as supporting the English during the Boer War, the New Zealanders seemed to express their longing for a home on the other side of the globe in the Victorian architecture of their cities. Even the country house of Mansfield's childhood 'was named "Chesney Wold" after the Dedlock mansion in Dickens's *Bleak House*, a name determinedly expressive of cultural loyalty' (Tomalin 1987: 16). Of course, the idea that the New Zealander of Mansfield's time merely 'imitates his brethren and ancestors at home' (1873: 474), as Anthony Trollope claimed in his travel reports, is in itself a biased point of view and does not at all capture the complexity of identity formations in the colonies of the early twentieth century. If we look at Mansfield's notebooks, we discover that she, for one, does not perceive New Zealand simply as a 'Britain of the South' (King 1994: 197), nor does she consider herself to be 'more English than any Englishman' (Trollope 1873: 16). While English values and modes of appreciation influence especially her early writing, her notes (and stories) also exhibit a range of decidedly un-English experiences and observations. A vignette focusing on a visit to the Botanical Gardens in Wellington illuminates the strangeness that pulsates through Mansfield's prose. Setting out, the vignette first describes the Botanical Gardens as a manifest example of British landscaping, complete with ordered flowerbeds and Wordsworth's daffodils:

> In the Enclosure the Spring flowers are almost too beautiful – a great stretch of foam-like cowslips. As I bend over them, the air is heavy with their yellow scent, like hay and new milk and kisses of children, and, further on, a sunlit wonder of chiming daffodils. (Mansfield 1997: 170)

As soon as the narrator leaves the Enclosure, however, she passes into a less organised area:

> And suddenly it disappears, all the pretty, carefully-tended surface of gravel and sward and blossom, and there is bush, silent and splendid. On the green moss, on the brown earth, a wide splashing of sunlight. And, everywhere that strange, indefinable scent. As I breathe it, it seems to absorb, to become part of me ... (171)

In this vignette we do not witness English landscaping overtaking the New Zealand flora, but rather the separate existence of a shaped area and a seemingly untouched one. Here, the overwrite does not succeed: The moment when the gardens' gravel paths disappear into the bush creates a sense of alterity that cannot be eradicated or even suppressed. As a result, this excerpt has three effects: It questions the image of New Zealand as an easily recognisable copy of England, it establishes a mixed space, where English horticultural endeavours blend with the New Zealand landscape and vice versa, and it establishes the narrator as a figure who is both aware of the spatial differences and at the same time able to cross over from the English space into the bush, a remnant of the densely forested areas which defined New Zealand before the first wave of settlers set foot on the islands. More importantly: The narrator is not only able to cross over, she seems compelled to do so. Splitting apart from the visitor crowd, she becomes absorbed by the bush only to make it a part of herself by inhaling its scent. This sense of being one with the landscape strongly points to a moment of identification, not with New Zealand as a facsimile of England but with New Zealand as other space. This allegiance is crucial in that it signifies both a transgression and a shift in the perception of the familiar and the foreign.

As a writer, Mansfield shows a keen awareness of the lines her country draws between domesticated and alien spaces. The characters of stories like *How Pearl Button Was Kidnapped* or *At the Bay* may have grown up in New Zealand, but even for them all those areas that have not been entirely transformed by colonising efforts retain the strangeness of foreign territories. Their homes, the places they define as familiar, are the Victorian buildings Tomalin mentions, with the bush set back far beyond the garden fences (for example, Mansfield 2001: 205). *Botanical Gardens* echoes this division when it restricts the children to the Enclosure and defines the bush as 'strange' (1997: 171). Further on in the vignette, the bush is also connected with Māori culture when the narrator imagines 'a great company ... wreathed with green garlands' (171) moving through the shadows of the trees. It could be argued that the inclusion of Māori in her notes and stories pays tribute to the fact that New Zealand has a history and indeed an identity that is not dependent on its English colonisers. Her method is not unproblematic, however. Mansfield's frequently stereotyped depiction of Māori shows that 'she too was a product of European colonialism' (Maxwell 2007: 37).[2] Nevertheless, texts like *Botanical Gardens* at least demonstrate an awareness of diversity as well as the persistence of otherness in Mansfield's self-definition. Thus in the vignette, we witness not only an acknowledgement of strangeness, but also the possibility that the strange landscape can 'become part of' (Mansfield 1997: 171) the self. Indeed, the image of the narrator inhaling the scent of the 'strange, indefinable' (171) bush implies an encounter with otherness not across a fence but within her own identity.

In *Landscape and the Foreigner Within*, Angela Smith suggests that for colonial subjects 'internalizing the landscape and finding a way to represent a non-European country' (2005: 142) are important steps towards the recognition of otherness without and within the self. Smith here refers to Julia Kristeva's *Strangers to Ourselves*, a book which proposes a shift from setting self and other apart as entirely different entities, to the recognition of the other as an integral if uncanny part of the human psyche. Locating division inside the

---

[2]   In *Botanical Gardens*, for example, Mansfield problematically describes the presence of Māori as 'passing', echoing nineteenth-century theories which (falsely) predicted that Māori culture would fade from existence, but she also worries that she herself might be 'the thief of their birthright' (1997: 171). For an in-depth discussion of Mansfield's interpretation of Māori culture see Bridget Orr's *Reading with the Taint of the Pioneer*.

subject, Kristeva's theory refutes any schema by which the diverse population of a settled colony could be separated into 'imperial subject and colonized other' (Orr 1993: 53). Because of this, the notion of the 'other with/in' (Orr 1993: 53) has become an important aspect in the analysis of Mansfield's work. When Kristeva proclaims that 'we are our own foreigners, we are divided' (1991: 181), her words almost seem to echo Mansfield when she writes: 'I am a divided being: I am always conscious of this secret disruption in me' (Mansfield 2008: 304). It seems to me, however, that Mansfield's texts do not only focus on the rifts that occur when a subject is pulled in two directions at once. Smith links the other within to 'a duality in the self' (2005: 152), by which she understands not only the condition of a self split in two, but the self being two things at once. The end of *Botanical Gardens* portrays an almost natural coexistence of the protagonist's two selves: After inhaling the 'strange, indefinable scent' (Mansfield 1997: 171) of the bush, the narrator returns to the Enclosure and quietly re-affiliates herself with the visitors who spell out the 'Latin names of flowers' (171) in the tradition of English botanists. Other passages foreground the rich and layered texture of her self, for example when her encounter with the bush is described in terms that suggest a connection on an instinctive level. In her own words, '[a]n inexplicably persistent feeling' compels her to 'become one' (171) with the forest. It follows that the word 'become' does not only suggest a process of the subject changing into someone else, it also signifies a moment of recognition, of becoming aware that those aspects of New Zealand that she formerly defined as other or, more precisely, strange and 'curious' (170), might well resonate with her subconscious. In this sense, the subject becomes a threshold where the already known and the yet to be recognised converge. This creates a sense of duality which the text further supports in its arrangement of spaces.

As she leaves the Enclosure, the narrator does not only transgress the border between the gardens and the bush, she also directs the reader's attention to the convergence of English and un-English spaces: The sound of swaying cabbage trees carries past the hedge that separates the Enclosure from the bush, European forget-me-nots intermingle with tree ferns, the 'smooth swept paths' segue into a clay track broken up by 'knotted tree roots' (171). Those fluent transitions develop into a sense of condensed distance which carries over into the end of the vignette. As the narrator returns to the central walk, she observes that '[h]ere is laughter and movement and bright sunlight – but, behind me ... is it near, or miles and miles away ... the bush lies, hidden in shadow' (171). In the end, the sense of the bush overshadowing the gardens, being both far away and close, evokes not only a side-by-side existence but a merging of landscapes. As a result, the vignette does not only describe a disruption of a binary order but a coming together, an overlap of spaces that, according to imperialist ideology, should be mutually exclusive. This, I would say, is a key feature of Mansfield's notes: They do not just express an awareness of difference as a line drawn by colonising forces, they also point out the fluidity of concepts such as familiar and strange. Thus at the end of the vignette, the narrator no longer focuses on the hedge that separates the garden from the outback, but on the shadow which blurs the transition between them.

Even though they emerge from a colonial context, Mansfield's notebooks work incessantly at an alternative to the binary topography of an English and un-English New Zealand. Steering away from absolute inclusions and exclusions, her notes produce spaces and identities that dissolve binaries. The moment of this dissolution, and the landscape that arises in its occasion, is particularly interesting. Taking a closer look at Mansfield's Urewera diary, the final part of this essay will analyse how the convergence of the familiar and the foreign facilitates not just discomposure, but composition.

A Map for the Self

In its search for self-knowledge, Mansfield's Urewera diary traverses a country of liminal landscapes. Employing images of mist and twilight, the entries blur landmarks such as trees, mountains and lakes and blend them at the edges. In this context, the word 'liminal', deriving from the Latin 'limen', refers to a border or threshold as well as a type of limbo, a place of suspension where limits and order unravel (see Smith 1999: 10). This concept can easily be applied to Mansfield's diary where not only the landscape but also its effect on the diarist shifts into an indefinite and ambiguous dimension:

> Next morning – mist over the whole world. Lying, her arms over her head, she can see faintly like a grey thought the river & the mist – they are hardly distinct. She is not tired now – only happy. Goes to the door of the tent, all is very grey, there is no sun first thing, she can see the poplar tree mirrored in the water. (1997: 145)

Opacity and dissolution mark Mansfield's description of the Ureweras: Mountains are 'hidden behind a thick grey veil' (137), willow trees are 'full of gloomy shades' (136), rain obscures the distant hills, mist distorts the manuka shrubs. Arriving at lake Taupo, Mansfield observes how '[t]he sky changes, softens, the lake is all grey mist, the land in heavy shadow' (148). These descriptions are all examples of liminality: Set during the morning or evening, the diary entries evoke a sense of transition just as mist, twilight and gloom turn the threshold-landscape into an environment that defies segmentation. Indeed the entries dissolve binaries like sky/earth or river/bank until they are 'hardly distinct' (145). The softening or smudging of distinctions is, however, only the first step to a mobilisation of spaces. At this point, another function of 'the wizard' becomes important. Continuing her entry on the morning campsite, Mansfield evokes a magician's ability to conjure up objects, or in this particular case, cities, from thin air: 'The grass is wet, there is the familiar sound of buckets. As she brushes her hair a wave of cold air strikes her, clamps cold fingers about her heart – it is the wizard London' (145).

With these lines, Mansfield composes a moment in which the New Zealand outback and the city of London mingle both outside and within the narrating I. As the text describes it, London takes the shape of air, a mobile substance which interweaves with the bush much like the mist, but it also manifests as fingers around the writer's heart. It is striking that this entry once again turns the subject into a receptacle, with London taking up the characteristics of the other who is incorporated by the diarist. Indeed, the image of places permeating the human body and thereby its cognitive apparatus is a recurring motif with Mansfield: We have already seen how the narrator inhaled the essence of the outback, now London squeezes her heart, to which we can add Mansfield's later assertion that 'New Zealand is in my very bones' (2008: 115). With Mansfield's personal writings, we frequently get the impression that she has photographed her self in double exposure with trees and hills and London gardens seen through the silhouette of her body. The fact that the landscapes that show through her are already doubled, moving in and out of each other like shadows or air and mist, again expresses multiplicity in the form of an overlap. To Smith's observation that '[t]he liminal greyness catches [Mansfield] between places, in the bush, but lured by the metropolis' (2005: 153) I would therefore add that her liminal con-fusion of selves and spaces catches her not just between places, it also locates her in two places at once. This technique becomes even more refined in later years. In 1919, for example, Mansfield writes from her house in Hampstead, in London:

> I am the little colonial walking in a London garden patch – allowed to look perhaps,
> but not to linger. If I lie on the grass, they positively shout at me. Look at her, lying on
> our grass, pretending she lives here, pretending this is her garden, and that tall back
> of a house, with windows open and the coloured curtains lifting, is her house. She is a
> stranger – she is alien. She is nothing but a little girl sitting on the Tinakori hills and
> dreaming: I went to London and married an Englishman and we lived in a tall grave
> house, with red geraniums and white daisies in the garden at the back. (1997: 166)

With its overlapping places, this entry subverts the idea of time and distance as linear and fixed concepts. Mansfield, in her own words, is 'never far away from' (32) the places she remembers, but the act of drawing them up in her notes and stories moves beyond nostalgia and turns into a specific method of life writing: Her notes conceive of places not as either/or, then or now, distant or far, but as slides put on top of each other, and her understanding of the self follows the same approach. As such, her writing contributes to a representation of human consciousness as layered instead of linear. The subjects she writes about do not emerge from a time- and place-bound home, instead they manifest on the seams where images, selves and places intersect.

What then can we gather from Mansfield's navigation of the threshold? For one, her notebooks not only locate their narrator in a zone between different cultural and geographic territories, they also create a narrative space which blends the places that shape the narrator's identity, invoking the Tinakori hills in a London garden and the wizard London in the Urewera bush. Retaining an awareness of the forces that disrupt every possibility of belonging through rejection and marginalisation, the notes do not depict the in-between as an easy position. In her diaries, Mansfield struggles with the label of the 'little colonial' (166) knowing full well that the category limits among other things her success as a writer. And yet, Virginia Woolf famously wrote that she was 'jealous of [Mansfield's] writing' (1980: 227). As the descendant of colonisers, Mansfield grew up on the border between a New Zealand fashioned as a facsimile of distant England and a country that, in some aspects, still felt 'indefinable' (Mansfield 1997: 171) to her. As a colonial moving to England, she experienced the bias of the English who discounted her as an outsider. It is exactly this sense of not quite belonging anywhere which marks her out as distinctive among modernists. For one, Mansfield's unique depiction of the liminal as a space where attributes like foreign and familiar overlap, defies hierarchies and foreshadows future developments in postcolonial criticism.[3] Giving both London and New Zealand room within the text as well as unravelling and rearranging their meaning indicates that both environments play an equal part in the formation of Mansfield's personae. As such, the notebooks subvert any dichotomy which conceives of England as a role model and of New Zealand as a piece of clay to be shaped in England's image. In addition, their description of New Zealand as both home and strange place creates a multiply determined narrator who –

---

[3]   For example, her engagement with the other within and her understanding of the self as an ever-shifting composite formed by the meeting of different cultures shows parallels with Homi Bhabha's concept of hybridity (see Bhabha 2005).

much like a figure composed of many shifting atoms – develops a kaleidoscopic approach to life writing.

In conclusion, the cartography we can draw from Mansfield's personal writings lays out the self as 'a strange land of borders and othernesses ceaselessly constructed and deconstructed' (Kristeva 1991: 191). In this sense, the notebooks 'problematise rather than consolidate identity' (Orr 1993: 58), but they also impressively present the emplacement of selfhood, to quote Eve Kosofsky Sedgwick, as 'a continuing moment, movement, motive – recurrent, eddying, troublant' (1993: xii).

References

Anonymous. 1903. *The New Zealand Colony: Its Geography and History*. London: Edward Arnorld.

Bhabha, H. 2005. *The Location of Culture* [1994]. London and New York: Routledge.

Gordon, I.A. 1978. Katherine Mansfield: The Wellington years, a reassessment, in *The Urewera Notebook*, edited by Ian A. Gordon. Oxford: Oxford University Press, 11–30.

King, M. 1994. *The Penguin History of New Zealand*. Rosedale: Penguin.

Kristeva, J. 1991. *Strangers to Ourselves* [1988], translated by L.S. Roudiez. London: Harvester.

Mahar, C.A. 2005. Landscape, empire and the creation of modern New Zealand, in *Landscape and Empire, 1770–2000*, edited by G. Hooper. Aldershot: Ashgate, 65–78.

Mansfield, K. 1988. *The Poems of Katherine Mansfield*, edited by V. O'Sullivan. Oxford: Oxford University Press.

Mansfield, K. 1997. *The Katherine Mansfield Notebooks*, edited by M. Scott. Minneapolis: University of Minnesota Press.

Mansfield, K. 2001. *The Collected Stories*. London: Penguin Books.

Mansfield, K. 2008. *The Collected Letters of Katherine Mansfield*. Vol. 5: *1922–1923*, edited by V. O'Sullivan et al. Oxford: Clarendon Press.

Mansfield, K. 2013. *The Collected Fiction of Katherine Mansfield, 1898 –1915*, edited by Geriri Kimber et al. Edinburgh: Edinburgh University Press.

Maxwell, A. 2007. Encountering the cultural other: Virginia Woolf in Constantinople and Katherine Mansfield in the Ureweras. *ARIEL: A Review of International English Literature*, 38(2–3), 19–40.

Murry, J. M. 1993. Katherine Mansfield, in *Critical Essays on Katherine Mansfield*, edited by R.B. Nathan. New York: Macmillan, 183–97.

Orr, B. 1993. Reading with the taint of the pioneer: Katherine Mansfield and settler criticism, in *Critical Essays on Katherine Mansfield*, edited by R.B. Nathan. New York: Macmillan, 48–60.

O'Sullivan, V. 1994. 'Finding the pattern, solving the problem': Katherine Mansfield: The New Zealand European, in *Katherine Mansfield: In From the Margin*, edited by R. Robinson. Baton Rouge: Louisiana State University Press, 9–24.

Sedgwick, E.K. 1993. *Tendencies*. Durham: Duke University Press.

Smith, A. 1999. *Katherine Mansfield and Virginia Woolf: A Public of Two*. Oxford: Clarendon Press.

Smith, A. 2005. Landscape and the foreigner within, in *Landscape and Empire 1770–2000*, edited by G. Hooper. Aldershot: Ashgate. 141–57.

Tomalin, C. 1987. *Katherine Mansfield: A Secret Life*. London: Viking Press.

Tordasi, K. 2012. Stevie Smith, Virginia Woolf und das Verlangen nach Vergessenheit, in *Potentiale des Vergessens*, edited by A. Blum et al. Würzburg: Königshausen & Neumann, 229–50.

Trollope, A. 1873. *Australia and New Zealand*. London: Chapman and Hall.

Woolf, V. 1980. *The Diary of Virginia Woolf*. Vol. 2. London: Harcourt Brace.

Chapter 9

Isaac Rosenberg's Life in Letters: Between the 'coil of circumstance' and a 'place for poetry'

Anne-Julia Schoen

The poet and painter Isaac Rosenberg was born in 1890 in Bristol as the second son of Lithuanian Jewish immigrants. His family had crossed half of Europe on an arduous journey and finally settled in the East End, the geographical and social periphery of London. By the time Isaac Rosenberg was killed during a German raid on the British trenches in northern France on the morning of 1 April 1918, he had travelled as far as South Africa. But he had not succeeded in establishing a reputation as a published poet or painter. It was only in the late 1930s that critics like F. R. Leavis and Jon Silkin began to bring his extraordinary poetry to a wider public's attention. To this day, his poems have not reached the same popularity as those of Robert Graves, Wilfred Owen or Siegfried Sassoon (Moorcroft Wilson 2008: 11–13). Unlike most other English war poets, and due to his different background, Rosenberg was never free from material constraints that limited his scope for action. Aspiring to devote his life to art and poetry, he used both as a means to assert his existence. His artistic endeavours removed him from his religiously observant family and enabled him to enter various locations on London's compartmentalised cultural map. However, he also encountered mechanisms of exclusion from culturally relevant circles. In this chapter I claim that his struggle to overcome intellectual as well as economic and social obstacles to his life as an artist considerably informed his writing. I argue that in writing letters to friends, patrons, fellow poets and his family, Rosenberg practiced what Frédéric Regard would call 'a poetic spacing of the self' (2003: 90). He created spaces for writing and responding to poetry in a cultural context that was socially and ideologically structured to prevent him from doing so.

This chapter focuses on some critical moments in Isaac Rosenberg's life as presented in his letters written between 1911 and 1918. Many of them suggest a great sense of unease and discomfort with regard to the different environments in which he lived, worked and socialised. They also relate his attempts to position himself as an Anglo-Jewish artist and poet in British society during the first two decades of the twentieth century. His correspondence records his journeys through the different social environments in literary London, which were determined by a cultural politics that set the standards for what was to be read, heard and seen in magazines, books, theatres and galleries. As an outsider to the cultural scene of pre-war London, Rosenberg often reported his efforts to defy 'the law of the place' (de Certeau 1984: 36) and inscribe himself in the cultural field. Art and literature were like a destination to him and his letters speak of his repeated attempts to create a place in which he could practise them and thus position himself in the literary and artistic world. Like many artists, Rosenberg had to confront the dilemma of adapting to pre-defined artistic standards without compromising his sense of difference (in Rosenberg's case his identity as a Jewish Whitechapel boy) from the groups he sought to commune with. The letters show how he resorted to a set of tactics to disseminate his work and achieve some sort of integration into the London cultural establishment, while making a strong impression as an artist. During phases of disorientation, the letters seem to have helped him navigate different trajectories between past and present, the engraver's and the poet's workshop, London and South Africa and, finally, between army and civilian life.

A considerable number of his papers have been lost in exchanges between family members, friends and editors, and thus could not be assembled in their entirety. My observations are based on the most recent and comprehensive edition of Rosenberg's works and letters by the late Vivien Noakes (2012).[1] To provide further contexts for the records of his efforts to find spaces for reading, writing and publishing poetry, I will also incorporate information from various biographies and sections of Joseph Leftwich's diary from 1911, which is available as a manuscript copy in the archives of the Imperial War Museum.[2]

---

[1]   The discovery of a package of unpublished letters and drafts of poems during the preparations to move the British Library to St. Pancras in 1995 enabled Noakes to assemble, compare, edit and revise all existing papers together with existing publications, so that the 2012 edition is so far the most authoritative source for scholarship on Rosenberg. For more information about the journeys of Rosenberg's letters, see Noakes (2012: xi–xx) and Liddiard (2007: 29–59).

[2]   Leftwich (1911), Noakes (2012), Cohen (1979) and Moorcroft Wilson (2004).

Writing Letters and 'making do'

Michel de Certeau refers to 'poetic ways of "making do"' as tactics to 'reappropriate the space organized by techniques of sociocultural production' (1984: xiv). By using the limited means available, the individual is able to find provisional and subversive ways of 'creating ... a space in which he can find *ways of using* the constraining order of the place or of the language' (1984: 30). I transfer this expression to Rosenberg's letters, which open up spaces not otherwise available to him, where he can approach different friends or acquaintances for criticism, books, advice and funds. Furthermore, these tactics consist in using both the enabling as well as the restraining aspects of his environment to present a self to his correspondents that is simultaneously aspiring, actively resistant but also passively exposed to his circumstances.

'Thanks so much for the Donne. I had just been reading Ben Jonson again, and from his poem to Donne he must have thought him a giant. I have read some of the Donne; I have certainly never come across anything so choke-full of profound meaningful ideas', Rosenberg writes to the school teacher Winifreda Seaton in autumn 1910 (Noakes 2012: 230). Meeting her through his friend John Amschewitz, who would later introduce him to several other future friends, Miss Seaton advises him what to read, sends him books and responds to his poems. This and other letters to her clearly show his attempt to map and chart the territory of English literature: he tries to cultivate his taste in poetry, establishing a spatial order in which greater poets are higher or larger in proportion to the number of 'meaningful ideas' they have to offer. Earlier, he had confessed to Miss Seaton: 'Anyway, if I didn't quite take to Donne at first, you understand why. Poetical appreciation is only newly bursting on me' (Noakes 2012: 229). The violent metaphor for poetical taste spilling into his uneducated mind resonates with one of his earliest poems, written in 1906 when he was still at school, 'In art's lone paths I wander deep': 'Yes many a time shall fade to gloom,/ Ere I can burst thro' the wild bounds/ That the pure realm of art surrounds' (Noakes 2012: 2). The metaphor of the 'wild bounds' is suggestive of the circles of critics, editors, publishers and educated readers, who protect the space of art from unsuitable intruders; he can only overcome this obstacle after 'poetical appreciation' has made him sufficiently educated to grasp the 'meaningful ideas' of giants like Donne. As in the letter, this poem portrays a speaker whose mind is too overwhelmed and untrained to be able to enter 'the pure realm of art' (2). He writes: art's 'dazzling star' is far away and yet it 'dims my eyes', but in the end 'e'en its drudgery I'm denied', which shows that he is fully aware that the real work only starts after having entered art's 'flaming sphere' (2).

After a considerable period spent reading and writing poetry, he writes to Miss Seaton with much more confidence:

> I forgot to ask you to return my poetry, as I mean to work on some. I agree the emotions
> are not worth expressing, but I thought the things had some force, and an idea or so
> I rather liked. Of course, I know poetry is a far finer thing than that, but I don't think
> the failure was due to the subject – I had nothing to say about it, that's all. (232)

As we can see in this reply, he takes up her criticism but is palpably hurt by it and tries to justify his failed attempt. I propose that this is an example of conducting an apprenticeship in poetry through letter-writing; the pattern of inviting criticism to his enclosed drafts of poetry and discussing them with Miss Seaton would continue with other correspondents but in different ways. In the absence of public education, letters such as these record his movements as well as his own positionings on the charted territory of literature.

The existential significance of poetry and painting is very explicit in Rosenberg's correspondence. In his encounters and relations with friends, writing blends with and is suffused by daily routines. Poetry and writing seem to belong to his sense of self. Early in their friendship, Joseph Leftwich notes in his diary: 'It is only in poetry that he feels himself worth something. It is true that in poetry he feels himself confident and thoroughly at home' (Leftwich 1911: 12 February). From this remark of a new friend we can infer a clear distinction and conflict between Rosenberg's material home and a kind of intellectual home (a space in which he had the time and opportunity to acquire and exchange knowledge). Although 'his people are very unsympathetic to him' (Leftwich 1911: 12 February) and his literary endeavours, he pursues them unerringly,

> going in his own way, running away to the libraries whenever he can to read poetry and
> the lives of the poets, their letters, their essays on how to write poetry, their theory of
> what poetry should be and do – everything he can find about poets and poetry. Poetry
> is his obsession. (Leftwich 1911: 12 February)

Leftwich conveys Rosenberg's obsessiveness in the breathless repetition of 'poetry' and 'poets' that characterises 'his own way', his mental and physical forays into literature. The acknowledgement of Rosenberg's 'singlemindedness' (Leftwich 1911: 12 February) is in stark contrast to his awkwardness, shyness and his capacity to be swayed by his economic obligations, all of which he discusses and struggles with in his letters.

From Whitechapel

Growing up in the crowded streets of Whitechapel was an unlikely provenance for an aspiring poet, and Rosenberg's letters tend to emphasise the deprivation of his upbringing. 'You mustn't forget the circumstances I have been brought up in, the little education I have had', he writes to his friend Winifreda Seaton in 1911 (Noakes 2012: 229). These circumstances provide him with an explanation for his limited absorption of English poetry that is only compensated by his voracious reading. He informs Miss Seaton about his unsystematic studies and appeals to her for support. His strong desire to escape the deficiency of his 'circumstances', where 'nobody ever told me what to read, or ever put poetry in my way' (Noakes 2012: 229), obscures the educative efforts of his family and school teachers in spite of scarce opportunities. Since there is no vacancy at the more sophisticated Jewish Free School, he attends a gentile institution where the headmaster recognises his talent for drawing, reading and writing. Rosenberg is allowed to draw instead of having to pay attention to the lessons that do not interest him. He wins several essay and drawing prizes. His sister Minnie later introduces her brother to the librarian of the Whitechapel Library, who reads his first poems and advises him on what to read. Until he is 14, the family supports him even though his adherence to the idea of becoming a painter and a poet alarms them (Noakes 2012: xii). The self-image he is constructing for Miss Seaton and other supportive acquaintances, however, complies more with Joseph Leftwich's version of the obsessed and misunderstood fledgling poet and has the function to elicit sympathy and a favourable response to his writing and painting.

For an aspiring artist, the ethnic diversity among the Jewish population, manifest in a multitude of communities, shops, shuls, housing estates and in a rich texture of languages, dialects and cultural practices, was both a restraint and a blessing. It was difficult for Jewish working-class people to rise above their station and move out of the confines of the 'ghetto',[3] but they often had family relations in Europe, or even in America, Africa or Australia, as well as connections to the wealthier Anglo-Jewish establishment, which enhanced social and geographical mobility. The latter provided a dense network of charitable institutions to

---

[3]   See the bleak and exoticising accounts from outside Whitechapel by Booth (1889–1903); for contemporary accounts see Zangwill (1892) and Leftwich (1911) as well as the socio-historical study by Fishman (1975). Whitechapel was not a ghetto in the strictest sense, because Jews lived there for mainly religious and practical reasons. After the massive immigration from Russia, Poland and Lithuania from the 1880s on, the East End became so overcrowded with Jewish refugees that the term was increasingly used, however. The publication of Zangwill's *The Children of the Ghetto* in 1892 seems to have established the term (see Vaughan 1994: 30).

foster the anglicisation of the masses of mostly orthodox Jewish immigrants from Eastern Europe.[4] Rosenberg would write about 'some wealthy Jews who are kindly interested in me' when Mrs Joseph Cohen pays his fees for the Slade School of Fine Art (Noakes 2012: 236). He would also benefit from the Jewish Education Aid Society that provided lodging, education, training and healthcare for members of poor Jewish families. Although Rosenberg's 'circumstances' would never match that of an English middle- or upper-class poet in terms of education, financial means and an easy access to influential social circles, critics and biographers alike agree that his experiences in such a diverse environment as the East End clearly informed and enriched his poetry.[5] It is also the case that these economic, social and educational aspects of his background gave him something to aspire against. As we will see, his desire for self-improvement and his wish to become a poet are often expressed in spatial terms, such as a journey to be made or other metaphors suggesting a lack of mobility and energy to paint and write. The descriptions of his 'circumstances' that keep him from practising and pursuing his arts are aimed at opening up an alternative space where he can 'wander deep' 'in art's lone paths' (Noakes 2012: 2) and transform himself from an avid reader into an active writer and peer of the poets.

From the Workshop

The abrupt ending of his school education in 1905, due to the necessity of supporting his family, marks the beginning of the struggle against those circumstances that prevent him from writing and painting. His letters from 1911 are a plea for liberation from the deprivation of the spaces he inhabits, and they vividly represent the terrible working conditions that stifle his vitality, highlighting a self-image subdued by hardship and the utter lack of freedom he experienced. Although he is employed in one of Carl Hentschel's engraving workshops in Fleet Street, synonymous with publishing and professional writing,[6] Rosenberg detests the work, which is badly paid and where he has to

---

[4]   There were institutions like the Jewish Board of Guardians, the Poor Jew's Temporary Shelter, the Jewish Association for the Protection of Girls and Women and the Jewish Education Aid Society, to name but a few (see Russell and Lewis 1900 and Feldman 1994).

[5]   See Moorcroft Wilson (2008), Hill (2008), Lawson (2006), Parsons (1979) and Cohen (1975).

[6]   Carl Hentschel owned a prestigious firm of engraving and printmaking and provided printing blocks and illustrations for many famous and popular press products; he was one of the most innovative and successful members of his trade (see Obituary 1930).

inhale toxic fumes during long hours of monotonous operations. He chooses to portray himself as a slaving apprentice who is unable to pursue his career as an artist, and prefers not to mention the opportunities such a position could offer in terms of becoming a writer. Despite working in the City and away from the East End, his letters to Miss Seaton could have been sent from any crammed sweatshop in Whitechapel:[7]

> I am bound, chained to this fiendish mangling machine, without hope ... of deliverance, and the days of youth go by ... I despair of ever writing excellent poetry. I can't look at things in the simple, large way that great poets do. My mind is so cramped and dulled and fevered, there is no consistency of purpose, no oneness of aim; the very fibres are torn apart, and application deadened by the fiendish persistence of the coil of circumstance. (Noakes 2012: 227–8)

The 'fiendish mangling machine' damages and crushes his body and mind, squeezing his vitality out of him with mechanical and relentless precision. The enumeration of 'cramped and dulled and fevered' echoes the movements of the machine, violent and repetitive, perforating and disrupting any 'consistency of purpose' or 'oneness of aim'. As in a version of hell, he is surrounded by the steam and the fumes of chemical substances used in engraving and lithography. The strain of the noise, smells and the monotony at the workshop undermine his mental 'vigour' (Noakes 2012: 227), thereby obstructing his scope for self-expression and movement. He needs to fulfil the tasks of an engraver, supervising the dangerous machines or processing the printing blocks during long working hours. By the time he writes to his friend he has worked there for five years; he is concerned that the work environment will have a lasting effect on his mind and body. He uses the complex metaphor of 'coil', which clearly resonates with Hamlet's famous monologue on death, 'when we have shuffled off this mortal coil' (III, i, 67). The mortal coil alludes to the skin and flesh that have to be '*shuffled off* at death' (Shakespeare 1994: 240; emphasis in the original), but it also denotes the physical and mental turmoil that marks our lives. The 'coil of circumstance' more particularly relates to Rosenberg's daily troubles and the physical and psychological shackles that prevent him from becoming a poet. His sense of a lack of linear progress in his life is reflected in the shape of the coil. This first surviving letter to Miss Seaton accounts for the immense effort needed to keep up his desire for sufficient 'purpose', free time, workspace and inspiring

---

7   In 1909, he is further apprenticed by process engraver Mr Lascelles in Shoe Lane in the City, but still under the patronage of Carl Hentschel (Noakes 2012: xxviii).

company to be able to 'look at things in the simple, large way that great poets do' (Noakes 2012: 228). To him, 'excellent poetry' seems out of reach because he cannot acquire that 'simple, large' perspective on things he needs in order to become a poet, an outlook he clearly senses when reading Keats, Shelley or Donne. Much later, when he is already at the front, he explains in a letter to a patron how he longs for 'more leisure in more settled times' so that he can work 'on a larger scale and give [him]self more room then' (305). However, when he is finally dismissed from Hentschel's workshop, the 'coil' is still in his mind, revolving around death and 'work, work, any work, only to stop one thinking' (228).

Luckily, he finds company in other young men from the East End, such as Joseph Leftwich, David Bomberg and John Rodker, and on endless daily ramblings they traverse spaces of philosophy, science and literature, and pursue their further education in Epping Forest, Hampstead Heath, Toynbee Hall, the Whitechapel Library and the Jewish Theatre. Rosenberg's training at the Slade School of Fine Art connects him to a wider social circle and to different parts of the cultural establishment and brings him closer to the aspired life of an artist than ever before. In autumn 1911 he writes to Miss Seaton: 'I am studying at the Slade, the finest school for drawing in England. I do nothing but draw – draw – ... ' (236). He informs another friend that 'I am now attending the Slade School of Art, being sent there by some wealthy Jews who are kindly interested in me, and of course I spend most of my time drawing' (236).

He also starts corresponding with more established poets, and the exchange of poems, criticism and opportunities to publish help him approach the spheres he wishes to be accepted in. To Laurence Binyon he writes in 1912: 'I must thank you very much for your encouraging reply to my poetical efforts. Rambles in the wake of the muse generally end in ditchwater – and I expected a good sousing for my boldness in way-laying so staunch an upholder of the Muse's honour' (236). Rosenberg tries to show modesty and to humour the addressee by impersonating a highwayman who steals time from an eminent member of London's cultural elite (Binyon was at that time also Keeper of Prints and Drawings at the British Museum) by imposing a long poem and an autobiographical sketch on him. He asks whether Binyon could introduce him to 'editors or people who might consider my things' (237), since Rosenberg's own attempts to disseminate his poems have not succeeded so far.

From Cape Town

In 1914, after the end of his training at the Slade, Rosenberg fails to acquire commissions or earn money with his first publication of poems. His health deteriorates and so does his financial situation. He plans to travel to Cape Town to visit his sister and, with the prospect of leaving London, his letters evoke utopian visions of a good life abroad and explain his aversion to the British capital:

> I am about to sail to Africa as I have been told my chest is not strong and I must live away from towns. If I get the chance I may work on a farm for a year or two as I am young enough to afford it. I might also this way get ideas for real things. One is so cramped up here ... (Noakes 2012: 255)

He identifies the crampedness 'up here', that is his life in London, as the cause of his failures and health problems. Furthermore, he hopes to 'avoid the rut' (52) he has encountered in his painting or writing practice, and decides the best way of achieving this is to leave the country. Applying for funds from the Jewish Educational Aid Society,[8] he envisions in his letter to the secretary 'heaps of good subject matter. The kaffirs[9] would sit for practically nothing. In a year I'd have a lot of interesting stuff, to send to England' (Noakes 2012: 254), thus emphasising the professional merits of his journey.

From Cape Town, where he lives at his sister's house in a Jewish neighbourhood very similar to Whitechapel, he writes to his patron Edward Marsh in July 1914 about the difference between London and South Africa:

> I am in an infernal city by the sea. ... We are walled in by the sharp upright mountain and the bay. Across the bay the piled up mountains of Africa look lovely and dangerous. It makes one think of savagery and earthquakes – the elemental lawlessness. You are lucky to be in comfortable London and its armchair culture. (Noakes 2012: 259–60)

Rosenberg depicts Cape Town as an antithesis to London. He describes the topographical features of Cape Town with a mixture of delight and mocking

---

[8]   The Jewish Educational Aid Society had already funded his last year at the Slade School of Art (Noakes 2012: xxx).

[9]   The term 'kafir' originally meant 'infidel' in Arabic and was used for non-Muslim black people encountered by Arab traders. Another denotation is that of a person belonging to a group of South African peoples, later transferred to any black South African or even to white persons who are thought to favour black Africans. Since the early 20th century it has been considered very offensive in the South African context and therefore avoided (see OED).

terror, exoticising them in order to impress his upper-class friend. His remarks
on the place and its population of white colonisers who own the goldmines
and other exploitative venues, resemble the Victorian colonial rhetoric about
bringing civilisation to invaded territories (Torgovnic 1990: 27). In Rosenberg's
case it was art, not Christianity, that would improve the minds of ignorant
men, 'millions of years behind time', their eyes and ears 'dreadfully clogged up'
by 'gold dust, diamond dust, stocks and shares' (Noakes 2012: 260). To correct
their profane, capitalist outlook, he presents himself, by contrast, as 'a creature
of the most exquisite civilisation, planted in this barbarous land', who will bless
them with a series of lectures on modern art. He is adamant to 'clear through
all this rubbish' (Noakes 2012: 260), a task that very much resembles charitable
(middle- and upper-class) efforts to educate the working classes to which he
had been exposed as a young man. Yet in some respects his ambitions are quite
similar to those of the gold-diggers he criticises. Being considered 'exotic' in
London does not seem to have prevented him from harbouring the exploitative
attitude of the white colonisers towards the black South Africans. He wants to
use the latter as cheap models, and will then go on to sell his exoticising paintings
to the white inhabitants of Cape Town or in England. Rosenberg desperately
needs to create a market for his art by 'cajoling and demanding interest' from
those to whom poetry and art are 'a luxury but not a necessity' (Hill 2008: 460).
Hovering between different geographical and social spaces, he is neither able to
distance himself fully from the former colonisers and gold-diggers, nor is he able
to spread the gospel of art in the midst of the 'elemental lawlessness' he sees.[10]
Staying with his sister and her family associates him with the Jewish population
in Cape Town, but he finds himself in a similar predicament as in London: 'I've
not been able to get away from my people here, to write. They don't understand
the artist's seclusion to concentrate' (Noakes 2012: 260).

From the Trenches

Physically and mentally recovered on his return to London from South Africa
in March 1915, he recognises that Europe is already in the throes of the First
World War. He repeatedly writes to different people about whether or not to

---

[10]   However, his efforts to get access to the cultural elite in Cape Town succeeded: His
lecture on art and two of his poems were published in the *South African Women in Council*, which
helped to acquaint him with the sister of the Speaker of the South African Parliament, Miss
Molteno. She invited him to her house and introduced him to the famous writer Olive Schreiner
(Noakes 2012: xxxi).

enlist. Writing seems to force him into a clear stance towards the war. Taking up arms will alienate him from the parents and siblings that he tries to support. To the poet R. C. Trevelyan he explains: 'My people are Tolstoyans and object to my being in khaki' (Noakes 2012: 296).[11] It seems important to him to make his friends realise the extent of his personal investment when becoming a soldier. Writing to Marsh, he describes his dilemma of becoming a soldier as a Jew from a pacifist family in the following way: 'I never joined the army for patriotic reasons. Nothing can justify war. I suppose we must all fight to get the trouble over' (Noakes 2012: 288).

The next section of this chapter explores the existential function of letter-writing in Rosenberg's life as a soldier. Writing to others about the abominable and harsh circumstances of army life, such as drills, long marches, eating inedible food, sleeping rough and being exposed to anti-Semitic assaults help him adapt to and endure these ordeals. Sending drafts of poetry, receiving and discussing books creates a productive space. To the poet Gordon Bottomley he writes from France on 23 July 1916:

> Simple *Poetry* – that is where an interesting complexity of thought is kept in tone and right value to the dominating idea so that it is understandable and still ungraspable. I know, it is beyond my reach just now, except, perhaps, in bits. I am always afraid of being empty. When I get more leisure in more settled times I will work on a larger scale and give myself more room then I may be less frustrated in my efforts to be clear, and satisfy myself too. (Liddiard 2007: 73)

Here, Rosenberg outlines his ideas about what poetry is and a vision of life in which he would have the space to work on the clarity of his poetry. I would suggest that 'settled times' and 'more room' to work on a 'larger scale' come close to what he imagines as being 'thoroughly at home' (Leftwich 1911: 12 February). In this passage, Rosenberg envisages the adequate conditions for poetry (and the poet), in which ideas and images thrive and transcend the commonplace. Thanking his patron Mrs Cohen for a copy of *The Poetry Review,* he criticises Rupert Brooke's 'begloried sonnets' for their 'second hand phrases' and insists on a more abstract approach, 'with less of the million feelings everybody feels' (Noakes 2012: 304). At the front, he feels these standards to be mostly out of reach and he is afraid that the inspiration and ideas for poetry might be drained out of him

---

[11]   The Tolstoyan movement based their principles of pacifism, socialism or communalism on the philosophical and religious views of Russian novelist Leo Tolstoy. However, Tolstoy himself was never a 'Tolstoyan' (Sanborn 1996).

by the conditions of war. Instead, life in the trenches seemed to have posed a productive challenge for him to create poetry under adverse circumstances. The sheer amount of poems and plays that he drafted, sent and got printed while at the front prove how successful he was in contesting the theatre of war.

The remaining years and months of his life in the army are characterised by the constant insecurity of never knowing when he would be transferred, sent to the front line, to hospital or on leave. It seems crucial to his self-awareness and sanity to inform his correspondents about the physical situations he is in. And so his patrons and friends always know whether he is 'on a long march' (Noakes 2012: 304), in a dug-out, 'doing coal fatigues' (286), crippled by perforated boots, or in action with 'bullets whizzing all over the show' (299). His gratitude for responses to his poems is an important feature of these letters from the trenches. He sends a poem and a sketch about 'the contortions we get into to try and wriggle ourselves into a little sleep' (300) to R. C. Trevelyan to continue discussing his own and other poets' works. Praise and news from London offer some consolation: 'your letter made me feel refreshed and fine' (300). Some letters seem to transport him out of the space of the trenches: Two letters arriving at once were 'like two friends to take me for a picnic' (305).

After a longer spell in hospital at the beginning of 1918, there is a dramatic change in his mood and outlook.[12] It is especially the lack of energy to write that worries him and his old fear of being empty reappears: 'Poetry seems to have gone right out of me, I get no chance to even think of it' (358). However, he keeps sending his drafts to Marsh and Bottomley. With his last letter to Edward Marsh from 1918, he also sends his last poem: 'I've seen no poetry for ages now so you mustn't be too critical – My vocabulary small enough before is impoverished and bare' (364). To the last moment, he needs to frame his poetry by hinting at the terrible context in which he was writing; the impact of his environment upon his internal world.

A rejection of his request to be transferred to the Jewish Battalion serving in the Middle East frustrates him deeply. He had hoped to escape the cold, the mud and the anti-Semitism in the army. He would at least be in the company of other Jewish soldiers and close to 'Zion', the homeland evoked in one of his earliest poems. In his last poem sent with his last surviving letter to Edward Marsh, he relates the fate of soldiers fighting on foreign soil to the fate of the Jewish people in the diaspora: 'like waifs their spirits grope/for the pools of

---

12   Noakes suggests in contrast to all other biographers that Rosenberg was treated for venereal disease, and that the extreme decline of his mental and physical state could be attributed to a series of injections of drugs that had unpleasant side effects leading to the deterioration of the patient's general well-being (see Noakes 2012: 436–7).

Hebron again –/For Lebanon's summer slope. ... They see with living eyes/How long they have been dead' (123). Without any hope of removing himself from the theatre of war, it seems as if he meant to extend the topos of Jewish exile to all the combatants doomed for death, disconnected from desired places.

Conclusion

Isaac Rosenberg's life seems to have offered no secure or fixed place that he could have inhabited without struggle. The streets of London, the hills and vales of Cape Town and the trenches in northern France were all defined by social codes and mechanisms of exclusion that he found difficult to negotiate. Rosenberg's life as it emerges from his letters is largely determined by his contestation of these codes that coordinated sociogeographical, psychological and intellectual space. Reading his letters reveals the extent to which he depended on the possibility of writing poetry as well as on the responses of his correspondents.

Sometimes he seems to have achieved the desired equipoise between the 'coil of circumstance' and the 'simple, large way' of poets (Noakes 2012: 225–6). Writing about his material circumstances that comprise working conditions, physical health, access to literature, leisure time and financial means, he is not merely recording them, but trying to adapt to them by reworking his responses to them in his poems. Geoffrey Hill states that 'one cannot come to an equitable valuation of Rosenberg's work without acknowledging his own recognition of the psychology of circumstance, of the interrelatedness of experience and language' (2008: 449). Rosenberg himself was highly aware of how much his experiences, the conditions in which he lived and worked, and his conflicting responses to his various contexts, impacted upon his poetry: 'I will not leave a corner of my consciousness covered up, but saturate myself with the strange extraordinary new conditions of this life & it will all refine itself into poetry later on' (Noakes 2012: 320).

Rosenberg saved some of his most remarkable work by sending drafts to his sister and to various other correspondents. His letters are, furthermore, rich sources for examining his appreciation of the relationship between writing and space. They served to generate instances and conditions for writing and sharing poetry. His correspondence also testifies to his attempts to find a way into the literary industry before and during the war years. In the footsteps of the Romantic poets, but also deeply entangled in the social and cultural politics of his time, his efforts to waste nothing remain evident and there is hardly a better place than the letters to see how he used and contested his provenance and circumstances to reach, and dwell in, a 'place for poetry' (Noakes 2012: 354).

References

Booth, C. 1889–1903. *Life and Labour of the People in London.* 3rd edition. London: Macmillan and Co.

Cohen, J. 1975. *Journey to the Trenches: The Life of Isaac Rosenberg 1890–1918.* London: Robson Books.

De Certeau, M. 1984. *The Practice of Everyday Life* [1980], translated by S. Rendall. Berkeley: University of California Press.

Feldman, D. 1994. *Englishmen and Jews: Social Relations and Political Culture, 1840–1914.* New Haven: Yale University Press.

Fishman, W. 1975. *East End Jewish Radicals: 1875–1914.* London: Duckworth.

Hill, G. 2008. Isaac Rosenberg: 1890–1918, in *Collected Critical Writings,* edited by K. Haynes. Oxford: Oxford University Press, 448–64.

Lawson, P. 2006. *Anglo-Jewish Poetry from Isaac Rosenberg to Elaine Feinstein.* Edgware: Valentine Mitchell Press.

Leftwich, J. 1911. *Diary 1911.* Imperial War Museum Archive, Doc. P 351.

Liddiard, J. (ed.) 2007. *Isaac Rosenberg: Poetry Out of My Head and Heart. Unpublished Letters.* London: Enitharmon Press.

Moorcroft Wilson, J. 2008. *Isaac Rosenberg: The Making of a Great War Poet. A New Life,* London: Weidenfeld and Nicolson.

Noakes, V. (ed.) 2012. *Isaac Rosenberg.* Oxford: Oxford University Press.

Obituary of Carl Hentschel, Engraver. *Jewish Chronicle,* 7 January 1930, 10.

Oxford English Dictionary [Online]. Available at: http://www.oed.com/view/Entry/102330?redirectedFRom=kaffir [accessed: 23 June 2014].

Parsons, I. (ed.) 1979. *The Collected Works of Isaac Rosenberg: Poetry, Prose, Letters, Paintings and Drawings.* London: Chatto and Windus.

Regard, F. 2003. Topologies of the self: Space and life-writing. *Partial Answers: Journal of Literature and the History of Ideas,* 1(1), 89–102.

Russel, C. and Lewis, H. S. 1900. *The Jew in London.* London: T. Fisher Unwin.

Sanborn, J. 1996. Review of William Edgerton. *Memoirs of Peasant Tolstoyans in Soviet Russia* [Online]. Available at: http://www2.h-net.msu.edu/reviews/showrev.php?id=312 [accessed: 21 March 2014].

Shakespeare, W. 1994. *Hamlet* [1603]. Oxford: Oxford University Press.

Torgovnick, M. 1990. *Gone Primitive: Savage Intellects, Modern Lives.* Chicago and London: University of Chicago Press.

Vaughan, L. 1994. *A Study of the Spatial Characteristics of The Jews In London 1695 & 1895.* Unpublished Thesis. London: UCL.

Zangwill, I. 1892. *Children of the Ghetto.* 2nd edition. London: William Heinemann.

IV
SPACE AND THE FORM
OF LIFE WRITING

Chapter 10

Spaces of Intervention:
Hélène Cixous's *Portrait of Jacques Derrida as a Young Jewish Saint*

Frédéric Regard

In traditional philosophy as well as in Lacanian psychoanalysis, the dead return because they have not been properly buried; the return of the dead is thus the symptom of a dysfunctioning in burial rites, and more generally in symbolic practices (Žižek 1991: 23). In order to contain the ensuing disorder, customs must be scrupulously observed. The dead may then rest in peace: dispatched for good this time, they will cease haunting the living, who will then resume their former occupations without having to worry about revenants. Proper burial rites ensure therefore that fundamental differences are restored – between the living and the dead, of course, but also between the here and the beyond, the present and the past, presence and absence. It is precisely this law of differentiation, this ontology of difference, that 'deconstruction' seeks to trouble. Jacques Derrida goes as far as to argue that the contestation of the ontological law of differentiation between the living and the dead is crucial to an understanding of the history of human thought and culture (1994, 1998). In this sense, Derrida's 'philosophy of the limit' (Cornell 1992) is indeed a 'hauntology', in opposition to classical 'ontology', and Colin Davis may convincingly argue that whereas psychoanalysis teaches one to do without ghosts, deconstruction on the contrary teaches one to do *with* ghosts (Davis 2007: 75).

I propose to push such a statement to its most logical conclusion. I suggest that by privileging simultaneity and coexistence over opposition, hierarchy and chronology, by installing a deferral of difference (what Derrida famously called a process of 'différance' [1978]), revenance and spectrality reinstall space as the dominant dimension of living. As a matter of fact, deconstruction may be said to ensure that the dead and the living are summoned on the same stage, to engage in what Derrida calls a 'choreography', that is to say an art of placing and replacing oneself and the other in space, which implies a blurring of individual postures, of gendered identities in particular, as dancing 'can carry, divide, multiply the body of each "individual"' (Derrida 1982: 76). I argue in this chapter that such choreographies do indeed characterise the deconstructionist practice of life writing, be it in the form of biography, autobiography, or literary portraiture, a still undertheorised, neglected subgenre of life writing.

My argument is based on Hélène Cixous's *Portrait of Jacques Derrida as a Young Jewish Saint* (2001), in which the French feminist philosopher and writer sought to explore the queer combination of Judaism and Catholicism in her friend Jacques Derrida's life and work, merging biography and textual commentary, thus overturning binary oppositions and blurring boundaries, in the typically deconstructionist fashion that is the hallmark of this now legendary intellectual couple. What will interest me more particularly is Cixous's use of an archival document, a dead textual body, a corpse-corpus – what I call a 'corpsus'– which should have remained a dead letter, but which Cixous chooses to recall to life in order to offer a portrait of her friend. The text in question is an unpublished draft of Derrida's, a manuscript, which can, as we shall see, be fairly easily identified as being part of his preparatory work for 'Circonfession' (Derrida 1991), Derrida's well-known autobiograhical meditation, appended as an immense footnote to Geoffrey Bennington's own portrait of Derrida, a scholarly, academic portrait of the philosopher (Bennington 1993). This archival document is reproduced only a few pages before the end of *Portrait of Jacques Derrida* (Cixous 2001: 110, 2004: 120, see Plate 2).

Before we can measure the importance of what is at stake here, a detour is in order, to briefly recontextualise Cixous's use of archival documents, and of Derrida's autograph in particular.

Canadian critics Robert Dion and Mahigan Lepage, two foremost specialists of life writing, justly remark that it seems to have been a claim of recent biographical writing that the archive should no longer disappear under the surface of the life narrative, that it should on the contrary be exposed as a central, destabilising point of resistance to hegemonic interpretation. According to Dion and Lepage, the result of such a tendency is that the archive has in fact come to 'dis-lodge' – Dion and Lepage use the French verb *déloger* – both the biographer's work and the archive's traditional function: the archival document, they therefore argue, has ceased to be a simple biographical *object*; it has now acquired the status of a biographical *subject*, 'in replacement of the biographee' (Dion and Lepage 2007: 11–12; my translation).

In deconstructionist terms, the dead body of archival matter, the 'corpsus', seems thus to have recovered a life of its own, with all the indeterminacy and unpredictability of a creature whose revenance causes trouble in the classic ontological order of writing, precipitating some kind of uncanny blurring of the demarcation line traditionally separating the living from the dead, subject from object, present from past, presence from absence. The archival document has now come to thrive on 'the limit', whereby roles are redistributed, places reshuffled, differences made to play again. The moment the archive is disinterred and brought back to full visibility, the 'corpsus' surprisingly gains a life of its own, which turns it into the real subject of life writing. Life writing then no longer consists in translating life, *bios*, through the mediation of writing, *graphein*: it might be argued that in today's most innovative biographies, writing reinstills life into the dead archive, resuscitates an inanimate corpus, resurrects a dead textual body, which it also allows to play the part of a haunting revenant, one that it is impossible to bury away and dispatch for good. The archival document thus concretely materialises the event of revenance; it spatialises it, inviting life writing to become what I, in a tribute to Homi Bhabha's theory of the 'third space', choose to call 'a space of intervention', the space of what takes place half-way between the two sides (Bhabha 1994: 10).

Cixous's art of literary portraiture is particularly emblematic of such 'intervention'. The specificity of her *Portrait* is that even before it presents Derrida's autograph to the reader, it also reads nine excerpts from the French edition of 'Circumfession', to which it again lends both a visual and spatial presence (for one short example see Plate 3, Cixous 2001: 31). It would be too long to give here a translation of Derrida's text, and probably useless too (the English translation does not attempt to do so, for any of Derrida's nine 'periods', which are grouped together in the middle of Cixous's essay, as a central unpaginated batch, positioned between pages 58 and 59). What matters is less to understand what Derrida is actually saying than to see what Cixous is doing to all nine excerpts, which are reproduced in facsimile, but irrespective of their initial order of appearance, and seemingly erratically disseminated in the original French edition (Cixous 2001: 14, 17, 23, 31, 43, 67, 75, 86, 93), not therefore fully integrated into Cixous's central essay. To a certain extent, they come in simply to loosely illustrate the literary portrait of Derrida, as supplements to its main body. *Portrait of Jacques Derrida* puts thus together ten supplements – the nine pages taken from 'Circumfession', culminating in, or crowned by, the unpublished autograph, a spatial layout which strongly suggests that the nine excerpts should not in fact be dissociated from the final autograph: they too acquire archival status the moment they are presented as bearing the marks of Cixous's manuscript, as having been copiously highlighted and annotated by Cixous's own hand, in red, blue or black ink. It should be noted here that even more explicit archival status would later be granted to those documents by

Cixous's remark that adding her heavily annotated draft sheets to the published *Portrait* had certainly not been her idea, but Michel Delorme's, the publishing director of Éditions Galilée, also known as an astute art collector and dealer, with an eye for neglected visual art works (Cixous and Jeannet 2005: 87).

How do Derrida's 'periods', augmented by Cixous's handwritten marginalia – a practice Heather Jackson analyses as the 'literal materialisation of the space of reading and interpretation' (2001: 44) – relate to the rest of the literary portrait? How does the margin relate to the centre? To what extent does the margin, occupied and animated by Cixous's handwriting, materialise the space of intervention? In his analysis of an annotated copy of Kipling's famous Anglo-Indian novel *Kim*, Alexis Tadié shows how one John Cresswell, a British colonist (of whom we know nothing), used marginalia to perform a colonial appropriation of an apparently ideologically neutral description of the Raj (Tadié 2008). Should we read Cixous's annotations as one such colonial reappropriation of Derrida's 'periods'? Or should we not rather consider her marginalia as a truly postcolonial rearrangement, making space for a non-violent way of reading the other's text, thereby inaugurating a 'spectral' relationship between subject and object, self and other, sameness and difference, biographer and biographee, man and woman? Another crucial question deserves to be addressed here: Do the pictures of such archival documents – both Cixous's annotated sheets and Derrida's autograph – take the place of the traditional photographic portraits almost every biography presents to its readers as one of its choicest moments? Or does the use of the image in Cixous's *Portrait* correspond to another logic of supplementarity, another logic of intermedial illustration, one that would here again introduce trouble into the classic text-image relationship of subordination? One final question: What kind of link is to be established between the Cixous archive and the Derrida archive? What takes place between the two? What intervenes?

On the 'period 8' leaf (reproduced as Plate 3), Cixous's hand's work seems to have consisted in highlighting two vowels in Derrida's text, and copying them down in the margins of the published page. The two vowels are a and i, which are, obviously enough, the two vowels to be heard or seen in Derrida's original first name, *Jackie* (not Jacques, chosen as a pen name, to sound more orthodoxically French). But while some a's and i's are clearly both seen and heard in the French text, as in 'veritas' (the Latin for 'truth') or in 'immortalité' ('immortality'), some others can only be seen, not heard, as their pronunciation varies depending on their contextual placing in specific phonemes, as in 'aimais' or in 'commençais' ('loved'; 'started'). Cixous's hand plays therefore a major interventional part here, as it signals to the reader's eyes and ears what would otherwise remain almost invisible and definitely totally inaudible (reading 'ai',

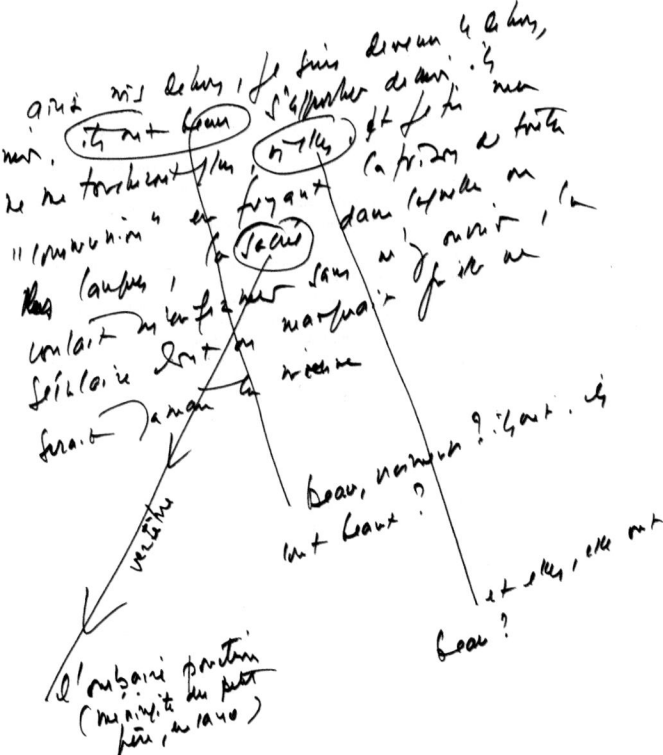

Plate 2 Untitled

Source: Hélène Cixous, Portrait de Jacques Derrida en Jeune Saint Juif, Paris, Éditions Galilée, 2001, p. 110. Reproduced by kind permission of Éditions Galilée

8 Comme si je n'aimais que ta mémoire et confession de moi mais qui serais-je, moi, si je ne commençais et finissais par t'aimer, toi, dans ma langue privée de toi, celle-là même, l'intraduisible, où le bon mot nous laisse à terre, gagnants et perdants comme le jour où une préméditation de l'amour m'avait dicté pour l'immortalité, non, pour la postérité, non, pour la vérité que tu es, *et lex tua ueritas, et ueritas tu*, « n'oublie pas que je t'aurai aimé », me croyant alors assez malin pour éviter le conditionnel en précisant à voix si haute « A 1, bien sûr », Jackie, les voyelles, ma voix de ton nom ou du nom de mon unique sœur, et ne percevant qu'après coup cette avance même ou ce retard par lesquels une haine s'efface en contrebande pour s'échanger avec l'amour de toi, avec le don de moi, *ego uero*

Plate 3   Untitled

Source: Hélène Cixous, Portrait de Jacques Derrida en Jeune Saint Juif, Paris, Éditions Galilée, 2001, p. 31. Reproduced by kind permission of Éditions Galilée

1 Le vocable cru, lui disputer ainsi le cru, comme si d'abord j'aimais à le relancer, et le mot de « relance », le coup de poker n'appartient qu'à ma mère, comme si je tenais à lui pour lui chercher querelle quant à ce que parler cru veut dire, comme si jusqu'au sang je m'acharnais à lui rappeler, car il le sait, *cur confitemur Deo scienti*, ce qui nous est par le cru demandé, le faisant ainsi dans ma langue, l'autre, celle qui depuis toujours me court après, tournant en rond autour de moi, une circonférence qui me lèche d'une flamme et que j'essaie à mon tour de circonvenir, n'ayant jamais aimé que l'impossible, le cru auquel je ne crois pas, et le mot cru laisse affluer en lui par le canal de l'oreille, une veine encore, la foi, la profession de foi ou la confession, la croyance, la crédulité, comme si je tenais à lui pour lui chercher dispute en opposant un écrit naïf, crédule, qui par quelque transfusion immédiate en appelle à la croyance du lecteur autant qu'à la mienne, depuis ce rêve en moi depuis toujours d'une autre langue, d'une langue toute crue, d'un nom à demi fluide aussi, là, comme le sang, et j'entends ricaner, pauvre vieux, t'en prends pas le chemin, c'est pas demain la veille, tu sauras jamais, la surabondance d'une crue

Plate 4   Untitled

Source: Hélène Cixous, Portrait de Jacques Derrida en Jeune Saint Juif, Paris, Éditions Galilée, 2001, p. 43. Reproduced by kind permission of Éditions Galilée

Elle y arrive
A la fin *Elie* *arrive*

16 Elle devient à présent, je suis près d'elle ce 18 juin, ce que toujours elle fut, l'impassibilité d'un temps hors du temps, une mortelle immortelle, trop humaine inhumaine, le dieu muet la bête, une eau dormante au fond désormais apaisé de l'abîme, ce volcan dont je me dis que je me suis bien sorti, *in istam dico uitam mortalem, an mortem uitalem, ? nescio,* elle bouge peu sur son lit, les doigts seulement, elle regarde sans voir, entend à peine et comme « les analyses sont bonnes », qu'elle « mange et dort bien », ce qui lui reste d'avenir, indéfiniment dirait-on car on ne peut plus compter, sur elle ni en quoi que ce soit et c'est donc la vraie vie, sa vie donc rassure et inquiète les autres, les siens, au seul signe d'évolution qui ait encore couleur de désir, d'histoire ou d'événement, autrement dit le sang, s'appelant d'un nom que j'apprends à apprendre, de fond en comble, l'*escarre,* un archipel de volcans rouges et noirâtres, plaies enflammées, croûtes et cratères, des signifiants en puits profonds de plusieurs centimètres, s'ouvrant ici, se fermant là, sur les talons, les hanches et le sacrum, la chair même exhibée en son dedans, plus de secret, plus de peau, mais elle paraît ne pas souffrir, elle ne les voit pas comme moi au moment où l'infirmière dit « ils sont beaux » pour marquer que leur être-à-vif, le caractère encore non nécrosé du tissu laisse espérer une cicatrisation, et j'essaie de la faire parler. « Qu'est-ce que tu me dis ? – Je sais pas. – ... – Quoi ? », ou « Qu'est-ce que tu me racontes ? – Qu'est-ce que je raconte ? – Oui. – Rien », mais elle répond mieux au téléphone, dont le dispositif revient à faire sombrer le monde pour laisser le passage de la voix pure vers le fond de la mémoire, et c'est ainsi qu'il y a peu elle a prononcé mon nom, Jackie, en écho à la phrase de ma sœur qui lui passait l'écouteur, « bonjour Jackie », ce qu'elle n'avait pu faire depuis des mois et ne fera peut-être plus, outre qu'elle sut à peine, au long de sa vie, l'autre nom : « *Élie* : *mon nom – non inscrit, le seul, très abstrait, qui me soit arrivé, que j'ai appris, du dehors, plus tard, et que je n'ai jamais senti, porté, le nom que je ne connais pas, c'est comme un numéro (mais lequel ! matricule allais-je dire en pensant à la plaque de l'Élie mort que porte Marguerite ou au suicide, en 1955, de mon ami Élie Carrive) désignant anonymement le nom caché, et en ce sens, plus que tout autre, c'est le nom donné, que j'ai reçu sans le recevoir là où ce qui est reçu ne doit pas se recevoir, ni donner aucun signe de reconnaissance en échange (le nom, le don), mais dès que j'ai appris, très tard, que c'était mon nom, j'y ai placé, très distraitement, mis de côté, en réserve, une certaine noblesse, un signe d'élection, je suis celui qu'on élit, ceci joint à l'histoire du thaleth blanc (à raconter ailleurs) et à quelques autres signes de bénédiction secrète »* (23 12 76), mon escarre même.

elle
ici *elle*

elle *lit*
ly
elle

el
el

elle
eli *ils*

elle *elé*

Jackie
el

Elie

L I
qu'arrive
Elie !

el
l'hi *le el*

10 Aléa ou arbitraire du point de départ, l'irresponsabilité même direz-vous, l'incapacité où je demeure de répondre de mon nom, de le rendre même à ma mère, reste que je suis ici, maintenant, supposons-le, car jamais je ne pourrai le démontrer, le contre-exemple en série de ce que j'ai jamais pu écrire ou de ce que G. peut en savoir, et la peur qui me tient depuis toujours, car à cela du moins je suis fidèle, se désaccorde, elle se menace depuis deux imminences apparemment contradictoires, celle de l'écrivain qui craint de mourir avant la fin d'une longue phrase, un point c'est tout, sans signer le contre-exemple, et celle du fils qui, redoutant de la voir mourir avant la fin de l'aveu, pour cette confession promise à la mort, tremble donc aussi de partir avant sa mère, cette figure de la survivance absolue dont il a tant parlé, mais aussi celle qui ne pourrait à la lettre le pleurer, ce serait excès de souffrance pour qui a déjà perdu deux fils, l'un avant moi, Paul Moïse, mort en 1929 à moins d'un an, un an avant ma naissance, ce qui dut faire de moi pour elle, pour eux, un précieux mais si vulnérable intrus, un mortel de trop, Élie aimé à la place d'un autre, puis l'autre après moi, Norbert Pinhas, mort à deux ans alors que j'en avais dix, en 1940, sans la moindre image de sa circoncision que pourtant je me rappelle, et je vis alors le premier deuil comme le deuil de ma mère qui ne pourrait donc à la lettre me pleurer, moi le seul remplaçant, me pleurer comme le devront mes fils, alors que mon seul désir reste de donner à lire l'interruption qui de toute façon décidera de la figure même, cette écriture ressemblant à la pauvre chance d'une résurrection provisoire, comme celle qui eut lieu en décembre 1988 quand un coup de téléphone de mon beau-frère me précipita vers le premier avion pour Nice, cravate, costume sombre, *kippa* blanche dans la poche, essayant en vain non seulement de pleurer mais je ne sais plus, de m'empêcher de pleurer, *et fletum frenabam*, de me soustraire à tous les programmes et à toutes les citations, quand l'imprévisible ne manqua pas de se produire, me surprenant absolument mais comme ce qui va de soi, l'inflexible destin, à savoir qu'incapable le soir de me reconnaître et devant au dire des médecins ne survivre que quelques heures, voici qu'au petit matin, à l'instant où, ayant dormi seul chez elle, j'arrivai le premier dans la chambre blanche de la clinique, elle me vit, m'entendit et revint, pour ainsi dire, à elle, comme immortelle, sA en fit aussi l'expérience, il en eut, il en fut le savoir Absolu, sA le raconte, *cito reddita est sensui*, et j'écris entre deux résurrections, la donnée puis la promise, compromise à ce monument presque naturel qui devient à mes yeux une sorte de racine calcinée, le spectacle nu d'une blessure photographiée – l'escarre cautérisée par la lumière de l'écriture, à feu, à sang mais à cendre aussi.

Plate 6   Untitled

Source: Hélène Cixous, Portrait de Jacques Derrida en Jeune Saint Juif, Paris, Éditions Galilée, 2001, p. 17. Reproduced by kind permission of Éditions Galilée

as in 'aimais' or 'commençais', a French reader will not see each vowel per se but immediately perceive that the conjunction of the 'a' and the 'i' are meant to be fused into a single phonetic sound /e/). What emerges from this handiwork is that Derrida's text seems to have been secretly coded by the presence of a's and i's: Cixous's work of manuscripture ensures therefore that each word, read to the letter, is perceived, visually perceived, as a trace of Derrida's name, as if each and every word in his confession contained the visible signature of his self-portrait: the self-portrait of a man of letters, proposing a portrait of himself as a spatial display of letters. Cixous's hand thus prevents the secret, most intimate life of her friend's autobiographical text from being suppressed; she prevents the spatially drawn letters from being muted in the constituted, coagulated author's final published text, underlining how each line is in fact haunted by the revenance of certain key vowels, which her hand helps save from oblivion and invisibility, resuscitating them in the spatial body of the text, while also salvaging them like precious remains as she transfers them to the margins of Derrida's 'period'.

This is not to assume something like a hidden truth in Derrida's autobiographical text, an unconscious confession within the 'Circumfession' – for example the permanence of the mother's voice calling her baby child 'Jackie', a disturbingly alien name (an Americanised version of 'Jacques'), one that also introduces gender trouble through its feminine ending (as in Jackie Kennedy). When Cixous highlights and annotates 'period 1' (see Plate 4, Cixous 2001: 43), her crop of letters, syllables, words or groups of words certainly do not produce a series of reassuring, ontological truths about her friend's identity, be they conscious or unconscious. On the contrary, the written signs she extracts yield a succession of questions which clearly establish that this 'hauntology' of the revenant letter is certainly not meant to recapture the author's intentions or expose his unconscious desires. Nor do they seek to retrace any kind of truth regarding the text's various agencies As a point of fact, the biographee's extremely complex grammar makes the biographer's work of reception and interpretation of the message a very risky, almost impossible operation.

Again, what is actually said in Derrida's original text is of no fundamental importance here. What matters is to see that Cixous, or rather the marginal enunciator, is clearly at a loss to identify the persons referred to by the pronouns given central stage presence in Derrida's text. Her manuscript annotations admit of no possibility for a clear-cut answer as to who is who: 'lui qui?'; 'ma mère? ou Dieu? ou bien lui?' ('who he?'; 'my mother? Or God? Or him?').[1] There is of course no

---

[1]   In the 2004 American edition of *Portrait*, Beverley Bie Brahic chose not to translate Cixous's marginalia. The translations given thoughout this article are therefore mine.

answering such questions since Derrida's grammar is ambiguous enough to make all answers equally plausible. And yet, the secret of the text would not be given to the reader/spectator were it not for the interventional work of Cixous's 'gaze-touch' (Segarra 2004: 34), the work of this eye that is also a hand, and vice versa. Whether made through a computer's processing software or through a felt-tip pen, Cixous's annotations explore the inner recesses of her friend's tongue, to find letters or senses in it which were not perceptible prior to her surgical operation. In other words, he who ran the risk of laying himself bare on the couch of his own 'Circumfession', of allowing himself to be caught and fixed in the deadly typography of a published confession, is quickened by Cixous's annotations, both revived and thrown back into motion, through the magic of his friend's handwriting.

This redefined relationship between text and marginalia is strongly reminiscent, it seems to me, of one of the most potent myths of gender production, which it of course manages to reverse and subvert: in the Sleeping Beauty tales, it is the maid that is reduced to inanimation, made into a beautiful, unmoving object of desire who can only be brought back to animation with the aid of the male Prince Charming. Here, the magic kiss that revives the sleeping beauty is bestowed by a female prince, whose presence is not central, but remains in the outskirts of the male writer's text, whose life and beauty nevertheless depend on what is taking place in the margins. The archive is not therefore presented as a refuse, a dead corpus, used to pay lip service to the biographer's work. The biographer's inscriptions function as reinvigorating kisses, with the traces of red ink as so many lipstick traces.

That is profoundly why Cixous's literary portraiture of her friend – Derrida as the real-life person whose daily life she often shared due to common political agendas, various professional obligations, or simply to frequent friendly telephone calls – is truly deconstructionist: her marginalia do not concern Derrida's life, his natural and social *bios*; they are all made to bear on Derrida's *written* utterances, on his art of the written sign: life here is *gramma*, life writing less a matter of biography than of 'grammatology', a science and practice of the unpredictable written sign. Inevitably, self-writing ends up deferring the revelation of Derrida's self while spacing it by the same token, the two concepts being understandably inseparable in deconstrutionist thinking (see Derrida 1978: 217). But it should be clear that from a deconstructionist point of view, Cixous's inscriptions thus warrant Derrida's survival: paradoxically indeed, self-deferral and self-spacing even grant him a surplus, or supplement of life, as becomes clear in Cixous's treatment of 'period 16' (see Plate 5, Cixous 2001: 15).

The highlighted letters and words in Derrida's text (in blue and red) are transferred to the column of marginalia, but, more importantly, they are gradually taken up to form a line of black ink which, in both the lateral and upper margins of the sheet, seems to offer a manuscript continuation to Derrida's published text, as some kind of 'excrescence' – an abnormal increase, but still a natural outgrowth or appendage. Cixous's handwritten sentences – 'elle y arrive' ('she gets there', or 'she manages to do it', which in French also sounds like 'Elie arrive', that is 'Elie [the French spelling of Eli] is coming'), and 'qu'arrive Elie!' ('may Elie come!',) – both work on the assumption that the name of Derrida's dead friend (by suicide), Elie Carrive (/eli:kari:v/), is the secret key of the confession: the profound, coded meaning of Derrida's autobiography would be a call for and an invocation to Elie, 'qu'arrive Elie' (/kari:veli:/) – a call which can only take place in French, as it is in fact untranslatable: 'Elie Carrive', the friend's full name, will indeed never lend itself to being inverted and transformed into 'qu'arrive Elie', 'may Elie come', in any other language but French, all the more so as this secret homophony also relies on the rather infrequent use of the French subjunctive ('qu'arrive Elie', 'may Elie come'), a stylistic feature that is characteristic of Cixous's own writing according to Derrida (Derrida 2006: 104).

What is made conspicuous here, however, is that Cixous's marginalia do not *introduce* meaning into Derrida's published text, from the outside of the autobiographical 'Circumfession'. To write a literary portrait of Derrida is to use handwritten annotations in such a way that the intervention only makes room for what has always already been *inside* the text: Cixous's marginalia are an intervention, therefore, only to the extent that they give right of way and passage to the 'à dire', the 'yet to say', which Derrida was also keen to capture in Cixous's own writing (Derrida 2006): that which has always already been present within the autobiographical text, in waiting for its subjunctivisation, so to speak. Cixous grants her friend's text a right of passage from death to life by granting it the power of its own subjunctivised call for Elie, by allowing the magic of its own homophonic might to *take place*, literally, that is to say: to find space for expression. Her annotations in the margins materialise and spatialise a taking place which can only happen in language, in the magic space opened up within the French idiom.

The idea that such marginalia could and should be considered marginal to what takes place inside the main text, namely Cixous's more serious portrait of Derrida and her exploration of his queer Judaism, is therefore no longer tenable. The heart of the matter cannot be said to reside in the 'central' essay of Cixous's portrait, which the various archival documents would come merely to 'illustrate'. What I have been suggesting, on the contrary, is that the heart of Cixous's literary portraiture sketches itself first and foremost in the marginalia, which do not therefore come second to the more serious portrait, but constitute its core (from the Latin *cor* and French *cœur*: the heart) – I did not say central – event. This is indeed where Derrida's real-life portrait is to be found, in the space of this cordial or cardiac system, constituted by the ten annotated documents, and in what ties them together. In deconstructionist terms, such documents constitute Derrida's closest likeness or resemblance, and in that sense replace the traditional photographs which biography-readers are keen to find in someone's life. To be more accurate, both Cixous's and Derrida's archives contribute to drawing this likeness of Derrida, Cixous's annotations of her friend's pages functioning as a portrait of Derrida, and Derrida's autograph as a portrait of himself, a self-portrait.

As has already been mentioned, Derrida's autograph (see Plate 2) is quite clearly a draft for 'period 54' of 'Circonfession' (Derrida 1991: 265). The eight handwritten lines – shortened to six in their published version – deal with exile, a historically dated experience caused as much by Derrida's ignorance of Hebrew as a child, as by his exclusion from a French school in Algiers under the government of Pétain. It should be recalled here that the facsimile of this as yet unknown draft is the last 'illustration' in Cixous's portrait, crowning so to speak the gradual movement of disclosure traditionally leading from one photographic portrait to the other (from the child to the adult, for example). Still, although it eventually lifts a veil on Derrida's own handwriting (no longer Cixous's), this last document does not constitute an ultimate revelation. This is not the final portrait of the author which the biographer would like his readers to remember, the true image of the biographee. Instead, this final archival document invites the reader to perceive the similitude, not to say kinship, between the two types of archives (the portrait and the self-portrait, the annotations and the autograph) and more precisely between the two operations of manuscript inscription.

Indeed, if one simply juxtaposes the two documents, one realises that making a distinction between Cixous's and Derrida's marginalia, their respective annotations, is a sheer impossibility: as a point of fact, Derrida's own comments on his text could very easily be replaced by Cixous's, and vice versa. What is suggested, therefore, is that Derrida's autograph simply illustrates how Derrida's autobiographical writing has always already sought to deconstruct itself, to draw a portrait of the autobiographer as a self-divided inscriptor, reading and interpreting his own utterances to the letter, using marginalia not as an afterthought or as a way of improving the initial text at a *later* stage, but as a necessary, *original* 'supplement' to (or spacing of) the text. The work of annotation sketches itself in the very time of writing, as Derrida spaces himself in writing, through his own textual operation, one that is always already perfectly phrased the moment it is couched on paper – there is absolutely no difference between the main text of the handwritten draft and its published version – and yet one that is always already imperfectly formulated, as it is immediately animated, revived, kissed awake, by its own wealth of marginalia, agitated by its own excrescences, disquieted by its own might, haunted by the revenants it itself fosters in the course of its own delivery.

Derrida's marginalia thus suggest that the very process of autobiographical writing constantly spawns unpredictable meanings, the scriptor having no other choice but to question his use of certain French idioms, or the gender-biased grammatical encodings of the French language. For example, as he reads what he has been writing, the word 'sacrée' ('sacred') immediately calls to Derrida's mind a medical term, 'les vertèbres sacrées', 'sacral vertebrae' (French allows thus a pun on 'sacral' and 'sacred'), which in turn reminds the writer of his younger brother's meningitis in 1940. Similarly, the use of the French idiomatic phrase 'ils ont beau' ('however hard they may try') brings about comments on the literal meaning of the words ('to have it good', or 'to be handsome'): 'beau, vraiment? Sont-ils tout beaux?' ('handsome, really? Are they really quite handsome?'); finally the enunciator perceives a contradiction as he keeps the idiomatic phrase 'avoir beau' ('beau' being an adverb but also a masculine adjective, as opposed to the feminine 'belle') even when using feminine pronouns: 'et elles, elles ont beau?' – to write or say 'et elles, elles ont belle' being grammatically impossible in French.

Once again, what matters here is not to follow Derrida's eminently complex, because eminently idiomatic, lines of thought; it is first and foremost to perceive the striking similitude between Cixous's handwritten inscriptions in the margins of Derrida's text and Derrida's annotations of his own text, as if Cixous had simply *replaced* the missing annotations in the final, published text, substituted her hand for Derrida's: as if, therefore, the biographer's role had been to retrieve the biographee's phantom marginalia and offer them a chance to be rearticulated again, although at 'second hand', so to speak. Seen from such a perspective, what characterises the biographer's relation to her biographee is not the temporal distance, or difference, that is normally established between subject and object, but rather the deferral, or spacing, of the difference between subject and object, that is also to say: between here and there, presence and absence.

Hence the general impression one derives from holding the two archives together: the nine portraits of Derrida as annotated text allow something to take place that is very similar to what takes place in Derrida's self-portrait as an autograph. What Cixous's handwriting does in fact is liken itself to Derrida's own handwriting, establishing a form of intimacy or kinship with the other's writing, whereby it manages to meet the other's writing's unconscious expectations and rearticulate its missing supplements. Obeying the same grammatological law, Derrida's and Cixous's marginalia become thus almost interchangeable, the signifiers not of a signified (the real life of the person), but of another set of signifiers, gesturing by the same token towards the possibility of a mutual replacement, between biography and autobiography, biographer and biographee, man and woman.

This contributes to a blurring of the identities of the subjects of the enunciation. Cixous's annotations of 'period 10' (see Plate 6, Cixous 2001: 17), which bears on issues of filiation, kinship and descendance, are emblematic of this. The marginalia give birth here to Cixous's first use of the 'I' ('je') pronoun (in the upper margin): 'reste que je suis, citation' ('remains to be said that I am, quotation'). As is made clear by the term 'citation' ('quotation'), Cixous's utterance explicitly lends itself to being read as a borrowed utterance – and indeed the sentence 'reste que je suis' may be spotted in Derrida's text (third line from top of the page). And yet, whether Cixous's annotation is really a quotation from Derrida's 'period' remains a matter of speculation since we may assume that a native French speaker will not read the annotation as a true quotation: the classic orthographic marks of quotation, inverted commas, are not used, so that the reader is left in a state of uncertainty as to whether the term 'quotation' should definitely be read as an acknowledgment of the annotation's source. To write 'quotation' in full while doing without the traditional markers of citation, especially in a handwritten text – normally the sign of personal signature – blurs the demarcation line that traditionally separates the source from the later utterance, thereby distributing the fixed identities of the subjects of the enunciation. It seems therefore that the 'I' that springs up here is in fact what I have already called an 'excrescence', an utterance that comes as a natural but still abnormal appendage, a surplus of life, a survival of, or supplement to Derrida's utterance. In other words, the 'I' we discover for the first time in the marginalia is *both* Derrida's *and* at the same time Cixous's, the source functioning as both the law of the new utterance and its departure point, both a reminder of irreducible alterity and an object inviting individual reappropriation.

Indeed, evidence of Cixous's reappropriation of the source utterance is to be found in the rest of the sentence: 'reste que je suis, citation, seul remplaçant, reste d'Ester' ('remains to be said that I am, quotation, the only replacement, remainder of Ester'); then in the lower margin, 'à la lettre reste d'Ester, nom des noms à partir' ('to the letter remainder of Ester, the name of names from which'); and finally, in the lateral margin from bottom to top, 'à partir duquel il fait tout descendre de tout des cendres' ('from which he has everything descend makes ashes of') (see Plate 6). In order to understand Cixous's annotations, it is not only necessary to speak French but also to allow the French language to play both anagrammatically and homophonically: Cixous's annotations do indeed rest on the assumption that 'reste' ('remainder') is to be read as an anagram of Ester, Derrida's mother's first name; and that the verb 'descendre' ('to descend') is to be heard as possibly meaning 'des cendres' ('ashes'), which is indeed the case in the French phonetic system. In other words, Cixous's marginal annotations expose the anagrammatic and homophonic magic of the first enunciator's style, which allows the second enunciator to affirm personal, creative reappropriation of the quoted material, and feel therefore entitled to subjectivise herself while at the same speaking in the name of the first enunciator.

To quote the friend's text is not here to establish a difference between two locutors: On Cixous's part, to quote is to recontextualise Derrida's words, not so much to reappropriate them (as I have said so far) as to *incorporate* them into her own marginal inscription, in the mode of a creative reiteration, or of what Derrida would have called 'a graft' (1981: 355). The red ink highlights what takes place in the biographee's text, which is then taken up by the line of black ink in the margins, and transplanted into an utterance which is neither the first locutor's nor the second one's, but a hybrid, resulting from the transplantation of a piece of corpus into the margins where the two utterances yield a mongrel form of enunciative identity. The simple fact that Cixous's utterance finally introduces a masculine third person singular, 'il', 'he' ('il fait tout descendre'), is a clear indication that the first 'I' of her handwritten text was not in fact to be confused with Derrida's, that this first 'I' was already that of Derrida's replacement, of an agency writing in his place, having herself 'descend' from his own inscription.

To conclude, it is now time to return to Dion and Lepage's claim that archives in contemporary biographical writing 'dislodge' both the biographee's archive and the biographer's work. Dion and Lepage refer their readers to the work of another Canadian critic, Frances Fortier, the author of an article devoted to the notion of 'filiation' in biography (2005), in which, drawing her inspiration from 'proxemics' – the science of measurable distances between people as they interact –, she seeks to identify the various kinds of distance between biographer and biographee. Dion and Lepage adopt Fortier's useful categories of possible 'postures' to apply them to the biographer's use of archival material, which leads them to contemplate three major possibilities: the biographer may observe a certain distance from the archive, which is then left to exist in all its opaque materiality; the biographer may start to grant a certain degree of importance and significance to the archive, so that there emerges a tension between what the archive has to say and what the biographer would like it to say; finally, the biographer may wish to use the archive to make it serve his/her own purposes and authorise him/herself through appropriation.

Notwithstanding the immense merits of this approach, it must be said that it does not seem to be suited to deconstructionist literary portraiture. What is the posture implied by Cixous's introduction of marginalia? Is the archive abandoned to its obtuse, uninterpretable materiality? Should we speak of a tension between the archive's potential significance and the biographer's purpose? Is the biographer authorising herself through 'appropriation', making the document speak in the required manner to serve her own intentions? I have in fact already answered all three questions negatively, so that what takes place in the margins of Cixous's *Portrait of Jacques Derrida* is an operation for which there would seem to exist no recorded 'posture'. This is not to say that Dion and Lepage's classification is inoperative or irrelevant, but that one more 'posture' should probably be added to their list: the (im)posture of interventional replacement, whereby a choreography of self and other is inaugurated as the symptom of the profound spectralisation of the relationship linking the biographer to the biographee in deconstructionist writing. Writing a portrait of the other is not here equivalent to a successful ritual of burial: it consists rather in the art of intervening in the friend's writing, to the point of writing in the friend's place. The burial is definitely defective, or more precisely, it needs to prove a failure for the absent or departed friend (Derrida was already seriously ill and would die in 2004) to be offered an opportunity to return, which is to say: to be inscribed back into life. Deconstructionist literary portraiture may then be said to constitute an art of exhuming the dead, or rather of granting them the full dignity of revenants, and nowhere better than in marginalia will such revenants find an appropriate space.

References

Bennington G. and Derrida J. (eds.) 1993. *Jacques Derrida*, translated by G. Bennington. Chicago: The University of Chicago Press, 1993.

Bhabha, H. 1994. *The Location of Culture*. New York: Routledge.

Cixous, H. 2001. *Portrait de Jacques Derrida en jeune saint juif.* Paris: Éditions Galilée.

Cixous, H. 2004. *Portrait of Jacques Derrida as a Young Jewish Saint* [2001], translated by B.B. Brahic. New York: Columbia University Press, 2004.

Cixous, H. and Jeannet, F.-Y. 2005. *Rencontre terrestre*. Paris: Éditions Galilée.

Cornell, D. 1992. *The Philosophy of the Limit*. New York: Routledge.

Davis, C. 2007. *Haunted Subjects: Deconstruction, Psychoanalysis and the Return of the Dead*. Basingstoke: Palgrave Macmillan.

Derrida, J. 1978. Freud and the scene of writing [1967], in *Writing and Difference*, translated by A. Bass. Chicago: The University of Chicago Press, 246–91.

Derrida, J. 1981. *Dissemination* [1972], translated by B. Johnson. Chicago: The University of Chicago Press.

Derrida, J. and McDonald, C.V. 1982. Interview: Choreographies. *Diacritics*, 12(2), 66–76.

Derrida, J. 1991. Circonfession, in *Jacques Derrida*, edited by G. Bennington and J. Derrida. Paris: Seuil.

Derrida, J. 1993. Circumfession: Fifty-nine periods and periphrases, in *Jacques Derrida*, edited by G. Bennington and J. Derrida, translated by G. Bennington. Chicago: The University of Chicago Press, 3–315.

Derrida, J. 1994. *Spectres of Marx: The State of the Debt, the Work of Mourning, and the New International* [1993], translated by P. Kamuf. London: Routledge.

Derrida, J. 1998. *Archive Fever: A Freudian Impression* [1995], translated by E. Prenowitz. Chicago: The University of Chicago Press.

Derrida, J. 2006. *H.C. for Life, That Is to Say ...* [2000], translated, with additional notes, by L. Milesi and S. Herbrechter. Stanford: Stanford University Press.

Dion, R. and Lepage, M. 2007. L'archive du biographe. Usages du document dans la biographie d'écrivain contemporaine. *Protée*, 35(3), 11–21.

Fortier, F. 2005. La biographie d'écrivain comme revendication de filiation: médiatisation, tension, appropriation. *Protée*, 33(3), 51–64.

Jackson, H. J. 2001. *Marginalia: Readers Writing in Books*. New Haven: Yale University Press.

Segarra, M. 2004. *Hélène Cixous y Jacques Derrida: Lengua por venir/langue à venir*. Barcelona: Icaria.

Tadié, A. 2008. A Kipling reader: Modes of appropriation of books in colonial India, in *Moveable Type: Book History in India*, edited by A. Gupta and S. Chakravorty. Delhi: Permanent Black, 79–93.

Žižek, S. 1991. *Looking Awry: An Introduction to Jacques Lacan through Popular Culture*. Cambridge, Massachusets: The MIT Press.

Chapter 11

Strandlines:
Eccentric Stories, Thoroughfare Poetics and the Future of the Archive

Hope Wolf

The Strand is a nice place. I was standing by the Thames which is just off the Strand, and some people came along and said to me: 'Good afternoon, we're looking for London Bridge'. And I said: 'Nobody looks for London Bridge, because it's just a lump of concrete, you're probably looking for Tower Bridge'. And he said: 'Oh, yes I'm Professor something from the University in Harvard'. And he said: 'Can you tell me what side it's on?' And I said: 'It's a bridge, it goes from one side to the other, Professor; have a nice day!'

This hitherto unpublished anecdote was recorded in 2010. It was given in response to the question: 'What do you think about the Strand?' While it might not at first seem to tell us very much about this Central London thoroughfare, it has a great deal to say about the context in which it was related. I begin this chapter with this anecdote because its interpretation brings together some of the main strands of my argument. It shows how life writing both produces spaces and contests those imposed by others. It also demonstrates how the spaces constructed are shaped by the forms of life writing used, and also by the spatial relations between participants. Before elaborating upon these points, a little background on the catalyst for the recording is required. I collected the anecdote as part of my work between 2010 and 2013 on *Strandlines,* an ongoing project organised by academics at King's College London. The principal work of the pilot part of the project, started in 2010, involved the creation of a new archive of life writing. Rather than collecting with a specific temporal period in mind, we focused on a particular place: the Strand and its environs. Residents, workers and visitors were invited to add texts, images, sound recordings and films to a project website (www.strandlines.net). Contributions were also collected at events held at local charity and residential centres. The 'bridge anecdote' (as I will call it in this chapter) was told during a first meeting with a homeless group at The Connection at St-Martin-in-the-Fields.

The anecdote allowed the speaker to contribute to the project without being fully complicit with it. It identified him as someone who would not dutifully answer any question asked of him: he refused to talk about the Strand. Conveying a sense of what was, and what was not, permissible to ask on this occasion and in this place, he was engaged in the production of space. That the anecdote staged the outwitting of a Professor – with there being academics in the room – was significant. In an understated way, the anecdote enabled the speaker to challenge the balance of power. The Professor in the anecdote was self-important, asserting his institutional identity before asking his question, and was ultimately found lacking in commonsense. Exposing the academic questioner within his narrative, the speaker was perhaps indirectly snubbing the academics that wanted to know about his experiences of living and sleeping in the area. The Professor in the anecdote wanted to find a bridge between places; the academics in the room wanted to find a bridge between people. In both cases it was forgotten that bridges have two sides. The speaker may have been suggesting that he should have been given a bridge to the academics too: the exchange had to go both ways. He did not make any of these points directly. Any objections to the demands they made of him were presented only through analogy (the Professor was from Harvard not King's). The anecdote spoke reflectively and critically only once it was interpreted. Like the bridge, it didn't take sides.

The guarded and provisional qualities of the speaker's response gave a sense of how difficult the central aim of the *Strandlines* project, outlined in the initial bid for funding, would be to achieve: 'the facilitation of a sense of community around a place that for many is just a thoroughfare' (Reimer et al. 2010: 2). How the exchange of life stories might lead to the development of 'a sense of community' was not explained. However, the rhetoric of 'sharing' on the homepage of the *Strandlines* website is suggestive: the site is described as 'a place where residents, workers and visitors can engage with one another by sharing stories and images'. In *The Gift*, Marcel Mauss famously wrote that the obligation to give and receive forges a 'bond of alliance and commonality' (2002: 17). Did contributing a story have this effect? The bridge anecdote raised the question of whether the exchange between contributor and collector was sufficiently balanced to establish strong bonds between them. The former might have reasonably asked: 'What will I gain from telling my story?' The people who asked for a story were being paid to do so, and they had their professional reputations to manage. Academics increasingly need to show that their work has relevance outside of the university – or, to use the current jargon, 'impact'. There was also cause to question who would benefit from the establishment of 'a sense of community' on the Strand. Would this be particularly meaningful to homeless individuals who were being encouraged to move from Central London into more permanent residences elsewhere?

The initial aim of the project organisers did not always correlate with contributors' motivations for participating. For some it was the transience of life on the Strand, rather than continuities of people and practices, that attracted them to it. Tom Collins, in a story posted to the website called 'Up in Town' (2010), described the Strand as a 'portal' through which he and his teenage friends once escaped the 'pallid death-thump of suburbia'. *Strandlines* created forums in which individuals could show, directly and obliquely, what they wanted from the Strand, the project, and working and living environments more generally. It provided spaces (digital and physical) in which people could encounter different perspectives on the area, and see it anew (on a group evaluation sheet made at the end of the project one of the contributors wrote: '*Strandlines* offers ways of now seeing the Strand area through new eyes'). Such spaces were hard to find prior to beginning the project. In her 'Story of *Strandlines*' (2010), Director of the project Clare Brant wrote: 'How little we know of the lives that criss-cross ours every day'. An institutional website is an ideologically loaded space for learning about the lives of others, but contributors' sensitivity to this generated life writing that reflected upon social tensions and prompted consideration of alternative venues for exchange.

To establish an archive inclusive of multiple perspectives required a flexible approach to both form and space. It will be noticed that the bridge anecdote did not present anything straightforwardly 'autobiographical'. Containing a joke (possibly adapted from somewhere else), it offered a kind of substitute for personal reflection ('What do *you* think about the Strand?'). The opening line ('The Strand is a nice place') is vague, and potentially, given the context, disingenuous. Participation was possible through a partial fiction. Had we been looking only for more documentary kinds of writing, the anecdote might never have been archived. It might have met with a similar fate had the only space offered for exchange been digital. At The Connection, the audience answered the speaker with laughter: The level of resistance tested by the anecdote, and tested again by the group's response to it, was shown to be permissible, and perhaps desirable (it had given a kind of pleasure). Although the speaker might have opened up a space for conversation by adding his story to the website, the possibility of receiving a response was less likely: Visitors were able to comment on posts, but they rarely did. Given that the website could be viewed by readers anywhere, the weight of reciprocity did not fall on any one person. This is not to idealise face-to-face relations: some preferred to write rather than speak (it gave them greater editorial control). Rather, the observation is made in order to emphasise that the contents of the *Strandlines* archive can be better understood through awareness of the different spatial and formal preferences of participants. Perceptions of distance (spatial, temporal and experiential) between speakers and listeners, readers and writers, influenced both the forms of life writing experimented with and decisions to contribute.

Replacing Non-Places

Writing on the *Strandlines* website, or coming to a meeting, irrespective of what was said, was already to begin constructing spaces and selves. The act of contribution distinguished writers, speakers and photographers from a group against which they defined themselves. The speaker of the bridge anecdote, in that anecdote, was standing still – he was available to people who might ask him for directions. Similarly, he showed a degree of openness to others by coming to the *Strandlines* meeting. One characteristic many of the posts currently on the website have in common is the way in which they construct the author as one who is able to break, or does not have, a routine. Attitudes to time are manifested in the ways in which space is traversed: the author's movements are contrasted with the motion of the 'tide' of people who are unwilling or unable to stop. Papa T, who lives near the Strand, used this 'tide' metaphor in his poem, 'Strolling along the Strand' (2011): 'A look at the clock says it's half past five / Presenting a situation I cannot abide / Walking through a mass of stampeding aliens / When you're going against the tide'. For the project organisers, one of the most difficult tasks was trying to involve people who worked in the Strand's major businesses. Business workers who did engage with the project had a prior professional interest in the history of the area (the archivist at the Savoy Hotel, for instance) or its community (the policemen). While it may be the case that many *Strandlines* contributors literally did have time to spare (some were retired, some unemployed), it is also important to recognise how the homogenisation of workers constituted part of the way in which they distinguished themselves. In Papa T's poem the commuters' movements aligned with national and global conventions: 'half past five' is recognised in many places as the end of the working day. His contrasting use of space and time – he was 'strolling', and not 'stampeding', in the opposite direction – established his identity: a resident, engaged with his immediate surroundings.

It was not only residents who presented themselves as 'going against the tide'. In an interview, policemen John Levy-Cohen and Tony Skidmore described an artist who took pictures of clock faces in the middle of the night, and a driver who stopped his double-decker bus to pick up horse chestnuts from a stall at the side of the road (Wolf 2013). Both individuals broke with conventional working practices, as the policemen left their beat to work with me. In each case the refusal of mechanised living was shown to be beneficial: Art and a good story were created. In some posts, stopping was also found to be enlightening. A post by 'emmakj', a former King's sociology student, illustrates this point. 'Kevin (Charing Cross)' (2011) depicts a meeting at a bus stop between the writer of the story and a teenager about to join the army. It presents a set of confounded expectations: she thought he wanted money, but he wanted to know how to get to King's Cross; she thought he was much older than he was, he thought she was much younger (presumably a comment on their different social backgrounds: 'Where I'm from, it's just drugs and jail', said Kevin). This was ultimately a welcome encounter for emmakj: it helped her to adjust her assumptions, and made apparent to readers that she was studying the right subject at university.

The *Strandlines* archive to this date concentrates the voices of people who are able and willing to make space for an encounter with someone unknown to them, and who are, in some respects, resistant to the rhythms of global capitalism. In this regard the archive could be seen as a means of countering the treatment of the Strand as a 'non-place'. Marc Augé has written that 'the word "non-place" designates two complementary but distinct realities: spaces formed in relation to certain ends (transport, transit, commerce, leisure), and the relations that individuals have with these spaces' (2008: 76). He contrasts the 'anthropological place' with the 'non-place': Where the former 'is formed by individual identities, through complicities of language, local references, the unformulated rules of living know-how', the latter 'creates the shared identity of passengers, customers or Sunday drivers' (81). The individual's experience of the 'non-place' is that of being alone, but at the same time similar to others passing through: 'The space of non-place creates neither singular identity nor relations; only solitude and similitude' (83).

Augé's examples of 'non-places' include 'airports and railway stations, hotel chains, leisure parks, large retail outlets' and 'cable and wireless networks' (64). In some respects the thoroughfare – a means of transporting traffic from one place to another – is a good candidate for an addition to his list. King's student Alex Belsey, in his contribution to the website, 'Friendships and Thoroughfares' (2011), wrote: 'As a pedestrian on the Strand, the predominant feeling is often one of swimming against a tide of people, one of having to anticipate the movements of the onrushing hordes in order to successfully permeate their ranks and emerge unscathed'. His abstraction of the individuals in the crowd ('tide', 'hoard') is reminiscent of the 'similitude' Augé describes. Belsey in the story was, like the visitor of the non-place, '[a]lone but one of many' (Augé 2008: 82). Although he distinguished himself from the crowd ('swimming against the tide'), the individuals that made it up are not said to distinguish him. His 'similitude' with others was broken only by a surprise encounter with someone he knew (a school-friend he had not seen since he was fourteen): 'as I approached, the two of us briefly jostled from side to side, exchanged wary glances, and then calmed in the knowledge that yes, we did recognise one another'. The thoroughfare does not, like the other 'non-places' Augé lists, require that the individual passing through enters into 'contractual relations with it', in the sense of buying a ticket, paying with a bank card, or signing-in (82). However, proof of 'innocence' is indicated, and 'anonymity' earned, by the way in which people behave in that space (82). Belsey drew attention to the speed of the crowd ('onrushing'), and remarked on how he was unable to distinguish the people who made it up (the term 'ranks' is associated with uniformed military).

This is not to suggest that the Strand is a 'non-place'. Rather than thinking of the 'non-place' as an embodied material reality, it can be more usefully understood as a perception of, and way of attending to, space. The Strand is treated as a 'non-place' when it is imagined and navigated as a means to an end: *a* thoroughfare (reproducible and indistinct), not as *this particular* thoroughfare (so, the 'tide' metaphor could be used to describe many congested city spaces). For people who work in particular airports and railway stations, or visit them often, relationships will be formed, 'know-how' developed, and 'local references' amalgamated. To call the Strand a 'non-place' would be to forget the people who live, or spend a considerable amount of time, there. For them, as the *Strandlines* archive makes apparent, the Strand is full of informal ritual and shared memory. In 'I miss Wayne' (2011), Richard Wiltshire, an academic at King's College London, described an insult sparking a long-term connection with a homeless Strand resident: 'For years thereafter we exchanged pleasantries, cash (more a one-way flow) and tales of police harassment (also a one-way flow)'.

If the Strand-used-as-thoroughfare is constructed as a 'non-place', the website on which Strand dwellers' life stories are gathered constitutes, to use Michel Foucault's term, a kind of 'heterotopia'. It can be seen as a 'counter-sit[e]': a space in which the perceived use of the Strand as a 'non-place' is 'represented, contested, and inverted' (1986: 24). What the posts added to the site often seem to be contesting are forces associated with modernity and capitalism, such as homogenisation, speed, efficiency and instrumental productivity. They may also be resisting the instability of what Arjun Appadurai, in *Modernity at Large* (1996), calls the 'ethnoscape'. By this term he means 'the landscape of persons who constitute the shifting world in which we live'; he lists the following examples: 'tourists, immigrants, refugees, exiles, guest workers, and other moving groups and individuals' (33). He reflects upon how 'ethnoscapes' contribute to the production of localities: 'The way in which neighbourhoods are produced and reproduced requires the continuous construction, both practical and discursive, of an ethnoscape (necessarily nonlocal) against which local practices and projects are imagined to take place' (184). Descriptions of the pace and direction of the crowd contextualise and distinguish the individual who seeks to halt the movement of others and develop longer-term connections. Remarks about the downcast eyes of the majority, and the upturned gaze of the individual, act similarly. Richard Davenport-Hines contrasted the two in a 2011 post written in memory of his son Cosmo, a former student at King's: 'He [Cosmo] loved the onrush on the pavements, he loved eye-contact with the one person in a hundred who wasn't hastening by with scared eyes downcast towards their feet'.

Images added to the *Strandlines* website encouraged readers to redirect or refocus their gaze. Artist Luce Choules's project, 'In Search of Flora' (2012), comprised a series of photographs of some of the Strand's smallest residents: the tiny plants growing out of cracks in pavements that often get trampled under foot. Pointing his camera lens at 'Strand Faces' (2011), Classics Professor Michael Trapp invited others to look up. His collection inspired a creative writing group at The Connection to imagine, in their collectively authored poem, 'Time's Eye', the Strand from the perspective of the gargoyles and statues that looked down upon it (submitted by Wolf, 2011). Clare Brant, in her 2010 post 'Count Peter and the Savoy', used history and literature to reimagine the Strand's most lavishly decorated onlooker: the golden statue at the top of the Savoy hotel. She wrote: 'One of the Savoy's famous guests was Oscar Wilde, and the statue of Count Peter reminds me of his story of the Happy Prince'. She constructed a palimpsest of the location, remembering that the Savoy was the site of a medieval peasants' revolt and a hospital for the poor. As a consequence of reading her account, each time I pass the statue a simple but necessary question asserts itself: Why hasn't (as in Oscar Wilde's story) the gold been redistributed? The stories from homeless Strand residents uploaded to the site do not suggest that the Savoy statue sees only riches below him.

In *The Practice of Everyday Life* Michel de Certeau argues that the story 'opens a legitimate *theater* for practical *actions*' (1984: 125). It can do so by setting precedents. Having read and looked at contributions to the website, I now upturn my gaze in the hope of seeing strolling Papa T; remembering the tiny plant life, I walk the Strand with a softer tread; I consider the stony and golden faces that overlook it and wonder what they have seen. These are of course autobiographical reflections. Perhaps they have to be. Those whose appreciation of the Strand was most affected by *Strandlines* may be those who read the contributions most closely. Attempting to facilitate the reading, as well as the writing, of contributions, events were organised where stories could be shared face-to-face. Were I to continue working on the project, I would place greater emphasis on these activities, giving as much time to the making of connections as collections. De Certeau used the rhetorical term 'asyndeton', denoting the omission of conjunctions, to describe the way in which a space is transformed, through the way in which it is traversed, into 'enlarged singularities and separate islands' (1984: 101). The metaphor of islands appeared many times in stories submitted to the site (see, for instance, Michael Caines's poem, 'Your three islands', 2011). Use of this metaphor may have been inspired by the etymology of 'Strand' ('beach'), and by the historic churches stranded in the middle of the busy road. But it also spoke of how the Strand was navigated by those for whom it was only a means to an end. When one student interviewer, Eva Fielder, asked a former college porter, 'What does the Strand mean to you?', he replied: 'King's for me is very fond memories' (EHF 2012). The pattern was repeated in many other interviews: it was the individual buildings where people worked that they wanted to discuss. Encouraging participants to read one another's posts offered a means of connecting the separate islands, and of increasing the visibility of people for whom the Strand was not 'just a thoroughfare'.

Eccentric Stories and Thoroughfare Poetics

The *Strandlines* archive is more accurately read as anticipatory (the stories setting precedents) than as representative. There are voices and spaces that are underrepresented. *Strandlines* contributions typically include an unusual encounter. The characters described are also often eccentric – a term with spatial resonances ('out of the centre'). The anecdote this chapter began with veers off the Strand. Other contributions depict people who veer from a perceived norm in their dress or gestures. The policemen spoke of a man who promenaded a pet ferret, another who walked around in complete riding gear, an artist who blowtorched bubblegum into the pavement and made miniature artworks, and men dressed up in ball gowns for a Gay Pride event (Wolf 2013). Some writers showed that quirkiness on the Strand had a long cultural history. Christine Kenyon Jones (2010) described a menagerie that was housed in a building on the Strand from the 1770s to 1829; she mentioned the story of an elephant who escaped in 1826 and was shot by soldiers from Somerset House. Jane Palm Gold

(2010) uploaded a picture of Joseph Johnson, a nineteenth-century ballad singer who sang with a model of a ship balanced upon his head; he was said to have bowed his head to 'give the appearance of sea-motion'.

This focus on encounters and eccentricity may be a common strategy for humanising an otherwise dehumanising social experience (mechanised and alienated living). Yet without sufficient care over the interpretation of the stories, they may be used to support what they are implicitly resisting. While the more regulated, grinding aspects of Strand life provide a background to more unusual occurrences, they are rarely represented in a sustained or substantial way. Replete with eccentrics and encounters, the stories present a selective portrait of the Strand. Time is foreshortened; connections and excitement occur more frequently than in lived experience. If the virtual Strand and physical Strand are thought to match up, the eccentric character of many of the stories might encourage complacency and complicity with the status quo. The *Strandlines* project might also be seen to participate in the commodification or marketing of the metropolis (see the activities of The Northbank, which includes the Strand in its 'Business Improvement District': www.northbank.org). The lighthearted character of many of the posts can appear to smooth over difficult issues. Stories might amuse with accounts of unusual behaviour, but where does eccentricity end and poor mental health begin? 'Obviously because we are a bit open we do get some odd people', said the Assistant Site Services Manager of one of the King's College buildings, 'I remember we had one lady who used to come in and have a shower in the first basement. And you always knew she was there because she used to sing Abba songs while she was in there' (Saunders 2012). The wish to entertain, accompanied by concerns that the posts were public, may have encouraged the suppression of observances of behaviour that steered too far from the centre: eccentricity tipping into violence. For professional and legal reasons the policemen described only minor deviations from social norms. There were visitors who kept removing the cigarette from Maggi Hambling's Oscar Wilde statue; rickshaw drivers and business workers who took sandwiches from soup kitchens; stall holders who told tourists that the Charing Cross was actually the top of a church sunk into the marshes (Wolf 2013). There were legal bars in the way of contributors offering an account that was truly out of place.

In light of these problems I would suggest that local archiving projects could benefit from experimenting with both the formal taxonomies that frame their collecting efforts, and also with the spaces in which these activities take place. Although digital life story collections have the capacity to be more flexible than paper archives, the terminology of their calls for contributions still encourages the production of older forms of life writing. One term that seems to be particularly in vogue at present is 'story'. It can be found in the titles of projects (for instance, London's 2012 Cultural Olympiad project, 'Stories of the World'), funding calls (the Heritage Lottery Fund 2012 programme, 'All Our Stories'), and academic conferences ('The Story of Memory: New Perspectives on the Relationship Between Storytelling and Memory in the Twenty-First Century', University of Roehampton, 2014). The use of the term 'story', as opposed to 'memory', may be expressive of scepticism about the accuracy of reminiscences. It might also contribute to projects' inclusivity agendas: accuracy, expertise and a 'good memory' are not required; 'everybody has a story to tell' says the *Bristol Stories* website.

According to the *Oxford English Dictionary* a 'story' can be 'real' or 'fictitious' depending on the context. One of the advantages of fiction is that it allows people to discuss difficult memories or point to social tensions indirectly. While distress is generally not explicitly depicted in contributions, its presence can be implied by means of analogy. So, a homeless woman I interviewed, 'Charlie', talked of knitting a nativity scene for a lawyer who worked for a firm near The Temple (an area just off the Strand which includes two of London's Inns of Court). Remembering the Biblical story of Mary and Joseph finding no room in the inn, her story could be read as a bitter comment on there being no room in his Inn (Wolf 2010). Drawing attention to this ironic parallel, she remarked that the only thing she did not knit, as part of the scene, was the stable (so refusing him a representation of what he refused her). One of the most complex images submitted to the project was a 'Sketch Postcard' by a homeless artist called 'thereindeer' (2010). It included a copy of Hans Holbein's illustration of the pilgrim described in Desiderius Erasmus's *In Praise of Folly*. The following words were written around the outside margins: 'Erasmus's pilgrim left his home behind / He went where he can nothing hope to find / This while his wife and children sadly pined'. The largest image on the card was of a sycamore leaf; the artist mentioned on the reverse side that the sycamore tree 'was brought to Britain and follows civilisation'. The card also included a fragmented pun: 'keyword "leaf/leave"'. It is tempting to read this card for autobiographical meanings: the story of how 'thereindeer' became homeless, and his feelings about his current situation and whom he left behind. However, it is significant that this interpretative work was left for readers – it was nowhere stated that 'thereindeer' and 'the pilgrim' were one and the same.

Had the project not allowed for experimentation with form it is unlikely that such voices would have been archived. Contributors were required to choose whether to add a 'story', 'image' or 'video' to the site. The metaphor 'strand' was the term used to describe any contribution ('add a strand!' appears on the home page). 'Strand' not only designated a location but a fluid form of life writing.

Linked with weaving, 'strand', like 'story', had associations with fiction ('to spin a yarn'). It encouraged writers to see their contribution as part of a collective effort, to weave their work together with others. 'Story' was more self-contained. While the term might seem relatively open and inclusive, it can also be seen to encourage the production of the paradigms of unusual encounters and eccentrics mentioned above. Although the *Oxford English Dictionary* offers many definitions of 'story', most include the idea that it denotes a narrative of one or more 'events' or 'incidents' – so not the more monotonous, repetitive aspects of life. According to one definition, stories are told 'in order to amuse or interest'. A 'good story' is 'often, an amusing anecdote', and the latter is defined as: 'The narrative of a detached incident, or of a single event, told as being in itself interesting or striking'.

In *The Practice of Everyday Life* de Certeau identifies 'singular and plural practices' that resist attempts to administer and control behavior in urban spaces (1984: 96). He includes stories amongst them: 'where stories are disappearing … the group or the individual regresses toward the disquieting, fatalistic experience of a formless, indistinct, and nocturnal totality' (123) – the description is similar to how the crowd on the thoroughfare is depicted. The *Strandlines* archive is full of records of 'singular and plural practices', because it is 'singular and plural practices' that are regarded as worth making a story about. For this reason it is necessary to be attentive to what local archives exclude lest the physical site is viewed as a disproportionately open, diverse, creative, fun and even funny place to be. A passage from Virginia Woolf's 1915 *The Voyage Out* was added to the site: 'In the streets of London where beauty goes unregarded, eccentricity must pay the penalty, and it is better not to be very tall, to wear a long blue cloak, or to beat the air with your left hand' (EThornton 2011). Where eccentricity does not find a place in London's conduits for Woolf, it finds a place in her story.

Perhaps to understand what lies outside of the *Strandlines* archive, it is necessary to look at other collections. Although 'strand' was the term used to describe *any* contribution to the *Strandlines* website, textual entries were categorised as 'stories'. A request for a 'story' was unlikely to prompt the kind of response that can be found at the end of *Stranded* (2011), a film made by The Connection Open Cinema. To the question 'Do you consider the Strand your street?', the speaker answered:

> I live on a little ball in a little bubble. I am on the ball. I am in the bubble. This is my home, as in, I live on planet home. Wherever this bit is, if it's living, then it's at home. The place where I live is this little ball. All of this little ball is my home, not any bit of it, all of it. I am only scared of one thing: homelessness. If this little ball can't support my life, I've got a problem, and so have you.

With this poetic fragment the speaker constructed an intimate space for himself: images of the 'little ball' and 'little bubble' are reminiscent of Gaston Bachelard's lyrical descriptions of 'nests', 'shells' and 'corners' in his 1958 study, *The Poetics of Space*. These might be contrasted with contributions to the *Strandlines* website that celebrated public spaces: spaces that surprise, delight and shock. Instead of narrating an exciting and illuminating incident, the speaker in the film dwelled on his general experience of living on the Strand. The form of the passage is expressive of his struggle, and narration itself can be seen to constitute part of the work of survival. With the repetition of 'ball' and 'bubble', 'on' and 'in', he wrapped himself in words. The 'ball' and 'bubble' appear womb-like: 'If this ball can't support my life, I've got a problem'. The closing words are ambiguous: 'so have you' might suggest that the listener was imagined to share in the speaker's suffering (the limited resources of the planet will affect all), however, it might also imply that the speaker would become a problem for the listener if the resources were not shared more equally. That he cycled away, having delivered his pointed last words, gives weight to the latter interpretation. Where *Strandlines* contributions showed their openness to encounters both in the content of their stories, and in the act of contributing a story to a website, the speaker in the film ultimately excluded listeners from his 'little ball'.

Such fragments are important to archive given how they counterbalance stories that give a lighter impression of life on the Strand. They are also significant for the way in which they highlight social tensions between archivists and contributors. To give a further example of this kind of post, 'Covent Garden Shopping Trip' (2011), written by 'Flame', who took part in a class I ran at a local housing estate, is quoted in full below:

> Recently returning from a shopping trip to Tesco, I passed the side of the Opera House laden with shopping & as I turned the corner I was met with a raucous noise & what seemed like a carnival atmosphere, but couldn't see where the noise was coming from. It reminded me of the protest march at the weekend & I just rushed on as all I wanted was home & a cup of tea.

Both in her writing and with her writing Flame kept herself to herself. Like the anecdotist quoted at the beginning of this chapter, she showed herself to be someone who would contribute, but on her own terms. She would not offer anything that might straightforwardly be described as a 'good story'. Her account is 'striking' precisely because she refused to offer anything 'striking'. So doing, she was perhaps negotiating with the institutional representative who was asking something from her. That week the class was exploring the theme of 'protest'.

Flame protested her brief by writing briefly, by not writing about the Strand (she chose a proximate area), and by emphasising her spatial and temporal distance from the subject she was asked to write about.

It may be significant that 'Flame' did not add the story to the website herself. She agreed to have it uploaded. This is revealing of what voices might be currently missing from the archive, and what kinds of life writing the *Strandlines* archive might have lacked, had it remained only a digital project. The contributions that most markedly contested the questions, taxonomies and spaces provided by the project organisers were gathered through face-to-face discussions. If listeners and readers were to be admitted to participants' inner spaces (the 'little ball' and 'bubble'), something needed to be given in return – at the very least, a longer conversation. They had to be willing to compromise and modify the questions posed and the spaces chosen in the light of the exchange. In some cases the contributor had to be able to choose the space in which the story would be told. That the speaker of the 'little bubble' fragment could cycle away may have facilitated the making of a submerged threat. Thresholds – from which speakers could leave quickly and avoid further questions – sometimes functioned as spaces for disclosure. The interview with the homeless woman who knitted the nativity scene was conducted at the Southbank Centre. It was only after the recorders had been switched off, when we were saying goodbye at the revolving doors, that she told me how she had become homeless.

Conclusion: The Future of the Archive

Strandlines is one of many digital archives collecting life writing relating to local places set up in the UK in recent years. There is also a website for the tourist destination and residential area adjacent to the Strand mentioned by 'Flame'. The *Covent Garden Memories* community website 'aims to bring Covent Garden people, both past and present, together to celebrate and share memories of our fascinating area'. The digital in both cases is being used to counter transformations that it contributed to. Digital technologies, making it possible to advertise goods and share ideas with people from different parts of the globe, can be seen to promote both a flattening and diversification of local cultures. That they are being harnessed as part of an attempt to rehabilitate, sustain, or establish the local is perhaps indicative of how far individuals are already thought to be detached from their immediate surroundings. This chapter has drawn attention to some of the problems with these kinds of projects. If, from the outset, they seek to emphasise local distinctiveness, then the archives will underrepresent some of the most grievous aspects of contemporary experience. The archived area tends to appear 'fascinating' – full of eccentrics and exciting encounters. This is why it is important to recognise that the life writing submitted to such sites does not straightforwardly provide documentary representations, but rather constructs counter-sites whereby participants can show others how they think an area could be imagined differently.

It is not only recognition of the ways in which digital and physical sites do not align that could offset the more complicitous characteristics of local archiving projects. I have also emphasised the importance of project organisers being flexible with regard to both the forms of life writing they ask for, and also the spaces for exchange they introduce. Making these points, this chapter has not sought to present a model of how an archive can be rendered comprehensive (if this were even possible). The project would have succeeded on its own terms had the eccentric stories and thoroughfare poetry collected constituted the beginning of conversations that were never archived. The aim has been rather to show how different forms of life writing, and different ways of collecting that life writing, might affect the way in which spaces are constructed, imagined and traversed. *Strandlines*' tagline is: 'Lives on the Strand: past, present and creative'. This chapter has discussed 'creative' uses of analogy and selective representation in life writing contributed to the project between 2010 and 2013. While stories, poems and images archived past and present experiences, the way in which these were shaped orientated them towards that silent term, 'future'.

References

All websites were last accessed 26 August 2014. *Strandlines Digital Community* [Online] is abbreviated as *Strandlines*.

Appadurai, A. 1996. *Modernity at Large: Cultural Dimensions of Globalization*. Minneapolis: University of Minnesota.

Augé, M. 2008. *Non-Places: An Introduction to Supermodernity* [1992], translated by J. Howe. London: Verso.

Bachelard, G. 1994. *The Poetics of Space* [1958], translated by M. Jolas. Boston: Beacon.

Belsey, A. 2011. Friendships and thoroughfares. *Strandlines*. Available at: http://www.strandlines.net/story/friendship-and-thoroughfares.

Brant, C. 2010. The story of *Strandlines*. *Strandlines*. Available at: http://www.strandlines.net/story/story-strandlines.

Brant, C. 2010. Count Peter and the Savoy. *Strandlines*. Available at: http://strandlines.net/story/count-peter-and-savoy.

Bristol Stories. n.d. About. *Bristol Stories* [Online]. Available at: http://www. bristolstories.org/about.

Caines, M. 2011. Your three islands. *Strandlines*. Available at: http://strandlines. net/content/your-three-islands.

Choules, L. 2012. In search of flora. *Guide to Here* [Online]. Available at http:// guidetohere.com/projects/in-search-of-flora.

Collins, T. 2010. Up in town. *Strandlines*. Available at: http://www.strandlines. net/story/town.

Covent Garden Memories. n.d. [home page]. *Covent Garden Memories* [Online]. Available at: http://www.coventgardenmemories.org.uk.

Davenport-Hines, R. 2011. Cosmo's Strand. *Strandlines*. Available at: http:// www.strandlines.net/story/cosmos-strand.

De Certeau, M. 1984. *The Practice of Everyday Life* [1980], translated by S. Rendall. Berkeley: University of California Press.

EHF. 2012. 'It's all showbiz' – Joe May interviewed for the Oral History Project. *Strandlines*. Available at: http://www.strandlines.net/story/its-all-showbiz-joe-may-interviewed-oral-history-project.

emmakj. 2011. Kevin (Charing Cross). *Strandlines*. Available at: http://www. strandlines.net/story/kevin-charing-cross.

EThornton. 2011. Maneuvering the Strand on 'The Voyage Out' (1915). *Strandlines*. Available at: http://strandlines.net/story/maneuvering-strand-voyage-out-1915.

Flame. 2011. Covent Garden shopping trip. *Strandlines*. Available at: http:// www.strandlines.net/story/covent-garden-shopping-trip.

Foucault, M. 1986. Of other spaces [1967 and 1984], translated by J. Miskowiec. *diacritics: a review of contemporary criticism*, 16(1), 22–7.

Kenyon Jones, C. 2010. Exeter 'Change. *Strandlines*. Available at: http://www. strandlines.net/story/exeter-change.

Oxford English Dictionary [Online]. Available at: http://www.oed.com.

Mauss, M. 2002. *The Gift: The Form and Reason for Exchange in Archaic Societies* [1950], translated by W.D. Halls. London and New York: Routledge.

Palm Gold, J. 2010. Joseph Johnson. *Strandlines*. Available at: http://strandlines. net/image/joseph-johnson.

Papa T. 2011. Strolling along the Strand. *Strandlines*. Available at: http://www. strandlines.net/story/strolling-along-strand-0.

Reimer, T. et al. 2010. *Strandlines* Digital Community Project Plan. *National Archives* [Online]. Available at: http://webarchive.nationalarchives. gov.uk/20140702233839/http://www.jisc.ac.uk/media/documents/ programmes/digitisation/strandlinesdigicommunityprojectplanv1.pdf.

Saunders, M. 2012. They transformed the Strand into Piccadilly Circus: Janice Savage, interviewed for the Oral History Project. *Strandlines*. Available at: http://www.strandlines.net/story/they-transformed-quad-piccadilly-circus-janice-savage-interviewed-oral-history-project.

The Connection Open Cinema. 2011. *Stranded* [Online]. Available at: http://vimeo.com/25502531.

thereindeer. 2011. Sketch postcard. *Strandlines*. Available at: http://strandlines.org/story/sketch-postcard.

Trapp, M. 2011. Strand faces. *Strandlines*. Available at: http://www/strandlines.net/image/strand-faces.

Wiltshire, R. 2011. I miss Wayne. *Strandlines*. Available at: http://strandlines.net/story/i-miss-wayne.

Wolf, H. 2010. Knitting under Blackfriars Bridge. *Strandlines*. Available at: http://www.strandlines.net/content/knitting-under-blackfriars-bridgemaking-knitted-nativity-scene-lawyer-temple.

Wolf, H. 2011. Time's eye. *Strandlines*. Available at: http://www.strandlines.net/story/times-eye-first-draft.

Wolf, H. 2013. Policing the Strand. *Strandlines*. Available at: http://www.strandlines.net/story/policing-strand.

Chapter 12
The Columbus of the Near-at-Hand: The Author as Traveller through the Everyday

James Attlee

All writers in some way or another process their experience into words on a page. Life writing is the subject of this collection, and I have been invited to consider the ways in which this relatively new term applies to my own practice, more specifically the way movement through the physical environment operates as a method of generating material in my work. However, as I begin I am very conscious that, as a writer, talking overmuch about what I do is a dangerous pastime. Why dangerous? Because, as the rock musician Neil Young once said, approaching creativity is like exploring a shadow with a flashlight. Pin it down and it's gone (I have no reference for this anecdotally gathered quotation, but like to believe its pithiness gives it veracity). To guard against such demons I am writing this at a place and time so inconvenient and outside my usual routine it cannot possibly become a habit: sitting on a rotting and rain-soaked bench in a small park not far from my front door where two streets meet and cars puff clouds of exhaust as they hit a speed bump, as the setting sun shines straight into my eyes on an afternoon in late October, turning the screen of my laptop into a mirror. A young man's assignation barked into a mobile phone, the feet of children on the pavement running home from school, the greeting from a passing alcoholic on his way to the store, the smell of petrol, sodden wood, leaves and the herbs growing in the brick-edged beds behind me are all there to distract me from my task. Instead they find their way onto the page, become part of the work. In miniature this illustrates a methodology that runs through three writing projects I wish to discuss: two books, *Isolarion: A Different Oxford Journey* and *Nocturne: A Journey in Search of Moonlight*, and a multi-platform project arising out of my time as writer in residence, or Writer on the Train, for the rail operator First Great Western. The first two of these are completed, published, and have taken their place in the global library, while the last is still very much in development.[1] All have involved putting myself physically somewhere else: moving through space, whether locally or internationally, propelled in a variety of ways from walking to high-speed trains.

Thinking about this, trawling back through my notebooks in search of clues as to my own motivation, I came across a quotation I transcribed a decade or so ago, the closing words of a novel by Saul Bellow called *The Adventures of Augie March*:

> Look at me, going everywhere! Why, I am a sort of Columbus of those near-at-hand and believe you can come to them in this immediate terra incognita that spreads out in every gaze. I may well be a flop at this line of endeavor. Columbus too thought he was a flop, probably, when they sent him back in chains. Which didn't prove there was no America. (1953: 617)

This quotation has a talismanic quality for me, and seems to apply to all three of the writing projects of mine I wish to discuss. While the significance of the rest of the novel may have faded, the impact of this paragraph remains as fresh as when I first wrote it out. What is it about this particular fragment that means that its resonance has remained undiminished? First, the idea the narrator of Bellow's novel has of himself as a 'Columbus of those near-at-hand'. A similar notion animated my book *Isolarion*: namely that the people we rub up against in our daily lives, whatever their background, are potentially just as fascinating and worthy of study as any living on the other side of the world. Second, the belief that our immediate surroundings, rendered spectral through over-familiarity, are a *terra incognita* awaiting discovery; and third, that setbacks and partial failures in the attempt to explore and report from the space that 'spreads out in every gaze' are inevitable, and should not be taken as indications of the validity or otherwise of the undertaking. The process of observing and recording is about more than the creation of an end product; instead it is a way of navigating and processing our own lives.

The Columbus comparison has unfortunate imperialist connotations for present-day readers, of course, but in Bellow's defence I believe the kind of conquest he was interested in was different to that of the usual colonial marauder. He was himself a sort of Jewish-Canadian Columbus, a double outsider, the son of refugees who had lost everything when they left St Petersburg; his goal was not the discovery of lost cities or seams of gold, but to turn America itself into his material.

---

1   This chapter was written prior to the publication of James Attlee's *Station to Station: Searching for Stories on the Great Western Line* (2015).

By the time we reach the second decade of the twenty-first century, none of this is very original, of course. Any would-be writer moving through the landscape, especially on foot, is preceded by a bedraggled army, some divisions conducting a countryside campaign in the footsteps of Rousseau, Thoreau and Edward Thomas, while urban units are headed up by the Situationists and their present day descendants. London-based author Iain Sinclair usefully defined writers as falling into one of two camps – the 'peds' or the 'pods': those who are 'naturally accessing material by walking, observing' and those who 'sit within cars, figuratively or actually, and … allow reverie and imagination to play over them in that way' (Barfield 2008). By his definition, I am clearly a 'ped'; pods make me claustrophobic. Thinking about my writing through the prism of the theme of this collection has made me realise how much of it is concerned with space of different kinds, whether physical or psychological: space contested, or passed through; space overlooked and rediscovered; space as an avenue of escape. All three projects begin with a physical representation of a particular territory. With the first book I want to talk about, the story of a journey down one multi-cultural street in my neighbourhood, the clue is right there in the title. I first came across the word *Isolarion* as the name of an exhibition by an artist called Sophie Tottie, staged in Lund in Sweden in 2005. The exhibition publicity online gave an explanation that I quoted as an epigraph at the front of the book: '"Isolarion" is the term for the fifteenth-century maps that describe specific areas in detail, but that do not provide a clarifying overview of how these places are related to each other' (Tottie 1995). I was gripped as much by the word itself – its presence in the world as a sound and as an arrangement of letters on the page – as by its definition: which was as well, as pinning down its meaning proved elusive. You won't find the word in any English dictionary. I know this because a few months before the book was due to be published, I checked – and subsequently panicked: what had I been thinking of, choosing such an obscure and apparently meaningless title? The relationship of artists with language is a notoriously slippery one; I could not help remembering Michael Craig-Martin's *An Oak Tree* in Tate Modern which is actually a glass of water on a shelf, or the pipe that is not a pipe in René Magritte's *The Treachery of Images*. Could I be sure in this case that the artist hadn't made both word and definition up as part of her project? Fortunately for my sanity I managed to contact Sophie Tottie through a mutual acquaintance. It turned out the objects she had been referring to were known as *isolario* (without an 'n') in Italian – she had used a Swedish translation as her title. I began to research isolario. In the fifteenth and sixteenth centuries, I discovered, mapmakers were known as cosmographers – world-writers – which, in an age of constantly-shifting understandings of geographic space, they effectively were. The times they lived in presented them with a professional problem. The world maps that existed had come down to them from the revered classical past. At the same time, explorers were bringing back charts of new territories that lay beyond the borders of these models, apparently contradicting their detail while still unable to provide an overarching framework for a new understanding. Cartographers addressed the problem by collecting individual charts into atlases called isolario in the hope that eventually, through a process of compilation, they would build a picture of the entire world. These fragments, each with its own perspective floating free of a unifying world perspective, nevertheless proved useful in the ongoing quest to exploit world resources. Perhaps the most famous surviving example of an isolario was created by Benedetto Bordone and printed in 1528; it includes images of parts of North and South America and an oval world map, a precursor of the flattened projections we are familiar with today. While some isolario were principally designed for practical use, others were compiled for an educated, aristocratic audience of armchair travellers and contained descriptions of places in the form of sonnets, some of which were real, some imaginary. According to Stefan Jonsson, a typical book of this kind 'might consist of the following: First engraving, Mallorca. Second engraving, Atlantis. Third engraving, Rhodes. Fourth engraving, Island of Giants. Fifth engraving: Babylon. Sixth engraving: England. Seventh engraving: Hell. Eighth engraving: Utopia. Ninth engraving: The Azores. And so on' (2007: 15).

In the twenty-first century it seems to me our challenge is almost the reverse of that facing the cartographers of the fifteenth and sixteenth centuries. Today we have almost too much information about the world. We know when floods kill elderly residents of a town in Kyushu, or a roadside bomb explodes in Afghanistan, as fast if not faster than we hear about something that happens a few streets away in our own town. The paradox of modern life is that with so much information at our fingertips it seems harder to know what's actually going on. I wondered if the way to understand the bigger picture might be, counter-intuitively, to turn our backs on it and look in detail at one place, mapping it thoroughly.

Oxford is a strange city. Arguably it is two cities, but the outside world only hears about one: the university town that has been sold to us in a thousand different ways – in the novels of Evelyn Waugh, Ian Pears, Philip Pullman and George du Maurier; through the *Inspector Morse* series on TV and as window dressing in the Harry Potter films. That version of Oxford attracts around nine and a half million tourists a year from around the world – roughly a million more people than make up the population of Greater London. But there is another story to tell. In the 1920s the population of the city doubled with the influx of workers attracted to the industry on its eastern fringe, notably the car factory founded by William Morris, which by the 1960s had grown into one of the biggest in Europe. I decided to follow the trajectory of the road that connects the university at one end to the Cowley Works, now owned by BMW, at the other, joining two very different poles of attraction that have shaped a substantial proportion of Oxford's population. My hope was that in doing so I could examine many of the factors that shape our urban spaces: immigration, gentrification, pressure on housing stock, local government, and the way different ethnic and faith communities interact.

At one level, my research lay in libraries and online. However, far more important as a means of investigation was getting to know the area as a physical space through walking it repeatedly, placing myself within the territory I had selected and laying myself open to encounters I might have within it. In the introduction to the book I laid out the history of Cowley Road, from its beginnings as a route across the marshland that lay outside the city wall to the old leper hospital at Bartlemas and the village of Cowley that lay beyond. In contrast I tried to capture some of the vibrancy of its current incarnation in a sentence almost as long as the road itself, as if by naming things I could give them physical presence in my text:

Today it is lined with businesses that seem to represent every nation on earth. Among them are Jamaican, Bangladeshi, Indian, Polish, Kurdish, Chinese, French, Italian, Thai, Japanese and African restaurants; sari-shops, cafes, fast-food outlets, electronics stores, a florist, a Ghanaian fishmonger, pubs, bars, three live-music venues, tattoo parlours, betting shops, a Russian supermarket, a community centre, a publisher, the headquarters of an international NGO, musical instrument vendors, butchers (halal and otherwise), three cycle shops, two video-rental stores, post offices, two mosques, three churches, a Chinese herbalist, a pawn shop, a police station, two record shops, two centres of alternative medicine, a 24-hour Tesco, an independent cinema, call centres, three sex shops, numerous grocers, letting agencies, a bingo hall, and a lap-dancing establishment that plies its trade on Sundays.

Why make a journey to the other side of the world when the world has come to you? (Attlee 2007: xv)

Of course, while compiling this exhaustive listing I knew I was making the book particularly susceptible to being rendered inaccurate by the passage of time. However, it was never my intention to write a guidebook; instead I wanted to capture a moment on one side of the world that might resonate on the other, following the dictum of the poet William Carlos Williams that 'the local is the only universal' (1954: 28). However international one's ambition, it is not possible to operate at the local level without attracting notice. During the course of my journey I got drawn in, inevitably perhaps, to local politics. One of the things I liked about the street was the way it flouts the planning regulations that rule the city centre. Asian shopkeepers pile their goods on the pavement and vans pull up throughout the day to deliver boxes of mangoes and sides of meat to the halal butchers. Shopkeepers stand in the street to smoke and talk on mobile phones. A significant proportion of the city's homeless and mentally fragile population is present, attracted by the busy methadone clinic and the plethora of mental health services situated here. All of this, I was to learn, was anathema to those wanting to rebrand the area to make it attractive to the large retail businesses that could afford the business rates charged by the city. Some of this homogenisation of urban space seemed so insensitive I found myself abandoning the role of neutral onlooker and adopting that of a protesting voice.

Another quite separate motivation for exploring the road was to combat a feeling of melancholy, to use an old word, or alienation, a more recent one, engendered by commuting every day to work in London. I had already lived in Oxford for almost a decade when I began working on the book but I didn't feel as though I had truly arrived. The commuter has the unsought privilege of being an outsider in two places at once; even the geography that lies between work and home is blurred by speed. Perhaps my wanderings in my own locality, a territory I sought to reconstruct on the page, might offer a way of overcoming this sense of disconnection:

> For seven years I have been getting up at an unholy hour to travel by train back to London, where I lived for most of my adult life, to work. In many ways I still feel more rooted there than in Oxford. I was used to inhabiting a city abundant in space and spectacle, large enough to lose myself in. A hyper-mobile man, I have to learn to travel more thoughtfully, to slip beneath the surface and explore more deeply. Space is relative. One aim of my pilgrimage will be to connect me to the neighbourhood in which I live. At the same time perhaps my journey will offer clues to a wider reality. Oxford is an untypical city, its centre preserved in aspic for the tourists, its biggest landlord an ancient institution that still owns an inordinate amount of its buildings. Much of the change and diversity in the city has therefore been concentrated into a small area, its visible expression squeezed like toothpaste from a tube along the length of the Cowley Road. Paradoxically it is this place, often overlooked or omitted from the guidebooks, that is a barometer of the health of the nation. It is both unique and

nothing special. It could be any number of streets in your town. For that reason alone
it seems as good a place as any from which to start a journey. (Attlee 2007: xviii)

So I wanted to learn to travel in depth. I took as an inspiration and
metaphorical model the methods of the conceptual artist Francis Alÿs, who
was born in Belgium but lives in Mexico City. Two works in particular seemed
relevant. For the first, *The Collector,* Alÿs constructed a magnetised dog, which
he took for a walk through the streets one night, pulling its simplified metal
body along on a string behind him. For the second, *Magnetic Shoes,* or *Zapatos
Magnéticos*, he strolled through the streets of Havana, Cuba wearing his specially
adapted footwear. You can see videos of both pieces on YouTube. Both, for
me, act as metaphors for the experience of walking through a city – the way
its sights, sounds and smells adhere to us, changing us in the process. On my
own expeditions I was armed with an old-fashioned cassette recorder on which
I could capture the voices of those I met. Even in 2005 such equipment was
wilfully antique, but it had a physicality I liked, its operation depending on the
organisation of magnetised particles on tape.

To travel in depth required me to peel back the layers of the city and take
note of the strange resonances that echo down the centuries. The medieval
miracle-working well, filled in by the Bishop of Lincoln when it was thought
to encourage pagan practices such as dancing and the consumption of ale, that
had a drinking fountain placed on top of it in Victorian times sponsored by a
local brewery. The charity dedicated to rehabilitating those with mental health
problems through providing them with employment that is sited where the
Victorian workhouse once stood. Or the manner in which the city expelled
the Jews at the end of the thirteenth century only to let them back some three
hundred and fifty years later, in time for a man named Jacob the Jew to open
England's first coffee house in 1651; while a few years after the millennium, the
first pool (*Mikvah*) used for ritual purification by orthodox Jewish women to be
built in the city since the middle ages opened a few yards from a mosque serving
the Bangladeshi community. The mosque is situated on the corner of Cowley
Road and Tyndale Street, the latter taking its name from the protestant reformer
William Tyndale who made an early translation of the Bible into English, for
which he was rewarded by being first strangled and then burnt for heresy. An
unremarkable British street, I came to realise through my researches, when
examined closely turns out to be as multi-layered and saturated in different and
overlapping histories as any in Jerusalem or Rome.

The book *Nocturne: A Journey in Search of Moonlight* begins, just as *Isolarion*
did, with a visual representation of space:

Strange indeed are the places that give birth to the ideas that later, for better or worse, find physical form as books. I first encountered my subject lying on my back in a dentist's chair. In an effort to distract the minds of those undergoing treatment, the dentist in question had attached a large photographic poster to the ceiling depicting the earth at night, seen from space. It is to this distant yet familiar world that his patients cast their eyes, sometimes blurred by tears, sometimes pre-naturally sharpened by the effort of ignoring their discomfort. What they learn is that much of the planet we inhabit no longer experiences 'night' as it was once understood. Ever-increasing swathes of it are bathed in artificial light twenty-four hours a day and glitter like amber jewels when observed from the air; only the great deserts and oceans offer large areas of darkness. Those of us who inhabit these regions of eternal day (most of us, in other words) are increasingly cut off from the movements of the silent satellite that controls the tides, linked in the human mind for centuries with love, melancholy and madness. So if you asked what it was that inspired me to write about moonlight I would tell you that it was not the moon at all but *an absence of moon,* as well as of stars, meteorites and the rest of the celestial lightshow rendered spectrally pale today by the intensity of our self-regard. (Attlee 2011: 3)

So the space of *Nocturne* is the abandoned field of the earth at night – a *terra incognita* lying close at hand – specifically when negotiated by the light of the moon. The way this alchemical light can transform space and reveal realities hidden in daylight has been an inspiration to artists and poets, composers and playwrights for countless centuries. This fascination has been displayed throughout history, from the eighth-century Chinese poets Tu Fu and Li Po to Shakespeare's *Midsummer Night's Dream;* from the nineteenth-century paintings of Caspar David Friedrich to contemporary artworks by James Turrell or Katie Paterson; from the seventeenth-century Japanese poet Matsuo Basho to Goethe's *Italian Journey* or Proust's *In Search of Lost Time.*

The first thing I did on deciding to undertake the project was to put the dates of the full moon in my diary and resolve to walk in its light, as well as to visit those places where the moon and moonlight are still important in the culture. The trajectory of my journey took in a trip to Japan for the *Tsukimi* (autumn moon) festival; a lunar eclipse in the snow-covered Welsh hills; and the site in the Arizona desert of The Interstellar Light Collector, a three-story high array of parabolic mirrors used to beam 'concentrated moonlight' onto people in an effort to cure a variety of ailments. At the same time I undertook a parallel journey into art. Depictions of moonlight were in fashion with British collectors of the eighteenth century, who were especially fond of paintings by the Dutch landscape master Aert van der Neer; this must be why the first two paintings exhibited by the young and ambitious Joseph Turner at the Royal Academy were both nocturnes. It wouldn't be because he found night scenes the easiest of subjects – he told his biographer 'moonlights' were the hardest thing of all to paint well. Examining the second of these works, *Moonlight: A Study at Milbank*, painted when Turner was around 22 years old, from a viewpoint on the north bank of the Thames in London near the current position of Tate Britain, the viewer can't help being struck both by how dark the city is before the advent of artificial lighting and how the full moon provides easily sufficient illumination to navigate the river by.

At the end of the nineteenth century the great cities of Europe were still crepuscular. The painter James McNeill Whistler was regularly rowed out on the Thames from the Chelsea shore by the sons of the boatman who in his turn had rowed Turner, to capture the effects of moonlight and fog on the water. As one century gave way to another, Proust could write in *Swann's Way* of the pavements of Paris suddenly glistening as the moon rose; the moon reminds the narrator of his lover's face, 'which had, one day, risen on the horizon of his mind, and since then had shed upon the world the mysterious light in which he saw it bathed' (Proust 1992: 284). During the day, he is the one with elevated social status while she is a humble actress. Moonlight acts as an emotional X-ray, revealing the true nature of their power relationship. The brightly lit twenty-first century version of Paris offers no such opportunity for revelation. Perhaps in response to this shift in human relations with the natural environment, the artist Katie Paterson has collaborated with the Osram lightbulb company to create her *Light bulb to Simulate Moonlight* [sic]. Viewers in a gallery space can withdraw into a closed room, lit only by a single bulb designed to have the same spectral register as moonlight. Collectors purchasing the work are supplied with enough bulbs to guarantee sufficient moonlit hours to last a lifetime.

For some the space opened up by moonlight has more than just emotional resonance. The poetry of Edward Young, when translated into German had a profound impact on a generation of Romantic poets and painters. It speaks of the superior state that lies beyond death, a condition hinted at when seeing the world lit by the light of the moon. This parallel world is embodied in the paintings of Caspar David Friedrich, who specialised in moonlit graveyards, but who also used the moon's forensic light to reveal the gothic ruins and tumuli of an ancient, once-united Germany, conveying a political as well as a spiritual message to his troubled times. The only illustration in my own book is a black and white image of Rudolf Hess, a still from a clandestine film taken while he was incarcerated in Spandau, standing in front of a large lunar map, pointing out the location of the American moon landings. Hess was fascinated with astronomy and space travel from boyhood as well as being well-versed, like most educated men of his generation, in the German Romantic poets – well into his old age he could recite long extracts from Schiller by heart. I argue that his own description of his solo flight to Scotland, recounted in a letter to his wife, charged as it is with the implied terror of being apprehended and shot down, but also with the exaltation of being suspended high in the air as he circles a moonlit loch, is an exposition of the sublime.

My current project also begins with an image of a human projection across space, but this time it is the map of a railway line. For over a decade I commuted five days a week between Oxford and London. This activity changed and shaped my life, in more ways than one. Many people regard the time they spend commuting as lost, the train itself a non-place, a necessary but irksome interlude between home and work. I quickly realised that if I was to keep my sanity I needed to find a use for the time I spent on the train, to regard it as something to be explored rather than merely endured. In this I was inspired by some lines from William Blake's epic poem 'Milton':

> There is a Moment in each Day that Satan cannot find
> Nor can his Watch Fiends find it, but the Industrious find
> This Moment & it multiply, & when once it is found
> It renovates every Moment of the Day if rightly placed (1993: 193)

Blake would have been aware that workers in the factories that grew up during the industrial revolution were slaves of the clock. They could not afford watches themselves and were therefore at the mercy of factory owners – or Watch Fiends – who could manipulate their working hours at will. The life of the commuter, by comparison, is regulated by the timetables of the nation's public transport systems. Perhaps Blake's words could provide me with the tools with which to survive my new life. The space that existed between work and home, despite the fact that I occupied it precisely because of my work commitments, was in fact one in which I was slave to no one; where, if I was 'industrious' in the sense Blake implied, I had the freedom to develop and explore my own projects. By getting accustomed to writing on the train I learnt to write or think anywhere; on park benches, in airports, on the tube, in busy cafes. Of course there were times I needed to be in a library or at a desk, but the moments I stole from my daily routine did indeed renovate the rest of life, just as Blake had promised. The routine my commute imposed and the space it offered proved immensely useful. However, like all commuters I dreamt of a time when I would no longer need to travel every day. How much more productive I imagined I would be if

I was not so exhausted from early rising and late returns, when I no longer had to battle my way through the city rush hour or cope with major disruptions to the system. When the opportunity arose for me to go freelance and work more from home, to my surprise I found myself apparently with less time to write than I had before. This was what prompted me to contact the rail operator First Great Western to explore whether they might be able to offer me some kind of residency. This is what led to my appointment as Writer on the Train.

Initially I experimented by producing a blog, itself called Writer on the Train. One unexpected consequence of this public platform was that I was approached by an academic who suggested I should join him in applying for funding in order to create an app. His idea was that it could use geo-location and smartphone technology to deliver my writing to passengers as they travelled, depending on their location; his role would be to observe the effect this new medium might have on what and how I wrote. This digital project resulted in a prototype that demonstrated a lot of potential, but has not, at the time of writing, reached a stage allowing it to be commercially released. Very new technologies often have something of the makeshift and the unresolved about them, as they attempt to build bridges between two worlds; in this case between a Victorian industrial space and a still-imaginary future in which we are all seamlessly online, all the time, everywhere. In contrast to these researches my exploration of the railway has resulted in a more traditional outcome, in the shape of a commission for a book to be published in 2015 by Guardian Books.[2] Being embedded in the great tides of people who wash in and out of the city each day still seems to me an excellent position for a writer, whether work ends up on a page, a computer screen or a smartphone. Work and travel are inextricably linked; after all, the word travel is derived from the French *travail* (work) and the French word for day, *journée*, hints that each day is itself a journey. *Journée* was also the term used for the mobilisation of the mob in the French Revolution. The crowds of commuters that surge in and out of the great railway stations of our cities are themselves no less revolutionary, part of the huge shift brought about by the combination of new technology and capitalism in the past century and a half. Once again, as in all my projects, my exploration requires me to put myself within the territory, remaining open to the thoughts, impressions and encounters that may follow.

I spoke at the beginning of this piece of the dangers to authors of drilling down too far into their own motivations and working practices. Writing about books already between covers is one thing. Pronouncing publicly about unfinished projects from a bench in a park, half-blinded by the sun, is foolhardy at best;

---

2   See Attlee (2015).

at worst it invites disaster. Writing for new media has brought unaccustomed challenges, both aesthetic and technological, as well as glimpses of exciting new possibilities. By the time these words are printed, the more experimental aspects of the Writer on the Train project may have resulted in tangible outcomes; on the other hand they may remain as ongoing research into territories opening up for literature in the digital age. That's the risk we run. Nevertheless, we are compelled to try. As Augie March tells us, even though Columbus's expedition ended with him being sent home in chains, it didn't prove there was no America.

References

Alÿs, F. 1991–2006. *The Collector*. [Online]. Available at: http://www.francisalys.com/public/collector.html [accessed: 14 September 2014].

Alÿs, F. *Zapatos Magnéticos*. 1994. [Online]. Available at: http://www.francisalys.com/public/zapatos.html [accessed: 14 September 2014].

Attlee, J. 2007. *Isolarion: A Different Oxford Journey*. Chicago: University of Chicago Press.

Attlee, J. 2011. *Nocturne: A Journey in Search of Moonlight*. London: Hamish Hamilton.

Attlee, J. 2012. *Writer on the Train*. [Online]. Available at: http://writeronthetrain.com [accessed: 14 September 2014].

Attlee, J. 2015. *Station to Station: Searching for Stories on the Great Western Line*. London: Guardian Books.

Barfield, S. (ed.) 2008. *Psychogeography: Will Self and Iain Sinclair in Conversation with Kevin Jackson*. [Online]. Available at: http://www.literarylondon.org/london-journal/march2008/sinclair-self.html [accessed: 14 September 2014].

Bellow, S. 1953. *The Adventures of Augie March*. New York: Viking Press.

Blake, W. 1993. Milton [1804], in *Milton a Poem and the Final Illuminated Works*, edited by R. N. Essick and J. Viscomi. London: The William Blake Trust/The Tate Gallery, 9–219.

Jonsson, S. 2007. The thinking eye, in *Sophie Tottie: Fiction is No Joke*, edited by N. Östlind et al. Ostfildern: Hatje Cantz, 9–20.

Proust, M. 1992. *Swann's Way* [1913], translated by S. Moncrieff. London: Chatto & Windus.

Tottie, S. 1995. *Sophie Tottie 'Isolarion'*. [Online]. Available at: http://www.e-flux.com/announcements/sophie-tottie-isolarion [accessed: 14 September 2014].

Williams, W.C. 1954. *Selected Essays*. New York: Random House.

Chapter 13

There's No Space Like Home

Clare Brant

... if I were asked to name the chief benefit of the house, I should say: the house shelters daydreaming, the house protects the dreamer, the house allows one to dream in peace.

Gaston Bachelard, *The Poetics of Space* (1958)

Mixed with the horror, with the kindness of the station-master, with the smell of cinders and the riot of sound, was the raw bitterness of a hope that she might never again in life have to give up so much at such short notice. She heard herself repeat mechanically, yet as if asking it for the first time: 'Poynton's *gone*?'

The man hesitated. 'What can you call it, miss, if it ain't really saved?'

Henry James, *The Spoils of Poynton* (1897)

I

On a dark winter's night in a bookish town, a professor of literature said goodnight to the world and went to bed. A habitual pattern of movement – downstairs, upstairs, bathroom, bedroom, bed – came to rest; with her deerhound comfortably asleep nearby, she turned in, inwards to pillowed sleep.

She woke to thick black smoke, so acrid and oily the air was barely breathable. The room was full of it. *The house is on fire – get out*. She could hear a terrible thunder approaching – *get out. Get Out. GET OUT.* Eyes stinging, throat choking, through the smoke she felt her way down the stairs to where the hall was and the front door – then back up the stairs to get deerhound who had to be led like a horse from a burning stable through terror of smoke and noise, the thump, crackle and leap of flames through a blistered and buckling door – – – –

They got out alive. Just. In the greyest of dawns, the professor could see the wreck that was her house, her home of thirty years. Downstairs was burnt out; upstairs was heavily smoke-damaged. There were great black holes where floor and ceiling had been. Two crews of firemen departed. The ground floor windows were boarded up; the first-floor windows had black eyes. Her neat front garden was an ugly pile of burnt, torn, tangled debris.

What was this crazed space? It had been her home, a castle with a drawbridge wherein she was everything she was besides professor: poet, diver, life writer. It was where she was lover and friend, listener, philosopher, artist. It was where she was most various and yet most herself. Entrance was by invitation only, unless you were an animal, insect or bird.

On this black dawn, the birds had fled.

II

The professor's house – *home* – was unusual in what it held. Full of treasures, quart into pint pot of terrace house. Beautiful things instanced in many arts, including the art of arranging. Books of course, abundantly in every room, and paintings, china, *objets d'art*. Kaleidoscopes, shells, glassworks. Apposite gifts, souvenirs from extensive travels and acquisitions from all sorts of adventures. The professor, an epistolary scholar, kept correspondence. All of it. There were boxes of letters, family photographs, papers of many purposes. The professor was also a life writer: there were everyday journals and journals devoted to life underwater. There were longhand notebooks with researches from archives, awaiting transition to an overdue professorial book. The professor was interested in film and had catholic tastes in music: those lengthy accumulations lived downstairs along with a library of art books. None of this was tidy, though there was an order to things which enabled the professor nearly always to put her hand on anything sought – movements in a space where familiarity was so assured it could be attended by a little forgetting.

All of this was burnt. Some of it was vaporised – *there were songs in the smoke* – and some of it half-remained. The professor's favourite painting, pride of place, was locatable on the wall in the form of a carbonised frame. Through a blackened kitchen in what had been the back garden, home to bluebells in spring, roses in summer, there was a tortuous mountain of remains. The firemen had dragged out what they could. A strew of feathers, as if from fox kill, trailed from what had been a fine chaise-longue which crashed brokenly and burnt across rose bushes. It was hard to say what was most unreal: the displacement, the violence of dislocation, the dismemberment of things ... what was this half-burnt dining room table doing in a flowerbed? Why were these once-handsome books flapping open to the wind and rain? What was this heap of molten burnt twisted jumbled broken blackened mess?

The professor had magical friends and they came to help. The garden had to be cleared, remains from upstairs stuffed filthily into bags and binned. The professor grimly consigned many black sacks to the deep of a skip. *Burial at sea.* She watched with a lump in her throat as a kind strong neighbour took a lump hammer to what was left of her dining table. At the start of that long day, the first skip had been cavernous. Three skips later, the fourth was brim full. *Enough.*

The professor, an atheist, learned of an inner space; it appeared, deeply, where some said soul was. *You are shocked to the core,* said a doctor. Words crossed the space, then vanished. *All my past life is mine no more.* One word stayed: *elegy.* A black spell enveloped her. Toxic smoke filth covered her skin in a pall.

III

Domestic, metaphysical, poetic space emptied. Several people told the professor she was a glass half-full sort of person and would pull through. *Make mine a pint.* But what if you feel full of emptiness? Trauma disorientates: place is unmoored, space drifts. We talk of disorientation, as if east wanders off from its place of sunrise; all compass points revolve uncertainly. The professor's home had been her deep taproot; now a spade had cut through it. She felt utterly lost.

The process of emptying the house – no longer *home*, the house – involved an archaeology in which space and time took turns to sit like crows upon a corpse. Anyone who has cleared a relative's house following a death knows something akin. Buried things came to light. The space of the house changed (emptied, it grew more spacious). The space of loss changed – it absorbed more particulars, which did not reduce a sense of emptiness but peopled it. The professor had a mystical affinity with cardboard boxes and much of her history was stacked in boxes, in places others considered strange. There was a logic: if all this is to hand, you need do nothing with it. It did however mean that layers of boxes unreviewed for several decades now had to be disturbed. This was very disturbing, especially since a large cache of boxes contained life writings associated with others. An over-sharp irony emerged: the professor was now guardian of more life writings by others, particularly one other, than by herself. Self slipped down the cracks between floorboards. *I write therefore I am – ergo, who am I if those writings are burnt?* The professor thought of T.E. Lawrence's immense manuscript left by accident in a taxi ... she thought also of Boswell, a different Boswell who over a third bottle of claret would say to his friends, 'I wrote this great biography of Johnson but it all got burnt ... '

Retreat, sanctuary, inner sanctum – religious imagery for home. The professor found it difficult to have people, even friends, in what had been her bedroom and study. *Retreat in search of sanctuary ... and there is none.* Difficulty expressed itself in being difficult, snappily bad-tempered, for which she was very sorry and unrepentant. *You are in my space*: a violation of that invisible force field, a decorum which by and large keeps people from looking into other people's private space uninvited. *Trespass*. It may be an unconscious part of why estate agents are unpopular: they treat no space as sacred; even when that suits us, we know it is inhuman. And similarly, why we revile traffic wardens, who treat all space under their control as sacred when we know it is not.

Smoke condensed by firemen's steam had made extraordinary patterns on the walls. This artistry of soot was so beautiful, perversely, that the professor photographed it. There was black-on-white patterning of winter tree, forest, feathers; cactus-shaped drip, charcoal abstractions; there was soft drift of smudge; there was stipple and sharp streak. The rooms upstairs had madness, as if vampires had run through with spray cans. *Figure and ground, a confusion*. It was analogous to the confusion between fire self and home self: functional, plain surface had become an aesthetic of distress.

Filth had another aesthetic property: outline. The professor had numerous small treasures; upstairs ones were covered in oily blackness and perhaps recoverable. Small things carried great symbolism, so lengthy hours were devoted to restorations, tender scrubbing, with mixed success. Taking some things from their accustomed place left a stark white shape. Essence in silhouette: square, circle, oval, rectangle. The place of space, indelible.

Some nights the professor went back to the house. She leaned in the porch or sat on the garden doorstep to watch Orion walk across the black sky. Some nights she went around burnt rooms. *I know my way torchless, touchless*. Breathing burnt air, charred smell, nonetheless she took in a sustaining sense of home. It soothed.

IV

Conventions of domestic space change. Take the function of rooms: dining rooms had become garden rooms; people ate, formally informal, in extended kitchens. The professor was told that people these days – *and who are they?* – hid lavatory cisterns behind concealing woodwork. They put refrigerators into cupboards, and dishwasher, washing machine, freezer, waste bin, all behind uniform doors. Everything in a unit, unitary. All this disguise was attended by mistrust of function. Even the coverings acquired disguise: there were soft-close seats for lavatories so that, as one supplier put it, you need never hear again the sound of a lid closing. The professor was astonished. Why banish a lid closing from the soundtrack of domestic life? It denies animal function. 'O Celia shits', she thought. Kitchen apparatus was to be invisible. *Where are pans, pots, spoons, spices? Hidden away.* Since she had last fitted out a house, there were curious evolutions. People now hang doors the other way. *Why?* It was gently explained to her. Bedroom doors used to be hung to open bedwards so anyone in that bed had a moment's grace to arrange themselves into respectability. Now bedroom doors opened unbedwards so as to make a room look bigger. Size is everything. A greed for spaciousness displaces a fear of indecency. We want our spaces to seem bigger. A conspiracy of interiors, mirrors, colours is dedicated to fooling the eye. We want everything bigger. We want everything.

Builders moved into the house – *the house, my home, their site.* Downstairs walls had been taken back to the brickwork. A prop under an internal beam had two new padstones settling in. Padstones: new word. You could see how the rooms were made, brick upon brick, joists nailed, roughly cast mortar. There was something handmade and crafted about it all, which was endearing. But it was dismal, chasm dismal, in the exposure of floorboards where carpet had been, the wrenching out of wood in broken spars. Worse things happen at sea, the professor told herself. People from Syria, in tents – *they fled their homes* – are not even able to return to home ground. People from Bosnia's broken villages return to desecration, bullets, scenes of murder. By way of relief she considered words, architecture of thought. The purpose of padstones is to distribute load onto surrounding bricks which would not otherwise cope with load. *Bricks that cannot cope with load* – as ever, the professor was on home ground in a turn to metaphor. *Coping stone.*

Why do we talk of chimney-breast? What maternal gift, what infantile suck, do we latch on to in fire? The professor became newly attentive to the presence of fire, pondering the resurgence of it in wood-burning stoves, which almost all her friends had installed. Why this desire for fire? What Zoroastrian tendency, what Promethean fascination, holds us still in thrall? Why do we worship live fire when we have central heating? For two, three generations, living space had been organised around a different focal point: the television. Hearth co-existed with it. Then digital evolution liberated viewing into mobile space, just as the fixed working point of desktop computer became laptop, transportable around the house. The fireplace – *place of fire* – never went away. It was out in the open now – not as open fire but as fire in a box or a flame on fake coals. *An open secret.*

James Krasner proposes that domestic space is a concept realised through movement:

> While the home is both a cultural formulation and a building, it is, more than either
> of these, a cluster of tactile sensations and bodily positions that form the somatic
> groundwork through which we experience its emotional sustenance. If we focus more

> on motion and location in domestic space rather than on geometric or spectacular function, domesticity ultimately becomes contiguous with the body's sensorium. Embodied identity at home cannot be defined by a clear edge or reduced to figure/ground distinctions; rather, it must take into account the body's intimate and dynamic engagement with the home's resonantly familiar materiality. The home ... emerges as a bodily operation rather than an architectural structure. (2010: 5)

Although Krasner suggests that tactile relations between body and home are most evident when one or other or both is at risk, he focuses more on risk to body than to home. Your home may be at risk from fire, from flood, from extreme weather, acts of war and acts of God; it is also at risk from small print. *Your home may be at risk if you do not keep up repayments.* Your home, asset and liability, is resonantly defamiliarised by disaster. *Burnt home.*

While the meaning and practice of home is created through body and movement, as Krasner explores, it is also created through constructions in language. Home is a padstone word: it bears extra weight. The professor loved words and was a devotee of etymologies – *etymological dictionary, friend since youth, burnt.* Why home country, home ground, home guard, home front, homeland security? Why institutions as homes, as in nursing home, foster home, retirement home, dogs' home or rehoming? Why homesickness, home page, home key?

If you look up any word online in the OED, you start on a page with a title that says 'HOME: Oxford English Dictionary'. That word, 'HOME', is undefined unless you look it up and find 'home page', whose first use is 1993. There are dozens of home-associated words and their timings are interesting. Thus 'homesick' is first used in English in 1748, where it appears in a hymn as 'homesick-feelingly', a translation from the German 'seiten-heimweh-fühlerlich'. Eight years later appears 'homesickness', again with a nod to German via the Swiss scholar Johann Jakob Scheuchzer, who gave it a pathology (mountain people imbibed fine air with an effluvia which got squashed in them when they descended to valleys where they felt ill). 'Home help' appears in 1883, a little after 'home wrecker' in 1878. The lexicon of home words is a history of ideas. The professor marvelled.

The professor moved into a generously-offered space which included a top floor room from where she could see her home – *home ground, how comforting* – from a house that was someone else's home. Deerhound could not manage to climb the alpine-steep stairs; only ground floor space could be shared. *More loss.* Understanding new space had to be learnt. How streetlight falls through the curtains at night. How water from the tap splashes. How to stack the dishwasher. Where dog lead, dog bowl, dog food is to be left. How cushions sit on sofa. Small accretions of things-in-space became a new mosaic of movement. The professor tried hard to be a good house guest and follow the tolerant script of her very kind host. *Do it this way.* Her habit of piling things crept into corners. *Don't do it this way.*

V

It was assumed by nearly everyone that reconstruction would be cheering. *Rebuild house, rebuild me.* All those *re*lated words – repair, renew, regenerate. The professor thought about starfish who can regenerate new limbs from bodies so damaged there is barely a sliver of disc. Underwater in her old life she had seen such regenerates, stumpy and aspirant. She thought too about salamanders. Symbolism crashed as the builders moved through the house. It turned out that various conveniences were illegal. You cannot have this put back as it was, said the builders, nor this, nor that. The professor was aghast. It was by now a minor matter to have yet more change forced on her where she had relied on continuity. What you do in your own home is subject to legislation decreed by the European Union. An Englishman's home is his castle and there must be 650 mm between a water source and an electrical point; the castle's bathroom is zoned and only zone-specific lighting permitted. The professor, normally pro-Europe, proposed various dodges. The builders were immoveable. Eurolaw requires extractors to be fitted. Extractor? said the professor – why can't you just open a window?

The unreason of such requirements was very provoking. If we associate freedom with space, law constricts, and here was law to constrict freedom in space. The professor took a deep breath, as if on a deep dive. *All my past life is mine no more.* Other movements are required, compelled – *by law.* No wonder we talk of protest *movements.*

After the builders had finished for the day, the professor slipped home – child's howl, *I want to go home.* Krasner glosses it thus:

> Grief, memory loss, psychological disorders, and disease all reveal the tactile aspects of our intimate, embodied relations with our loved ones, caregivers, pets, and prized objects. Physical and psychological dysfunction threatens the graceful motion of the body through the home, reorganizing the boundaries and valuations of its spaces, to threaten both body and domestic order. (2010: 2)

Moving half-purposefully became loose choreography of grace. There was homework – *home*work – to do in sourcing fixtures and fittings, an interminable tedious process. Doors, windows, coving, tiles, taps, basins, floors ... there was now no inch of home space of which the professor was not fully cognisant and conscious. Wandering included getting to know the many trades which went into each inch – carpenter, plasterer, electrician ... and wandering also restored some sense of touch, a touch repossessively personal. Self-possession and home – *hurt, burnt* – in ghost's light touch.

Gaston Bachelard proposes that movement underlies the poetics of space: 'the word habit is too worn a word to express this passionate liaison of our bodies, which do not forget, with an unforgettable house' (1958: 15). He locates unforgettability in an *ur*-house, the house we were born in. That's pushing it, thought the professor, who had been born in a nursing home in quite another country and who had lost count of how many houses she had passed through since infancy. *Until this house, home.* Bachelard outlines a psychological space premised on lived-in domestic space:

> Of course, thanks to the house, a great many of our memories are housed, and if the house is a bit elaborate, if it has a cellar and a garret, nooks and corridors, our memories have refuges that are all the more clearly delineated. All our lives we come back to them in our daydreams. A psychoanalyst should, therefore, turn his attention to this simple localization of our memories. I should like to give the name of topoanalysis to this auxiliary of psychoanalysis. Topoanalysis, then would be the systematic psychological study of the sites of our intimate lives. (1958: 8)

Bachelard's model begs questions – for a start, is not his house modelled on a historically and culturally specific type of property? Yet he understands movement – 'we come back'. A house that is a home has comings and goings.

Let us take Bachelard more metaphorically. What is born in you when you think of a house as home? There is a hefty politics in Britain to home ownership, a phrase that accomplishes dreamwork by its conversion of house to home. The dream of owning your own home was a key policy of Thatcherism in the 1980s and is still a popular metonym for class mobility and autonomy. What if the house returned to was a house of adult choice? A dream of refuge realised in ownership? Houses are bought, homes are repossessed: mortgage companies deal in the slippery distinction. House purchasers become home buyers through a creation of psychoanalytic capital which disappears in transfer. In tackling the rebuild of her home the professor was very aware it was not her dream home, either past or future. The dagger-sharp end of loss was expressed in Bachelard's present tense: 'the house shelters daydreaming, the house protects the dreamer, the house allows one to dream in peace' (1958: 6). Whilst it had capaciously stored meanings from her past and cheerfully housed her hopes of future, it had been as present tense as heart beat. *Tick tock this is why clocks are at home*. What now? Would she ever put her hand on a door and not feel fire's terrible heat behind it? *As safe as houses. Or not*. What if your house turned into a nightmare? Horror films may prove Bachelard's model, in that many horror films involve the mutation of home space into nightmare place where owner or occupier is not sheltered and protected but attacked. Hammer *House* of Horror ... vampire tracery of soot.

VI

Krasner proposes domestic space as a site of self-spreading: 'our domestic lives tend to materialize and externalize our subjectivity in tangible self-representations and material engagements' (Krasner 2010: 5). We have things. Theburninghouse.com is an art project by Foster Huntington which arranges attachments into photographs of preternatural neatness. He asks: 'If your house was burning, what would you take with you? It's a conflict between what's practical, valuable and sentimental. What you would take reflects your interests, background and priorities. Think of it as an interview condensed into one question' (2011). The professor was not impressed by this. *You don't get to choose*. Violent dispossession of possessions, the actuality, features much in online forums for people who have experienced house fires: survivors, self-styled, of what one blogger refers to as 'the HELL that is losing your home in a fire' (Linville 2013: 2 February). The subtitle of this blog, 'Redefining Home', gestures to a process involving memory, language, materiality and space. One piece of advice the blogger offers is Inventory your Home:

> Even if you don't create an entire list of everything you own, take pictures and store online. Take a picture of each room, open drawers, document your clothes/shoes/jewelry. And please please take pictures of your garage and attic. It was far easier to recall the items I passed every day. It was not so easy (read: impossible) to figure out what was in the boxes in the garage. Insurance cannot compensate you for things you don't remember you had. (Linville 2011: 2 November)

The professor pondered. *I own therefore I am*. Professional declutterers, a class of persons the professor considered bizarre, recommend taking pictures of belongings before casting things away. A photograph thus becomes a sign of possession, substituting for an act of possession, or, for declutterers, an act of dispossession. That determines existence in purely visual terms, thought the professor: does not touch feel just as important in determining what a thing is? And smell? In the months after the fire, she came to think touch was more important than she had realised. For instance, how an empty space frustrates touch. *The not there of there.* And sound: the squeak of a floorboard, creaks of the stairs ... *gone*.

The life-after-fire bloggers point to language as an aggravator of trauma. Platitudes of 'well at least you're ok' (when you are not) and 'it's just stuff' (but it is very personal stuff) add to distress by denying distress (Linville 2010). One post discusses how best to help, practically, after a fire:

> After the first week, I started asking: 'what do you miss most?' I got some rather surprising answers: my Beatles albums collections, my legos, my cookbooks, and one teenager even said she missed her alarm clock! The gentleman who lost his wife in the fire asked for a pair of nice shoes to wear to her funeral. Perhaps we should ask ourselves, 'What would I miss most?' (Linville 2010: 5 April)

What would you miss most?

VII

Three weeks after the fire, an insurance company sent a loss adjuster to see the professor. Loss adjuster, thought the professor: *how can you adjust my loss, adjust me to loss*? He arrived with an air of intelligence hardened by long experience of flood, fire and fraudsters. When he saw the wreckage and the evidently pale professor, he expressed some sympathy. His parents were professors, he said, and he knew from his mother that some were unworldly enough not to insure possessions for their proper value. Not just professors, of course, and things of value to professors – *half my research is burnt, archives, longhand notes, writer's journals* – had anyway a value that did not figure in insurance. Ok, he said, tell me what was here. The professor took a deep breath. *How mad this is: I am describing things not here, phantoms, ghost objects*. There was also a sinister script: the loss adjuster was being paid to assess what least sum could be given; every missing object had to be given a monetary value. The professor pointed out that you could hardly know the current cost of possessions because living with old ones meant you didn't buy new ones. Have a guess, said the loss adjuster, with a slippery actuarial smile.

So they went round the house, room by room. The professor pointed her rescued torch – *my diving torch, lighting up the ribs of wreck* – at black holes, burnt spaces, charred remains, so the stranger – *in my home* – could inspect for himself the variously material proofs of her words. On this shelf was ... item by item, place by place, space by space. Three hours later, they were in the garden. Here, said the professor, by now drunk with the grief of description, mad with the irony of writing in air a life that was no more, here is corroboration: this half-burnt book, this blackened chair leg, this charred pot.

I like your stuff, said the loss adjuster.

VIII

How do you acquire a taste for things? A taste for things you think fine? The professor had learnt a great deal from one of the finest people in the universe, and many of the things in her household had come by way of that person. Thus things attached her to sentiments. In describing objects, what she dispassionately omitted from their descriptions was that passionate meaning in things which was intrinsically and permanently a large part of their value. *This was given to me by. I found this with.* Little narratives of acquisition, short stories, were attached to things. She kept some things she did not like aesthetically because she loved the givers. What we mean by sentimental value is also a valuing of sentiment itself. Things attach us to sentiments. Little narratives contained keys, musical tools to reconnect things to people, places, events, times, wet afternoons of excellent company, midnight revels, dawn revelations, flea markets and auctions, birthdays and second-hand bookshops, chance discoveries, off-road travels, encounters, human conversations. Things grew into things that belonged, expressions of self, adornments of nest. The professor was not so much owner as custodian. Their destruction by fire destroyed her as their guardian.

> When you've lived as long as I you'll see that every human being has his shell and that you must take the shell into account. By the shell I mean the whole envelope of circumstances. There's no such thing as an isolated man or woman: we're each of us made up of some cluster of appurtenances. What shall we call our 'self'? Where does it begin? Where does it end? It overflows into everything that belongs to us – and then it flows back again.

So says Madame Merle in Henry James's *Portrait of a Lady*. She elaborates:

> I know a large part of myself is in the clothes I choose to wear. I've a great respect for *things*! One's self – for other people – is one's expression of one's self; and one's house, one's furniture, one's garments, the books one reads, the company one keeps – these things are all expressive. (James 1978: 201)

Consumerism constantly pressurises us to buy things for domestic space. The psychodynamics of capitalism, however, do not make appurtenances a straightforward means of self-expression: self must express in relation to social. Norms, expectations, fashions shape consumption. Somewhere around 1960 there emerged the term lifestyle. The OED quotes *The Guardian*, 22 March 1961: 'The mass-media ... continually tell their audience what life-styles are "modern" and "smart"'. The professor was certainly not immune to ideological blandishments – *who is?* – but her tastes were formed with little reference to mass media. One of her favourite children's books – *burnt* – was Kenneth Grahame's *The Wind in the Willows*. It can be read as a story all about homes (as in Smyth 2006), which begins with a Mole spring-cleaning his home and ends with a Toad restored to his ancestral home, Toad Hall. Section V is titled Dulce Domum. What would Bachelard make of that? Mole has been staying with his amiable friend Rat. On the road, Mole catches the scent of his home and becomes desperate to return to it:

> Now, with a rush of old memories, how clearly it stood up before him, in the darkness! Shabby indeed, and small and poorly furnished, and yet his, the home he had made for himself, the home he had been so happy to get back to after his day's work. And the home had been happy with him, too, evidently, and was missing him, and wanted him back, and was telling him so, through his nose, sorrowfully, reproachfully, but with no bitterness or anger; only with plaintive reminder that it was there, and wanted him. (Grahame 1908: 98–9)

With a great effort Mole accompanies Rat back to his house, but sobs overcome him. Finally he explains: 'everything came back to me with a rush – and I *wanted* it! – O dear, O dear! – and when you *wouldn't* turn back, Ratty – and I had to leave it, though I was smelling it all the time – I thought my heart would break' (1908: 102).

What Mole *wants* is not possession but occupation, occupation with the presence of possessions. Appurtenances abstract themselves into the space of home, a concept so powerful that body and language combine to make an eloquent instinct. Space becomes meaningful even when shabby, small and poorly furnished. It reciprocates projection. *It was there, and wanted him.* The ever-amiable Rat proposes they go at once to Mole's home. They arrive to find all as it was, outside and in:

> Then, while the Rat busied himself fetching plates, and knives and forks, and mustard which he mixed in an egg-cup, the Mole, his bosom still heaving with the stress of his

recent emotion, related – somewhat shyly at first, but with more freedom as he warmed to his subject – how this was planned, and how that was thought out, and how this was got through a windfall from an aunt, and that was a wonderful find and a bargain, and this other thing was bought out of laborious savings and a certain amount of 'going without'.

Little stories, attachment to sentiment through things. Life in the key of home.

His spirits finally quite restored, he must needs go and caress his possessions, and take a lamp and show off their points to his visitor and expatiate on them, quite forgetful of the supper they both so much needed; Rat, who was desperately hungry but strove to conceal it, nodding seriously, examining with a puckered brow, and saying, 'wonderful', and 'most remarkable', at intervals, when the chance for an observation was given him. (Grahame 1908: 110)

In recognising the power of appurtenances, the kind Rat makes home a place of interaction and a space of emotional values. Mole's stuff is not just objects but things animated by sentiment. Animation, moreover, is contextualised by space itself appurtenative. It is striking how space features in the description of the forecourt to Mole's house. By one side of the door is a roller:

On the walls hung wire baskets with ferns in them, alternating with brackets carrying plaster statuary – Garibaldi, and the infant Samuel, and Queen Victoria, and other heroes of modern Italy. Down on one side of the forecourt ran a skittle-alley, with benches along it and little wooden tables marked with rings that hinted at beer-mugs. In the middle was a small round pond containing gold-fish and surrounded by a cockle-shell border. Out of the centre of the pond rose a fanciful erection clothed in more cockle-shells and topped by a large silvered glass ball that reflected everything all wrong and had a very pleasing effect. (Grahame 1908: 106)

Amusing – *a Mole an admirer of the Risorgimento!* – and charming, the description answers Madame Merle's question – *Where does it begin? Where does it end?* – by its movements around space, its indication of flow via narrative. There are ideological affinities; a taste for pleasures; a taste for ornament; artistic tendency. There's a visual pattern too, of straight lines and curves. There are different shapes, moulded, flat, spherical. The topography is clear: side, middle, centre. It also treats space as revelatory. *Might there be a bust of Garibaldi underneath every molehill ... ?* What is impossible in underground space is possible in the space of fantasy. It is possibly what defines home – *Redefining Home* – that home is a place where fantasy may live most comfortably, may be at home. 'I dwell in possibility' (1970: 327), as Emily Dickinson puts it in her 657 poem which represents writing poetry as an undomesticated space within a domestic space.

IX

In Henry James's short novel *The Spoils of Poynton* (first published under the title *The Old Things* as a serial in 1896 and then as a book in 1897), a woman devoted to the exquisite contents of her grand home is first compelled to give them up, then gets them back again in a smaller house, then dispossesses herself of them in the hope that her son will marry not Mona, the woman who wants them, but Fleda, the woman who appreciates them but also values her son. Half way through, Fleda, a subtle and complicated character, thinks she has lost the man she loves and the beautiful house. She reflects:

> ... her love had gathered in the spoils. She wanted indeed no catalogue to count them over; the array of them, miles away, was complete; each piece, in its turn, was perfect to her; she could have drawn up a catalogue from memory. Thus again she lived with them, and she thought of them without a question of any personal right. That they might have been, that they might still be hers, that they were at all – too proud, unlike base animals and humans, to be reducible to anything so narrow. (James 1897: 170)

Where declutterers propose substitute possession through photographs, Henry James suggests an immaterial actualising free from possessiveness. The idea of appurtenances in its medieval original was '[a] thing that belongs to another, a "belonging"; a minor property, right, or privilege, belonging to another more important, and passing in possession with it' (OED). The idea of passing on changes the concept of possession: you do not own a thing. You are in temporary possession of it, a guardian or custodian; you preserve rather than possess. In conserving it, you may confer meaning and value upon it and it may confer meaning and value upon you but, like the sense of home, it is a cultural capital that will transmute upon passing into the hands of another. Being too conscious of conferral may enjoin a spoiling: hence the *spoils* of Poynton alludes wittily to material goods and to the corrupting effect of material goods upon their temporary possessors if emotional investment in those goods exceeds what is good for social functioning. *I like your stuff*: if admiration becomes envy, possessiveness clogs relationships. Fleda is a heroine because her profound admiration of other people's things does not drive her relationships with those other people.

Fleda visits Mrs Gareth, the creator of Poynton's exquisiteness, who is now relegated to a cottage. Mrs Gareth has brought out the cottage's original furniture which belonged to a maiden aunt. Fleda acclaims its effect as just as lovely, indeed lovelier, because it manifested 'the impression, somehow, of something dreamed and missed, something reduced, relinquished, resigned: the poetry, as it were, of something sensibly *gone* ... It's a kind of fourth dimension. It's a presence, a perfume, a touch. It's a soul, a story, a life' (James 1897: 180). Adjusting aesthetics to accommodate loss – *how do you do this with burnt things?* – Fleda and the redoubtable Mrs Gareth live on at Ricks. Then Owen, Mrs Gareth's now-married son, writes to Fleda, who still loves him. He offers Fleda the gem of the collection from Poynton: whatever she wishes, her choice. It is an act of love, or so she interprets it. She considers the offer at length, then travels down to Poynton. It is a wild December night, stormy and ominous. With the smell of smoke. Poynton is burning down. *On fire.*

> Mixed with the horror, with the kindness of the station-master, with the smell of cinders and the riot of sound, was the raw bitterness of a hope that she might never again in life have to give up so much at such short notice. She heard herself repeat mechanically, yet as if asking it for the first time: 'Poynton's *gone?*'
>
> The man hesitated. 'What can you call it, miss, if it ain't really saved?'
>
> (James 1897: 192)

X

The professor observed how many literary classics closed with fire. Charlotte Brontë's *Jane Eyre* and Daphne du Maurier's *Rebecca* both end with conflagrations in which a fact of material loss is counterpointed by a conjecture of emotional gain. *You lose the house, you gain the man. Or something.* The house can be destroyed – *burnt* – and turned into memories both painful and sustaining. Or a reverie, expansive and protective. Discussing the house as a symbolic concentration of being, Bachelard proposes that 'we live in it in alternative security and adventure. It is both cell and world ... A house that is as dynamic as this allows the poet to inhabit the universe. Or, to put it differently, the universe comes to inhabit his house' (1958: 51).

The professor learnt that rebuilding her house was not quite the same as rebuilding herself. There was overlap, true; there was also difference, in the part that required symbolism rather than cement. With so much burnt, smoke-ruined or damaged, what was needed was a language of not giving up. What can you call it if it ain't really saved?

The ironic context of this composition was not lost on the professor: an essay about home, written in someone else's home, by a life-writing practitioner homeless, homesick and grateful for shelter. In that temporisation, her domestic space – elegiac, ideal, burnt – was both imaginary and forcibly real.

There's no space like home.

References

Bachelard, G. 1958. *The Poetics of Space* [1964], translated by M. Jolas. Boston: Beacon Press.

Dickinson, E. 1970. 657, in *The Complete Poems of Emily Dickinson*. London: Faber and Faber, 327.

Grahame, K. 1908. *The Wind in the Willows*. London: Methuen & Co.

Huntington, F. 2011. *The Burning House*. [Online]. Available at: http://theburninghouse.com [accessed: 26 January 2014].

James, H. 1977. *The Spoils of Poynton* [1897]. Harmondsworth: Penguin.

James, H. 1978. *The Portrait of A Lady* [1881]. Harmondsworth: Penguin.

Krasner, J. 2010. *Home Bodies: Tactile Experience in Domestic Space*. Columbus: Ohio State University Press.

Linville, B. 2010. What to do when someone's house burns down, in *Life After the Fire*. [Online]. Available at: http://www.lifeafterthefire.com/2010/04/what-to-do-when-someones-house-burns.html [accessed 26 January 2014].

Linville, B. 2011. Family emergency plan, in *Life After the Fire*. [Online]. Available at: http://www.lifeafterthefire.com/2011/11/family-emergency-plan.html [accessed 26 January 2014].

Linville, B. 2013. Scentsy flameless candles, in *Life After the Fire*. [Online]. Available at: http://www.lifeafterthefire.com/2013/02/scentsy-flameless-candles.html [accessed 26 January 2014].

Oxford English Dictionary. [Online]. Available at: http://www.oed.com [accessed: 26 January 2014].

Smyth, G. 2006. 'You understand what domestic architecture ought to be, you do': Finding Home in *The Wind in the Willows*, in *Our House: The Representation of Domestic Space in Contemporary Culture*, edited by G. Smyth and J. Croft. Amsterdam: Rodopi, 43–62.

Index